CCCCCCCCCCCCCCC

C000077562

About the Author

Born in South Wales in 1946, Sonia is the eldest daughter of Rosina and John, the main characters in this book. She has wanted to tell this story for many years. Sonia now lives on the West Coast of Scotland with her husband Bob. Retired, Sonia enjoys craft projects when not writing. She has a son and daughter, and three teenage grandsons, whom she adores.

Dedicated to you, Mum.

Sonia Murgatroyd

WAITING TO DIE...
BASED ON A TRUE STORY

Not many lived a life like Rosina

AUSTIN MACAULEY PUBLISHERS™

LONDON • CAMBRIDGE • NEW YORK • SHARJAH

A CIP catalogue record for this title is available from the British Library.

ISBN 9781398451339 (Paperback)
ISBN 9781398451346 (ePub e-book)

www.austinmacauley.com

First Published 2022
Austin Macauley Publishers Ltd®
1 Canada Square
Canary Wharf
London
E14 5AA

Acknowledgements

I have wanted and tried to write this book for years but it was only after Alison Speirs read my draft and reacted so positively to it that I had the courage to finish it.

I am indebted to many friends and family who have helped me: Particularly my family from Belgium, Andrea Atkinson, Rosalind Creighton, Angela Duffy and my son-in-law, Eric Wyllie, for their involvement with the story.

Elaine MacDonald and my daughter, Andrea Wyllie, for help with the technical aspects and for moving this project along. Also, my grandson, Ben Wyllie, for designing the cover.

Lastly, I would like to thank my husband, Robert, who has encouraged me from the very start and allowed me to pick his brains by answering my many questions.

I am grateful to you all.

It has been a long and difficult journey but I got there in the end.

Table of Contents

Chapter One
Wales, 1988

Rosina sat on the edge of the bed, her hands still tightly gripped around her cup of coffee, the contents long grown cold. She stared out of the window, not seeing the rolling green hills dotted with sheep, nor hearing the muffled rumble of traffic from the nearby motorway. She caught a glimpse of herself in the dressing table mirror and thought how gaunt she looked. Her small frame had become even smaller; she felt she had lost more weight, but that didn't matter now. Her priority was her daughters.

"How am I going to tell them?" she asked herself over and over. "They need to know the truth."

Rosina had felt unwell for some time but insisted on continuing her work as a carer in the community. Rosina wasn't one to admit defeat but now, with such severe pain, she was confined to her bed; she knew in her heart something was seriously wrong.

Doctor Samuels had given her a thorough examination and she couldn't help but notice his grim expression. He recommended that Rosina be admitted to hospital immediately so that tests could be carried out as soon as possible. Doctor Samuels sat at the bottom of the bed and wrote a short letter for the hospital.

"Do I have to go in to the hospital right now?" she asked.

"I'm afraid so. Would you like me to arrange for an ambulance to pick you up?" Doctor Samuels cast an anxious eye upon Rosina's ashen face.

"No, my daughter will take me in." She sensed an awkward urgency in his manner and it worried her.

The doctor rang ahead to let the hospital know that Rosina was coming. Before he left, he administered intravenous pain relief and gently squeezed her trembling hand.

The drowsiness soon filtered through Rosina's body and she longed to succumb to the luxury of rest.

"Not now!" she told herself sternly. "I need to think." Rosina suddenly felt an overwhelming need to embrace her two daughters and tell them how much she loved them and hoped they would both understand when they heard about her devastating past, which had led to such tragic circumstances that changed Rosina's life forever. So many times she'd wanted to tell them, but could never find the right words.

Now, she felt the time had come when she must confess all. Her daughters were now old enough to recognise the dark despair that had engulfed so much of her life and why she had so often tried to take her own life. Remorsefully, Rosina recalled the day-to-day misery and distress her girls had suffered whilst growing up.

Guilt-ridden, Rosina felt the need to do this before she went into hospital.

"Don't forget to ring the girls, John," she said to her husband.

"Okay, one thing at a time, Rosina, I'm looking for your dressing gown."

"Don't worry, the girls will do all that. John, come sit with me." She patted the bed with her hand. "Hold me, John, hold me tight, I want to savour this moment." She hesitated before continuing, "John, listen to me, I need you and the girls to be strong. I don't know what's wrong with me but I have never felt as ill as I do now; I don't know how I am going to do my job."

"Oh Rosina, thinking about others again. Your job is the last thing you should be thinking about, you need to rest. You'll get over this as you have done many times in the past."

"Well, I hope you're right, John, but I don't feel as confident as you seem to be. I know you will disagree with me, but I feel the time has come for the girls to know what really happened when I was a young girl."

"Don't you think you have enough to deal with, and you're only going to upset them and yourself again. Let it go, Rosina." John pleaded. He got up and kissed her on the forehead then moved over to the chair.

"I can't," Rosina muttered, choking on her tears. "I have mentioned it briefly to them over the years but now that they are older, they will fully understand the reasons for our constant rowing and the depression. God knows they had a miserable childhood and the girls need to know they were not to blame. I must do this, John, and I need you to understand the importance of what I am asking." She closed her eyes and tried to relax.

"I understand what you are trying to do but the past is dead and gone. Why do you have to rake it up now? It's ruined your life. Do you want it to ruin theirs too?" John looked annoyed.

"I must do this," she whispered again. With her strength ebbing, grasping for every mortal breath, Rosina looked to John for help as she managed to sit herself up. She studied his weary face and thought how cruel time can be: deep-centred lines masked his once handsome face. His lean physique now portrayed a hunched figure of an elderly man.

Rosina recalled the very first time she had laid eyes on John—it was the most memorable moment of her life. He was so good-looking: his stance and military uniform aroused passion she had never experienced before. For Rosina, it was love at first sight, and throughout their stormy relationship, her love for John never faltered.

"How would he cope if...?" she couldn't finish the sentence. He mustn't see her anxiety. "John! I'm talking to you, John. When the girls come, we'll tell them I'm just having some tests done and it's probably nothing serious. I don't want to worry them needlessly."

"Okay, if that's what you want. I'm going downstairs now to ring the girls." John left the bedroom.

Exhausted from the doctor's visit, Rosina flopped back onto the pillow and turned towards the window.

The weather looks like I feel, she thought: gloomy and depressing. It was late February and the coming Spring was anticipated with great apprehension. Alone and tearful, she was glad when she heard John's footsteps on the stairs.

"Susanna will take us to the hospital, I've also spoken to Louisa." Gasping for breath, he sat on the bed.

"Don't rush, John," she told him crossly but with a warm smile.

"I should have realised you weren't well," John's voice softened, "when you stayed in bed. At first I thought the depression had returned but I saw the look in your eyes, which you so desperately tried to hide, when the doctor examined you. Why didn't you tell me you were in so much pain? If you'd only said something, I could have helped."

"You've never had much sympathy, so why start now?" Rosina retorted but then relented. "Look, this is no time to be bickering. There are things that have to be said and done while I still have some strength left."

John pulled the quilt cover over his sick wife.

"Try and get some rest. I'll go down and make us both a cup of tea."

"Tea—why did the Welsh think it was the answer to everything? Coffee was the drink in Belgium," she murmured. As the tears slid down her cheeks unchecked, she suddenly felt a compelling need for her birthplace.

As the soporific effect of the sedative began to work, maudlin thoughts of her childhood in Oostende came unbidden to her mind. *I was happy then*, she thought. *For that short time in my life, I was happy.* With that thought, she drifted off into a drug-induced sleep.

Chapter Two
Belgium, November 1939

"Come on, Monica, or we'll be late again!" I cried. My sister, Monica, and I went to the gymnasium three times a week, but every day after school, we had to look after our younger sister, Sara, who was 7, and the twins—Louisa and Jack, who were only 6—until Mamma came home from her cleaning job. I was one of 9 surviving children. Marie and Ada, who were in their early twenties, were both married, as was my brother, Pieter, who was in the army with Marie's husband, Eduard.

My other brother, 16-year-old Joseph, was away at sea most of the time working on my Uncle Abeel's fishing boat. Monica and I were the oldest two still at home: Monica was 14 and I was 13 but we were considered well old enough to look after the younger ones.

On gym days, it was always a rush because Mamma was often late and we couldn't leave the little ones until she arrived home, but it was worth it because we loved gymnastics. Before a major competition, Monica and I would use every spare moment to practise. Our teacher, Miss Blommaert, was a perfectionist. She was very petite with short cropped hair and big brown eyes. She wanted us to excel, so we had to work very hard at our routines. Very often we were exhausted but we didn't mind, as we could see that we were improving and my dream was to become a successful gymnast at the highest level.

"I hope you've got my leotard, Rosina, because I don't have it." Monica rummaged through her bag as we ran down the road. It was raining—it hadn't stopped all day, and we were soaked to the skin.

"Yes, I've got both our leotards and a towel each but please, hurry, Monica, I don't want to be late tonight. You know what Sophie Beck and Colet Kins are like. They're always looking for some reason to complain to Miss Blommaert about us," I said sharply.

"Don't take any notice of them," my sister retorted.

Monica was my best friend as well as my sister. If you didn't know any different, you'd think we were twins: same colouring, same build, same blue eyes and short mousey hair cut in a fashionable bob. The only difference was that Monica was a little taller than me but my early puberty meant that my breasts were more developed than hers, even though I was a year younger. Miss Blommaert often remarked how they got in the way of my best moves, much to my embarrassment and the amusement of the rest of the team!

Monica gave me a reassuring hug before we entered the big wooden doors that led to the gymnasium but sure enough, as we ran to our lockers to get changed, Sophie Beck sneered at us.

"The Callen girls are late again! Why can't you both be on time like everyone else?" Sophie mocked and Colet Kins laughed as she looked around at the others for their response!

"Ignore them!" my sister whispered in my ear. The fire in my eyes let them know they weren't going to get away with it but I soon forgot their unkind teasing as the lesson began in earnest.

"Vaulting tonight, girls," called Miss Blommaert. "I want you to try something different. When you jump onto the springboard to mount the horse, instead of pushing off with your hands, I want you to push off from a handstand position. Watch me as I demonstrate, it may look frightening but the more you practise, the easier it will become. The tournament is in the last week of February and we must have the edge on our competitors if we're going to win again this year."

Sophie was the first to try the new move. Monica muttered under her breath, "I'd like to wipe that silly grin off her face. Just because she was chosen to go first, she thinks she's the best." I shook my head and told Monica to keep her voice down. I had to concentrate if I was ever going to get this jump right.

Sophie began her approach to the jump but I could see that she hadn't picked up enough speed so when she reached the springboard, she stopped dead.

Everyone laughed, but I felt sorry for her. When Miss Blommaert asked her to try again, she refused. *That's not the attitude of a winning gymnast,* I thought to myself.

When it was my turn, I felt nervous and my mouth was dry but I remembered all we had been taught. I ran as fast as I could, leapt onto the springboard, landed on the horse and pushed off from a handstand position. I had done it!

"Well done, Rosina," said Miss Blommaert, "but remember to keep your feet together when you land." Now it was Monica's turn. I prayed with all my heart that she would do it, and she did.

When we were back in the locker room, Sophie shouted, "Think you're clever now, don't you?"

"I've had enough of this, Monica! This has been brewing for a while; keep an eye on my things!"

"Be careful, Rosina. Or you'll be thrown off the team."

"I don't care, Monica. I'm sick of her snide remarks."

I marched over to them, eyes blazing, ready for battle. When they saw me coming, a look of panic passed over their faces and they stood up, but suddenly a voice pierced the air, "Aren't you girls ready yet? Do hurry up. I have to lock up soon." Miss Blommaert looked first at me, then at the other two. I'm sure she knew what was going on but she just clapped her hands and told us to be quick about it.

"You wait!" I whispered menacingly. "You won't be so lucky next time."

Despite the Feast of St Nicholas, which was always a happy time, being only a few days away, I noticed my married sister, Marie, wasn't her usual self. Mamma and I had braved the cold winter wind to go on a shopping trip to the market and Marie came with us. Mamma was hoping to find some cheap ingredients for her baking day. She had warned all us children she wanted peace and quiet to get her baking done. I tried to make conversation with Marie.

"I love this time of year, don't you, Marie?"

She shrugged her shoulders and said, "I used to, but this year it's different; I'm not a bit excited, in fact I feel quite disheartened. It's very worrying to know there are people suffering in other parts of Europe and it's getting worse."

Mamma tried to reassure her. "You mustn't think like that, Marie. We won't be involved. Belgium is neutral. You must think about Ellie. She's three now and she will be looking forward to St Nicholas day."

"That is precisely why I'm unable to relax and enjoy the festivities. I'm worried about Ellie and what life will be like for her if Belgium is involved." Fear was etched on Marie's face.

Although Marie was married with a three-year-old daughter, she was finding life very stressful since her husband, Eduard, was away serving in the Belgian army.

We jostled our way through the crowded market stalls where, in spite of the decorations and bustling shoppers getting ready for the Feast of St Nicholas on 6 December, the usual happy excitement was missing.

The effects of the War recently started in Europe were beginning to be felt in my beloved Belgium. Hitler's forces had invaded Poland in early September 1939 and were now turning their attention to the west. That's all everyone was talking about in school and on the streets. Papa had the wireless on constantly, listening for news of the war, and for the first time in my young life, I felt threatened in my own country.

Marie's voice could barely be heard above the crowd.

"Look closely, Mamma! Can't you see the fear in people's eyes? I can—it's all around us, the same thing that is happening in other parts of Europe. It's so worrying. The elderly people must be thinking, 'Not again!' It isn't that long since the Great War ended and people are just getting over it."

"Oh, Marie, don't be so dramatic!" Mamma looked quite upset by Marie's outburst.

"It's true, Mamma. I'm not being dramatic. It's a fact and everyone is dreading who's next on Hitler's list. Don't get me wrong, Mamma, I love Oostende; it's my home, the place where I was born, but now I look at it with different eyes. With the future so uncertain, I feel restless here. Everything is changing rapidly and I know I've changed."

"What do you mean, you've changed?" Mamma queried with wide eyes.

Marie stood her ground and cleared her throat. "Mamma, I think we should all leave Belgium before Hitler destroys our city, and us with it."

Mamma stopped and stared at my sister in amazement, as the crowd pushed and heaved around us. "Oh Marie, you're getting ahead of yourself, now calm down and don't speak like that in front of Rosina!" She made eyes at Marie not to continue. Mamma turned towards me and forced a half-hearted smile.

"Let's go to Zeger's café on the seafront for a coffee, I think I can even stretch to a cake as well."

As we sat waiting to be served, I was still shaken by Marie's sudden outburst.

"Mamma, if we leave Oostende, all my hard work in the gymnasium will have been for nothing. Mrs Blommaert says I am talented and maybe one day I could—"

Mamma interrupted me, "Don't be silly, Rosina! No one's going anywhere! Look in the window and choose which cake you would like."

I knew they didn't want me to hear what Marie had said. Why did they still treat me like a child? I was thirteen now and able to understand the dangerous situation all around us. Feeling frustrated, I pretended to check-out all the cakes in the display case near our table but I could still hear snippets of their conversation.

Marie spoke in a hurried whisper, "I've heard stories, Mamma. Do you remember Alexandra Hynrick? Her husband is in the army with Eduard. She and her three children are moving to England straight after the holiday."

Mamma looked shocked. "Is that what you want, Marie? You want to run away? I remember not so long ago when you married Eduard, you said you would never leave Oostende while he's in the army." I could hear the smile in Mamma's voice as she remembered how radiant and stunning Marie had looked in her wedding gown. We had all envied her good looks. Ellie, my little niece had arrived sometime later. I recall Mamma joking, "When is someone going to give me a grandson? That's three granddaughters now!" Everyone had laughed.

The coffee arrived and Marie called me to hurry and choose my cake. When I returned, we sat and sipped the steaming liquid in silence.

"I know how anxious you are about this war, Marie. We all are." Mamma's voice was full of compassion, as if she sensed something else was troubling my sister. Marie turned to look out of the window. The November sky was beginning to darken in the late afternoon and a trapped fly buzzed at the window. I sensed that Marie was trying to hold back tears that were threatening to spill. I kept as quiet and still as I could, hoping that perhaps they would forget that I was there. I picked up an advertising leaflet someone had left on the next table, then slid down in the chair and pretended to read it.

"I haven't heard from Eduard for over three weeks," Marie finally blurted out. "I'm sorry, Mamma, I didn't want to worry you with Pieter being in the same regiment as Eduard. Have you heard from him?"

"No, I've heard nothing," Mamma replied. Pieter was only 18 and married to Isabella, who was expecting their first child in a few months. He was the eldest surviving son in our family and I knew that Mamma worried about him being away in the army. Her consolation was that he and Eduard were together and would look out for each other.

Marie blew her nose noisily. "Eduard always writes so regularly to me. I don't understand what's going on in this wretched war. What if something has happened to him? I can't live without Eduard."

Mamma leant over and gently touched my sister's arm. "Look, you're probably worrying over nothing. You know what army life is like. Even under normal circumstances it's difficult to communicate, but Marie, the whole of Europe is in turmoil. He's probably on an assignment and not able to make contact with you or anyone else." Mamma never showed her own worries in her concern for others.

"Anyway I don't think this war will last long. Britain and France will soon put a stop to Herr Hitler's plans and, as I said before, Belgium is neutral. We won't be involved."

Marie couldn't contain herself any longer, "Haven't you been listening to the wireless, Mamma? The reports from the BBC are terrifying! I can't sleep for worrying." Marie ran her fingers through her long black locks and pressed the palm of her hand across her forehead. Her voice quivered with emotion as she said, "What's happening in Eastern Europe is frightening, Mamma. Hitler's sending out alarm signals to every one of us. He's made me stop and think. Do I want to be here when all hell breaks loose?"

Fear clouded Marie's face and she bit hard on her bottom lip to stop it trembling. "I don't think the British can stop Germany invading our country; they're already tracking west and I'm so worried for Ellie." Blinking back the tears, she shook her head, "It's just her and me now and I dread to think what will happen if they invade our country. I can't see any future here in Oostende." Again, Marie was being dramatic.

"Oh, Marie." Mamma gave her daughter a reassuring hug. "Don't ever feel you're on your own. You know that Papa and I will always be there for you, don't you? I don't think you've thought this through. Where would you go with a three-year-old? Be reasonable, Marie." Mamma's eyes searched her daughter's face.

"I don't think *you* have thought it through, Mamma. Why do you think I am so upset? I'm the one being realistic," Marie emphasised.

"It's not fair on Ellie. You can't just up and leave like that. You're not…you're not thinking of sailing off to England, surely?" Mamma anxiously asked.

The question hung in the air. I had been sitting so quietly they had almost forgotten I was there but I couldn't contain myself any longer.

"Please don't go, Marie! I couldn't bear it here if you left Oostende," I cried. "It wouldn't matter where you went; you would still be on your own with Ellie to look after. At least if you stay here you'll have your family all around you? Please think hard about this, Marie."

"It's not enough, Rosina. We will still be living dominated by an harsh enemy with no freedom," Marie replied.

Mamma drained her coffee cup and looked at her eldest daughter quizzically, but said nothing.

The café was quieter now as people began to head home. The clock in the corner ticked loudly.

At last, Marie looked at both of us and took a deep breath. "I'm sorry, Rosina, but yes, I want to go to England, but not just me; I think we should all go. The whole family. I'm sure the Germans won't get as far as England and we'll be safe there." Tears trickled down my sister's face and she made no attempt to wipe them away.

"I'm being torn apart, Mamma; I don't want to leave Oostende, but as the weeks pass and I hear more and more of the destruction of our neighbouring countries, I feel more and more certain that we must leave."

For the first time, I felt a dark cloud of fear and anxiety pressing down on me, some foreboding that I couldn't express; something inside of me was churning like a distant memory of a long-forgotten tragedy. A warning! But who would listen to a thirteen-year-old girl?

Abruptly, Marie stood up and shrugged on her coat. Wiping her eyes with the back of her hand, she shook her head and forced a smile.

"Come on," Marie said, as she looked at both of us. "Or we'll never get this shopping done."

Mamma and I were both surprised at the sudden change of subject but sensing that the discussion was only over temporarily, we followed Marie's lead.

The bill paid, the three of us left the warmth of the café to brave the biting cold November wind.

Mamma shivered and pulled her coat more tightly around her. Arm in arm we walked down the street seemingly without a thought in the world except Volaeren, the delicious sweet honey bread we would eat over Christmas.

Chapter Three
Rumours of War

When we got home, I went through to mamma's bedroom. Leaving the door slightly ajar, I could hear her bustle over to the open fire to warm her hands.

"It's so cold out there, Jakop," she said to Papa, who was already home. "That northerly wind coming off the sea is bitter. Do you want a hot drink, Rosina?" she called through to me.

"No, Mamma, I want to get on with my homework," I lied.

She lowered her voice but I could still hear her. I wondered what Papa's reaction would be when Mamma told him of Marie's wayward plan, and not only her plans for herself, but that she expected all of us to go to England as well. This would have a huge impact on my life and I wanted to know Papa's opinion; it meant a lot to me.

"I don't know what to think, Jakop. Marie's convinced this war will spread to Belgium and she's making herself ill with worry. She's talking about running off to England and she thinks we should all go. As if we could just leave everything behind! Honestly, Jakop, she's obsessed with the idea!"

Papa busied himself with pouring them both a coffee.

"Well, it's understandable," his strong, calming voice took on a reasoning tone. "She's on her own with a three-year-old which must make her feel very vulnerable. Having to make all the decisions herself and barely out of her twenties. She's not as strong as you, Hanna, but she'll come to her senses. Now, come and sit down and drink your coffee. I have something to tell you."

Mamma did as she was told but I knew from Papa's voice, the news wouldn't be good. "Hanna, I know you were looking forward to Pieter and Eduard coming home for the holidays but I've just been listening to the wireless and Belgium is on high alert. All leave has been cancelled."

"Oh, Jakop! Perhaps Marie is right."

Sipping the warm coffee, she cast an eye on Papa's drawn, tired face. Through the kitchen door that I had left ajar, I could just about see them both.

"I can't go through another war, Jakop." I could hear the tension in Mamma's voice, as she relived the nightmares of war. "I don't know about you, but memories of the last war are still so fresh in my mind. What haunts me most is the memory of the constant hunger pains—I'll never forget that feeling as long as I live. Do you remember the dreaded knock on the door? Can you remember, Jakop? When the soldiers demanded that we get out of our own home and they rummaged through our personal belongings, as if they were looking for something. I felt like retching, the thought of their filthy hands everywhere. I would have bleached the whole house if I'd had any bleach left."

I heard Mamma's voice quiver and knew she was close to tears. "Maybe we should go to England, all of us, you too, Jakop."

"Me? I can't leave: what about the house, my job? Not that I'll have a job for much longer," he retorted.

"What do you mean, you won't have a job?" Mamma gasped. "I don't know how much more bad news I can take, Jakop." Mamma dabbed her eyes with her handkerchief.

Papa continued, "When I arrived at the building site this morning, Yan Bryssinck, you know, the foreman, called a meeting. He told us that building materials were in short supply and as from the beginning of the new year," Papa intoned hesitantly, "I'm on a three-day week. Yan has already had to lay men off because of the shortage of materials and he thinks we're on the brink of war too, and from the wireless report just now, I don't think he's far wrong."

Mamma put both hands over her face. "Oh Lord, I knew this was going to happen!"

I couldn't believe what I was hearing and the despair in Mamma's voice was evident.

"How will we manage?" she moaned. "We're struggling now, we'll never cope with so many mouths to feed. I dread to think what the future holds, Jakop."

I heard a scrape on the floor as Mamma pulled her chair nearer to him. I knew that, despite her anxiety, she would be trying to reassure Papa and not express her own feelings too forcibly.

"We're not going to let this madman Hitler ruin the holiday season. Not a word of this to the children! Let them enjoy the feast of St Nicholas. Who knows what the future will bring? This could be the last year we all spend Christmas together as a family, in a free, democratic country." Mamma gulped down the remains of her coffee. "Jakop, promise me, not a word. Not even to Marie, about your job."

"Yes, yes, you're right, we'll try to keep everything as normal as possible. I wish I had your strength, Hanna. You never let anything keep you down for long."

I felt the blast of cold air as the door opened, before I heard Marie's voice call, "Have you heard the news, Mamma? Eduard won't be home for the holiday, it was on the wireless. All leave has been cancelled."

"Yes, I know," Mamma answered. "We heard it too."

"This is such disturbing news, Mamma. We could be at war soon. Do you still think the British can stop Hitler's armies invading Belgium? What more proof do you need, Mamma, that war is brewing and there's nothing we can do about it?" There was a mixture of panic and sadness in Marie's voice.

"This will be our first festive season apart since we met," Marie's voice quivered with emotion. "Ellie will be heartbroken too. Only this evening as she was going to bed, she asked when Papa was coming home." Marie smiled sadly as she recounted how she had to hold up her three fingers to count the days till St Nicholas would come.

"Well, with the both of you coming to us for St Nicholas, you won't feel so lonely," Mamma replied.

"Oh, Rosina!" Marie exclaimed. Seeing me at the bedroom door, "I didn't notice you there." Turning to Mamma, she pointed to the corner of the room. "I see you've planted the wheat candles."

I knew she was changing the subject because of my presence.

"Well, it is the first Sunday of Advent. Haven't you done yours?" Mamma asked.

"I just haven't had time, but I'll do it this very night. I can't stay, my neighbour is looking after Ellie." She kissed Mamma on both cheeks as she bade her goodnight.

Since the Christmas shopping trip, I realised they had no intention of including me when the conversation had anything to do with the war in Europe. Well, I'd had enough. I wasn't going to be ignored any longer.

"Marie, before you leave, I'd like a word with you and Mamma," I said. I ignored the eye contact between them and sat down on one of the kitchen chairs.

I held my chin up although my knees were trembling. I had to pretend to be confident even though I wasn't.

"Mamma, if I'm old enough to look after my younger brother and sisters while you go out to work then I think I'm old enough to be included in any discussions regarding the war in Europe. Monica and I are not young children anymore. I wish the two of you would realise that. I probably know more about the war than both of you. Whenever I walk into the room, you change the subject. I realise you're trying to shelter me from the horror stories sweeping through Europe. But Mamma, what you don't seem to realise is it's all around me in school. That's all everyone is talking about."

I glanced at Marie. "Since you decided you want to leave Oostende, the atmosphere in this house is so tense. Mamma and Papa are on tenterhooks. They're worried sick about you!"

"That's enough, Rosina!" Mamma interrupted.

"No Mamma, Marie needs to hear this." I was determined to have my say. "None of us want to leave Oostende—only you, Marie. Mamma's been so unhappy since you told us in the café. She's worried you'll go and we'll never see you again. Please don't do this or you'll split the family up. I have a very bad feeling about this."

I could hear my voice rising and expected some response from them. As Marie made her way to the front door, she turned to look at us both.

"I didn't realise I was the main topic of conversation in this house!" Marie snapped.

"Oh, Marie, don't say that." Mamma followed her to the door but she left without saying another word.

After Marie had gone, I expected Mamma to give me a row, but she didn't— she just stared at me.

Then she spoke: "With everything that's going on here lately, I've completely ignored the fact that you're growing up before my very eyes. You're right: you should be involved in all family discussions and in future, you and Monica will be."

The cold December wind howled around the house but at least the promised rain hadn't materialised. The hard winter months meant we children were confined to the house most of the time and easily bored. Mamma shooed us out of the kitchen.

"I need peace and quiet. I have warned you all." Mamma smiled. "It's nearly St Nicholas Day and I must get the baking finished today."

Outside, Papa was working in the back yard, building up a stock of firewood and filling the coal scuttles. Mamma was at her happiest cooking; the kitchen was her domain. I could hear her humming to herself as she gathered the ingredients together. The delicious smell of fresh bread filled the house and we were soon drawn back into the kitchen by the tantalising smell.

Papa's head appeared around the open door. "Is that fresh bread I can smell?"

He took off his boots and moved across to the sink to wash his hands. "I've just filled three scuttles and two buckets with coal. That should see us through for the next few days."

Mamma smiled her approval. She now had her mind on the six loaves of bread she had just taken from the oven and was turning out on to cooling trays.

Papa stood back and watched in admiration as another four loaves went into the hot oven.

For a moment the war was forgotten. As I felt the love and devotion of my family surrounding me, I felt safe and secure and I didn't want this feeling to ever end.

"Well, that's all the bread done," Mamma said wiping her hands on her apron. She turned around just in time to see Papa winking at me as he broke off a corner of one of the loaves and popped it into his mouth.

"Mmm! My favourite—cornbread. How many loaves are you making, dear? If I didn't know better, I'd think the whole street was coming for tea!" he said with a grin.

"Well, you know how many visitors we get over the holiday period. And this year, the whole family will be here, although maybe not Eduard and Pieter."

Tasting the soup, Mamma added the dumplings. "Just the spice cookies and the honey cake to make and that's everything done." Mamma flopped onto one of the chairs. "I'm exhausted!" she sighed. She took her shoes off and lifted her feet on to a stool as her ankles were very swollen.

"No wonder—you've been cooking all day," Papa responded.

"Shall I make us all a cup of coffee?" I asked.

"That would be lovely, Rosina." Mamma looked so tired and drained. We all wondered how she managed to juggle two jobs and look after all of us.

"I wonder where Joseph is?" Mamma sounded worried.

Papa put his paper down on his lap. "Hanna, Joseph did say he would be home for the festive season, but the weather has been rough lately. Don't be surprised if he is delayed."

Abeel, who was Mamma's brother-in-law, was the captain of a big fishing trawler which made long trips out at sea and Joseph was on his boat. We all knew Joseph would be safe with his uncle, but Mamma still worried about him.

Papa's big blue eyes appeared above his newspaper.

"You worry too much, Hanna," he said gently.

Marie and Monica had taken the younger children to see St. Nicholas arriving at the docks. I was just thinking how peaceful and still the house was when the door burst open and my little brother, Jack, and sisters, Louisa and Sara, tumbled into the kitchen, all laughing at the same time.

"Mamma, Papa, we've just seen St Nicholas!

Everyone was going wild when the steam boat came into the docks," Sara said excitedly. Seven-year-old Sara's pretty blue eyes were like saucers. She could hardly contain her excitement. "When the boat blew its horn, we all clapped. Even the old people were shouting." Hardly stopping for breath, she rattled on excitedly, "You should have come with us, Rosina, it was great fun."

"Marie gave us some speculoos and tarts to give to St Nicholas' Reindeers," interrupted little Louisa who was only six.

"And Sinterklaas's helpers, Zwarte and Piet, gave us some pink candy," Jack, her twin, joined in, not to be outdone by his sisters.

"You must have been frozen standing down by the docks," Mamma said as she helped them out of their coats and ushered them over to the fireplace to warm up.

Chapter Four
Christmas

The Day of St Nicholas finally dawned, crisp and cold. Mamma returned from morning mass to find us all up and dressed.

"My goodness, St Nicholas should come every day!" she laughed as she sat down to remove her shoes.

The excitement in the children's eyes was magical; the feeling of exhilaration that associates itself with this time of year, was quite wonderful.

As the day got under way, the eagerness and determination of us all drove the threat of war away from our house for the time being. Sara, Monica and I were busy getting the table ready for the biggest feast of the year, when Marie and Ellie arrived. Joseph had arrived home from sea late the night before and was still asleep. The cries of welcome and the children's excited chatter soon put an end to his peaceful slumber and he made his entrance, stretching and yawning.

I counted the places at the table. "I don't think we've got enough spoons, Mamma." I checked again.

"It's okay, I brought my set," countered Marie, reaching for her bag.

We all noticed that Papa just could not get into the festive mood. He went through the motions, but the sparkle was missing and, although nobody said anything, everyone felt it. With the prospect of a three-day week and the threat of a Nazi invasion, it took all his strength to get out of bed each day. He spoke of his memories of food shortages from the first war; it sent shivers down our spines. He told us how he would walk the streets for a pocket full of food and a cup of milk for his young babies. The unbearably painful memory of the death of some of the babies almost broke his heart. Hunger and shortage of medicine had all taken their toll. He never wanted to be put in that position again.

At six o'clock, almost everyone was seated at the table. One chair remained empty. Marie had hoped with all her heart that Eduard would have last minute leave and had insisted that a place be left for him.

Mamma began to dish out the home-made soup. She had also managed to find some paper hats for us all to wear.

"This soup is delicious, Mamma, it has such a rich, savoury taste," Marie voiced what we were all thinking. Mamma could produce such wonderful food even when there was very little in the cupboard.

The festive meal had just begun when there was a loud knock at the door which startled us into silence. Mamma's nervous look at Papa stirred mixed emotions in all of us. The German army hadn't arrived in Belgium, as far as we knew, but Mamma, being Mamma, had nervously locked the back door once all of the family were seated inside.

Papa stood up as Mamma started to nervously clear the soup dishes.

"Who can be knocking at this time?" he said.

Papa slowly opened the back door and to everyone's relief and delight, the tall, handsome soldier who stepped into the kitchen was wearing the Belgian uniform.

"Am I in time for dinner?" queried Eduard, as he removed his cap and threw it on the chair.

"It's Eduard!" everyone shouted at once. Only Marie was speechless as she flung herself into her husband's waiting arms with tears streaming down her face.

"Papa, Papa! We kept a chair for you!" Ellie pushed herself between the embracing couple, arms lifted high. Eduard picked up the little girl effortlessly and the three of them held each other tight, crying and laughing at the same time.

Mamma finally spoke: "It's wonderful to have you home with us, Eduard, and in time for the feast." She ushered Eduard to the empty chair and hurriedly ladled out another bowl of soup, then brought in more bread. Soon, we were all tucking into the meal and everyone declared it a great success. Joseph, ravenous after his time at sea, was on his third helping of soup. Mamma wondered aloud if he ate enough on his days away from home.

"Make sure you leave enough room for the rest of the meal," she laughed. "I'm so happy that Abeel managed to bring the boat back home in time for the festive season and I'm so glad I made an extra saucepan of soup!" Mamma kissed the top of Joseph's head as she gave him an affectionate hug.

After we'd eaten our main course of duck and vegetables, Mamma brought out the mouth-watering desserts she had made according to custom: some sweet, some savoury and some spicy. As the family ate, Mamma cleared her throat, and asked, "Tell me, Eduard, did Pieter have leave too?"

Eduard leaned across the table and patted her hand reassuringly.

"Yes, he's fine. He went straight to see Isabella at her parents' house. With her being five months pregnant, he thought it wiser that she stay with them while he's away on duty. He asked me to tell you they'll be over tomorrow." Tension was etched on Eduard's face. "We didn't know what was happening. One minute we were on high alert and the next we were being told to go home and enjoy some quality time with our families before..." he left the sentence unfinished.

"How long will you be home?" It was Marie who asked the dreaded question.

"They've given us two weeks but our sergeant said we could be called back anytime at short notice. We have to tune into the wireless regularly."

The younger children, bored with adult talk, were eager to open their presents. Mamma managed to find two little gifts each for the younger children, while we older children received just one gift. It took Mamma many months of saving and sewing to make or buy gifts for all the family. As we grew in number, she found it more and more difficult to be as generous as she would have wished, but with her determination and hard work, she always managed to make ends meet.

Monica and I both had new, black leotards, ready for the gymnastic tournaments scheduled for early in the New Year. Monica and I had won a number of medals already and we worked hard and practised regularly so our teacher had high hopes for us. It was my dream to represent Belgium. We hugged and kissed Mamma. We were old enough to understand that money was hard to come by and could appreciate the cost of our presents.

New Year, 1940

New Year's Day passed and all was quiet on the home front. My brother Joseph went back to sea and the rest of us went back to school. Papa started his three-day week. Mamma spoke to me and Monica one evening after the little ones had gone to bed and explained to us that the little money they now had coming in would have to be spent very wisely. She spoke hesitantly and avoided our eyes. "You have to understand, girls, these are difficult times for all of us.

I'm not sure if we can afford to pay for your gymnastics lessons any more now your Papa is on short time as I mentioned yesterday."

Oh, the selfishness of youth! We ranted and stamped our feet!

"But Mamma, we have a tournament coming up soon," we both shouted. "It's not fair! We can't stop now!"

Tears of anger and frustration fell unchecked. I didn't care. I worked hard at school and did more than my fair share of work around the house.

"The gym is all I have, Mamma. If you take that away, I have nothing and if Marie gets her way, I won't even have a home either."

I stormed out of the kitchen, ran up to my room and thumped my pillow with my fists out of frustration and anger.

The following morning, I didn't want to go to school.

I felt so miserable and didn't want to face anyone. But Mamma insisted I get up which I did, but I sat in stubborn silence at the breakfast table.

"Look, Rosina. I thought you, of all my children, would understand the situation," Mamma said.

"But Mamma, I have a tournament coming up soon and I've worked so hard for it. It's my life Mamma." I knew I was being selfish and horrible to her but I couldn't help myself.

When we came home from school that afternoon and after the chores were done, Mamma sat us both down.

"Papa and I have been discussing the tournament." Her face softened and her heart-warming smile shone through.

"We do know how much this means to you both and we know how talented you are, Rosina, and how much you've set your heart on this. Papa has agreed that we will continue to fund the programme but only until the tournament is over. After that, I can promise nothing."

"Oh, thank you, thank you, Mamma." We both jumped up and threw our arms around her neck. "We won't let you down, we'll work harder than ever, just you wait and see."

Chapter Five
Dashed Hopes

For once, Monica and I were early at the gymnasium. In fact the big doors were still locked but we didn't have to wait long as the caretaker arrived soon after us.

"You girls are eager tonight," Mr De Vooght said, unlocking the big wooden doors.

"Yes, it's our first night back after the holidays," Monica shouted as we ran down the corridor to our locker room. We were getting changed when the rest of the girls strolled in all chatting about Christmas. I immediately sensed a more relaxed atmosphere. It was only when we were in the gym that I realised that Sophie and Colet hadn't turned up. Miss Blommaert, our teacher, soon confirmed our suspicions.

"Sophie Beck and Colet Kins have pulled out of the competition," she told us. We all must have looked perturbed. "But not to worry, girls; Remy Speeck and Amelia Van Hoost who just missed being selected for the team were kind enough to step in. Before we start, I would like to remind everyone that if it hadn't been for Remy and Amelia, there would be no competition and with only eight weeks to go, penalties against us would have prevented us from entering next year. So a round of applause would be appreciated, don't you think, girls?"

We all clapped and thanked them for stepping in.

Despite Eduard's presence, Marie became more and more restless and unhappy. Mamma didn't know how to comfort her. Marie had only been a child when the Great War ended but she would have heard about the fourteen thousand brave Belgian soldiers who had given their lives for their country, not to mention the fifty-four thousand wounded. She would still remember seeing some of the maimed standing at street corners and seeing the horror of their missing limbs and empty eyes. Was it those early memories that were haunting her now? Mamma thought that Eduard might try to change her mind about leaving

Oostende but he seemed noncommittal and wouldn't talk about the way the war was going. I don't think he was allowed to.

Mamma reasoned with him, "Belgium is a neutral country. Surely even the Germans will respect that! We won't be dragged into this war, will we?"

Eduard just shrugged his shoulders. "You know I can't talk about it but if, or when, Belgium is involved then all leave will be cancelled. I don't know when I will be home again. Marie knows all this. It's all she wants to talk about. She knows the danger more than anyone, and yes, Belgium could be at war sooner than we think. I won't be around to support her then. Maybe that's why she's so keen to leave Oostende. But I've already said too much." And he refused to discuss it further.

It was January 1940 and Papa was, as usual, listening to the radio when he suddenly shouted, "Did you hear that, Hanna?" He sat up in his chair and turned the wireless set up louder. I was just about to go to bed as I had been at the gymnasium all evening and was worn out. "They've just announced that all Belgian soldiers are to report back to their units immediately, all 80,000 of them. It looks like Yan Bryssinck could be right. This could be it, Hanna. I don't think we can remain neutral any longer. It's War! Here!"

Mamma wrapped her dressing gown tightly around her thick waist.

"It's ten-thirty! What are they thinking, broadcasting such important news at this time?" Mamma put both hands to her face. "Not again! Please, Lord."

Papa reached for his boots and started to put them on.

"I should let Eduard and Pieter know," he said.

"No!" Mamma grasped his arm. "You're not walking the streets at this time of night. They'll no doubt get a telegram. Let them have this last night with their family. Come to bed, Jakop."

Papa shook her off impatiently. "Don't you realise, woman? Attack could be imminent! Their duty to their country must come before their families."

Papa was out of the door before Mamma could reach out and stop him. She moved over to the door and shouted at his quickly receding back, "Take care, the pavements are very icy!" He didn't turn around but lifted one hand in acknowledgement. Mamma returned to the kitchen shaking her head. She shooed us children off to our beds and settled down in front of the fire to keep her lonely vigil until his return.

It was five-thirty the following morning when Papa came home from Marie's apartment. I woke to the sound of voices and crept down the stairs. He was so upset that Mamma persuaded him to take the day off work but as much as she wanted to stay and comfort him, she had to go to her first cleaning job. She had also taken on two other cleaning jobs since Papa was on a three-day a week. That meant Monica and I had to pitch in and help more around the house.

"Mamma, I'll stay home with Papa today," I said. I followed her out to the kitchen. "I don't think he should be on his own. I don't have much on in class today."

Papa had gone out to the shed to fill the coal-scuttle.

"You're right, Rosina; he's had such a shock."

When Mamma had gone, I prepared the coffee and made him a slice of toast and then Papa began to open up to me.

"When I arrived at Marie's, Pieter and Eduard had already left. Apparently they had been expecting the order and as trained soldiers, they were fully ready to leave at a moment's notice. I was glad, however, to have been there and offer Marie my clumsy words of comfort."

I was touched and somewhat surprised by Papa's sensitivity.

"Marie was almost incoherent. She doesn't want to live in Oostende without Eduard and was sobbing uncontrollably. I couldn't leave her in that state, Rosina. She's convinced the Germans will be here sooner rather than later and she doesn't want to be here when they arrive."

I had never seen Papa cry before and I felt so sorry for him. I got a handkerchief from the drawer.

"One way or another, Marie is determined to take Ellie as far away as she can from this country. We must make her see sense; we can't stand by and do nothing. She finally fell asleep through exhaustion and that's when I left."

This was the first time Papa had seen my sister so distressed. Although Mamma had told him how worried she was about Marie, I think Papa thought she was exaggerating. Now he could see the situation for himself and he was so desperate to stop her leaving Oostende.

"I want her to give up the apartment and for her and Ellie to come back home to us until we have some definite news about this damn war. I told her to think about it and warned her not to let Ellie see her in this state again."

I got the children up and dressed and gave them breakfast. Monica wanted to go to school so she took the little ones with her.

When Papa had calmed down, he fell asleep in the chair. That gave me a chance to go and see Marie. I knocked on her door and waited.

"Oh Marie, you look dreadful," was my greeting to her as she slowly opened the door. I guided her through to the bathroom. "Why don't you wash and dress and I'll see to Ellie."

I didn't want Ellie to see her Mamma in such a state, and the poor soul was now repeatedly shouting from her bedroom: "Where's Papa? I want Papa!"

Marie threw her arms in the air: "How do I explain to a three-year-old, Rosina, that her Papa has gone back to the army and we may never see him again?"

Marie looked awful; the evidence of a harrowing night was etched across her face. She was obviously not coping.

By February, apart from the tension at home, the war hadn't really affected me too much until the day Monica and I went along to the gymnasium as usual and found it all boarded up. There was a handwritten message pinned to the wooden door which said: CLOSED UNTIL FURTHER NOTICE.

"What can this mean, a week before the tournament?" I asked some of the other girls who were standing outside. But they didn't know either; they just shrugged their shoulders. No one seemed to know what was happening.

Monica and I felt angry, puzzled and upset. We couldn't face going home so we walked along the promenade. The angry westerly wind blew across from the channel, stirring up the sand and throwing it, in its fury, at our faces. We moved closer together to shield ourselves from the onslaught and tried to protect each other from the storm as well as the grave situation we found ourselves in which was breaking our hearts.

I looked at Monica. "Do you think this has something to do with the war?" I asked.

"I hope not, Rosina, because if that's the case it may never open again," she replied.

"Oh, Monica, don't say that. What are we going to do? All my life I've dreamt of becoming a professional gymnast."

"I know," Monica replied.

"I could scream! This is all because of that evil monster in Germany. I feel my life is spiralling out of control and there's nothing I can do about it. We might as well go home." We slowly made our way up the road in a melancholy mood.

"Is everything alright?" Mamma asked when we let ourselves into the warm kitchen.

"Yes, of course," we chorused but I couldn't keep up the pretence so we told her what we had found.

"I don't know what to do! The gym is my life!" I could hear my voice rising in frustration and anger again. I knew I was overreacting but I couldn't stop myself. "Why is this happening? Now of all times. It's just so unfair!"

I took the stairs two at a time; I was so furious. Monica and I shared the attic bedroom and I threw myself on the bed and shouted, "I want things to go back the way they were!" I put my fist into my mouth to stop myself from screaming.

Chapter Six
Germany's Plans

Papa came home from work early one day and Mamma noticed something was wrong; he seemed quieter than usual. I was helping Mamma to make our evening meal.

"I don't know how true this story is," Papa said. "Yan heard that a German plane crash-landed a couple of weeks ago just south of Antwerp, due to engine failure. The soldier who was on board the plane was caught trying to destroy documents by burning them. He was turned over to the Military who alerted the Dutch and French armies, because the papers gave details of an imminent invasion of our countries." Papa ran his fingers through his hair.

"Hanna, I can't bear the thought of those Nazi boots trampling through our country," he cried. "That could be why the soldiers had to return to their units so suddenly. Something in those documents must have warned the military of an imminent invasion." Papa looked as if he bore the whole world on his shoulders.

"I have more bad news," Papa continued. He fumbled with his cigar, glanced at Mamma, then me, and said in a quiet voice, "I'm no longer employed. Yan has run out of materials so he was forced to terminate the few men he had left. This is my last pay." Papa handed over his wages to Mamma.

"Oh Jakop, this is so worrying! Maybe we should be seriously thinking about leaving Oostende. I don't want to leave but we have to be realistic about this; we cannot ignore the warning signs." I could hear the fear in Mamma's voice.

One evening, I felt so fed up I wanted to be on my own. I walked down to the seafront and as I turned the corner on to the promenade, the wind took my breath away. I wrapped my coat even tighter around my waist. I sat on one of the benches and thought how bleak and deserted the town looked. We weren't even at war and yet the cafés were quiet with empty tables and lonely chairs. The hustle and bustle of everyday life was already disappearing.

Tears pricked my eyes as I remembered fleeting moments of childhood, running and splashing along the water's edge with my brothers and sisters with not a care in the world.

They were now distant memories and I felt a feeling of panic and hopelessness as I waited for the onslaught of war. I had no idea what to expect. Some buildings were already boarded up as if they weren't taking any chances. I only knew that once again our country was threatened by yet another war. My birth place, the town that I loved so dearly would fall into the hands of an evil dictator. There was much to reflect upon but right then my emotions were in turmoil; I could no longer hold back the tears and I don't know how long I sat there sobbing.

Suddenly, someone was shaking me and calling my name.

"Rosina, Rosina, what's wrong?" I looked up to find Papa's worried face staring back at me. "I've been looking everywhere for you. What's wrong, are you hurt?"

"Look around, Papa, and you tell me what's wrong."

Papa sat down beside me on the bench, and held me in his arms.

"This war is really getting to you, isn't it?" he said.

"Yes it is and without the gymnasium, I have nothing. I don't think it will ever open again."

"Oh don't talk like that, Rosina, you are my gifted little girl. Look, this war may not come to anything. Most of Europe is against Germany and with odds like that, this war should be over before it's begun. Come on, Mamma's worried sick about you, let's get you home."

Hitler seemed determined to conquer the rest of Europe.

The Americans called it the "phoney war" because nothing was happening as both sides took time out for reflection. But Papa didn't believe for one moment that the Fuhrer, as they called him, would stop until he had achieved his objectives. Certainly the Belgian army seemed to be on full alert. The air of uncertainty continued and we were all glued to the wireless reports every day, wondering where Hitler's forces would strike next.

Papa became more and more concerned for his family. Every conversation in the house seemed to be about Hitler, about the Nazis, about War! Marie was constantly threatening to leave Oostende and still no sign of her moving in with us. I just wanted it to be over and for things to go back to the way they were before. I usually found somewhere quiet in the house to sit and read my book but tonight I stayed in the kitchen while Mamma did the ironing. Papa had that faraway look on his face again. These days it seemed to be his permanent expression.

"You're very quiet tonight, Jakop. Are you still worried about Marie?" Mamma put the iron back on the hob over the fire to warm up again.

"Yes I am. I've seen a drastic change in her over the last few months. I'm worried how she'll cope when we're under German occupation, which I'm certain will happen soon," Papa said sadly.

These days Papa wanted to speak his thoughts aloud more often than not. Often he spoke about his memories of the Great War.

"Belgium became the battlefield of Europe but the people worked so hard, side by side, patiently repairing the ravages of war when it was over." He shook his head as he said, "Was it all for nothing?" What Papa said next astonished both Mamma and me: "With having more time on my hands, I've been considering the future and listening to the wireless; I don't think any of us will have a future if we stay in Oostende."

"Whatever do you mean, Jakop?" Mamma asked.

He fiddled about with his pipe and then he gave us both a brief look.

"I'm hearing gut-wrenching stories of atrocious acts the Nazi soldiers are inflicting on innocent people. What worries me is that their victims are randomly chosen from the villages they march through; it's just awful, Hanna. It makes me sick to think what these men are capable of." Papa lit his cigar and after puffing on it a few times, he lowered his head and from his sombre expression I knew I wasn't going to like what he was about to say. "It made me think, it may not be a bad idea for you to leave Oostende."

"What, are you serious, Jakop?" Mamma was quite taken aback.

"I've never been more serious in my life. Marie won't survive a day once we're under Nazi rule. Maybe Britain is our only hope of freedom."

"But, Papa, I don't want to leave my home," I cried. "I want things to go back to the way they used to be." I seemed to weep easily these days and much as I tried to hold back the tears, the floodgates opened and I sobbed uncontrollably.

Papa put his arm on my shoulder; his tone softened but was still masterful: "My darling Rosina, life will never be the same once the Nazis get their filthy hands on our beautiful country, you might as well get used to it. You said you wanted to be involved, well, now you are." Despite the gentleness with which he spoke, I couldn't ignore his underlying bitter tone.

There was a moment of hope when news of the battle of the River Plate reached us: the destruction of the great German armoured ship The Admiral Graf Spee. And her captain, Langsdorff's subsequent suicide greatly boosted our confidence in Britain's naval power but Marie was now more convinced than ever that England would provide shelter for all of us.

One morning Marie burst into the kitchen, eyes blazing, not realising the little ones were still having their breakfast, laughing and giggling as children do. I could hear the hysteria rising in her voice, but then she took a deep breath and calmed herself, realising all eyes were on her. Mamma put a cup of coffee down in front of her, saying, "Here, drink this!" Then she looked at me and said, "Take the children upstairs, Rosina. They've all finished their breakfast now."

I did as I was told but I crept back down and sat on the stairs to listen as Marie said, "I cannot stay and watch everything fall apart, Mamma! Every day that passes is a day nearer to an invasion!"

The pitiful cry from Marie overwhelmed me as I sat on the stairs with tears streaming on to my lap.

Mamma was quite stern. "Do you realise what you'd be giving up, Marie? Do you think I haven't thought about leaving too? I don't want to live under Nazi rule either but what can we do? I've been thinking about it. In fact, I've thought of nothing else."

Mamma swilled back her coffee and slammed the cup down on the table. Marie lowered her voice so that I could barely hear her.

"Mamma," she paused, "I thought maybe you would ask Uncle Abeel if he would take us to England in his fishing boat. Now that he has a bigger one, it could be done and I know he would do it. But you would have to ask him. Please Mamma!" Marie pleaded.

"Are you mad?" Mamma was horrified. "Uncle Abeel would never agree, he's far too busy with the fishing industry to be taking mothers and children across the Channel to England. What are you thinking, Marie?" Mamma was astonished.

"Well, I think he would do it." Marie was determined.

"I'll have to think about this. I will not make any rash decisions and I'll have to speak to Papa first. We could lose everything we've worked so hard for: our homes; our lives as we know them. We'd be refugees in a strange country, is that what you want?"

"Yes. Mamma. Yes! I would rather that than be a prisoner in my own country."

After Marie had gone, I tip-toed down the stairs and opened the door slowly. Mamma had her elbows resting on the table, her eyes were closed and she was holding her head in both hands.

She opened her eyes when I walked into the kitchen. "I suppose you heard everything?" she said. I nodded. I had wanted to come down the stairs and have my say but I had felt so sorry for Mamma. She was under tremendous pressure and I didn't want to make it harder for her.

"If it helps, Mamma, I'll go along with whatever you decide. But why didn't you tell Marie what Papa said the other day about us all leaving Oostende?"

"Because Papa and I haven't really discussed it properly and there's a lot at stake here. We need to organise a family gathering and find out what everyone's views are," she replied.

Mamma was quite a robust woman. She'd had to be: she had given birth to fifteen children and seen six of them die before, and during, the Great War. She was a big woman with a big heart and her brown eyes exuded warmth and comfort. She had a round, motherly face and her long thick locks were always worn neatly in a bun. I loved her so much and I didn't know what I would ever do without her.

She wore her clothes down to her ankles and her skirt was covered by a pinafore. She and her house were always spotlessly clean. She had brought up all nine surviving children in this tiny narrow three-storey building with only two bedrooms and a small attic room. Could she say goodbye to all those memories?

Chapter Seven
To Stay or Go?

February's frosty nights slipped their way into March's blustery winds. Mamma still hadn't arranged a family gathering. Normal home life had disappeared and in its place, domestic chaos reigned. Papa had the wireless on, constantly reminding us of the maniac who was terrorising Eastern Europe.

Mamma was under considerable pressure from us all and sometimes found it extremely difficult to stay calm. I sometimes felt I would go crazy if I stayed in this environment much longer. If only the gymnasium hadn't closed!

One day Mamma asked me to call around and see if Marie and Ellie would like to come for lunch. I found Marie to be very anxious when I arrived.

"I'm afraid to go out shopping," she said. "The Germans may be here any day and I'm worried what they may do to Ellie."

"Look, shall we go to the shops now so you can stock up on some food so you won't have to go out so often." Marie seemed pleased with that idea, so I continued, "Then we can go to Meme's for lunch. Would you like that?" I glanced at Ellie.

"Yeah, Meme makes the best bread in the world!" Ellie shouted.

As we walked down the road past the boarded up gymnasium, shuttered furniture shops and empty office buildings, I suddenly felt insecure and vulnerable. Soon, every town and city in Europe would be under the mighty force of Nazi Germany.

"I must stop listening to the wireless," I muttered to myself.

It didn't bear thinking about, and I certainly wouldn't mention my thoughts to Marie. Everyone was in a hurry; no one stopped to pass the time of day. There was Mr Vandenbosch walking his dog on the other side of the street; he kept pulling at the dog's lead as if to hurry him along. Poor dog, he doesn't know why everyone is so frightened.

When we arrived at the butcher's, there was a short queue. We had to stand outside but with a cloudless sky and a lukewarm sun we couldn't grumble, after all it was still only March. No one spoke or asked after anyone's health, and certainly no one mentioned the dire problems in Europe. We were lucky the butcher had almost everything Marie needed.

On our return home, Marie voiced her thoughts aloud: "Isn't it sad to think that our beautiful Oostende will soon be overrun by those evil Nazi soldiers? I can't bear it, Rosina!" Marie glanced down at her daughter.

As we turned the corner, the low sun shone directly into our eyes. We were almost home, when there was a horrific noise that assailed our ears. Marie and I looked at each other in terror over the head of Ellie, who had started to cry. The thunderous noise grew louder and louder. Marie scooped Ellie up into her arms then from a side cobbled road came two huge army lorries.

As they made their way towards us, my first thought was if they were German lorries. But Marie reassured me they were Belgian with their flag flying high. With a sigh of relief, I smiled.

"Wave Ellie. Look, they're waving to you? Wave to our brave Belgian soldiers."

But Ellie just buried her head in Marie's shoulders, screaming, too frightened to look.

"This is just the start," Marie argued with Mamma. "Next time, it could be German tanks and I don't want to be here when that happens. I won't be here!" Marie thumped the table with her fist.

"I don't think Mamma and Marie will ever agree on the situation in Europe," I muttered to myself.

Mamma asked me to take Ellie across to the park but I flatly refused—to everyone's surprise. The trucks had really shaken me too and I was still too fearful to leave the house. I agreed to take Ellie upstairs to see her Pepe who was repairing a bed. When I came back downstairs, Mamma had already given Marie an ultimatum.

"As I said, if you give up the flat then I'll go and have a word with uncle Abeel and I'll also arrange a family gathering. You cannot stay alone in that flat any longer. Look at Ellie—she's crying for the least thing; that child isn't happy anymore. If you carry on much longer, you'll end up having a nervous breakdown. And what happens to Ellie then? Papa's repairing one of the spare beds and Monica and Rosina have offered to give up their attic bedroom for you and Ellie. The children don't mind sharing with their older sisters. End of discussion! I don't want to hear another word!" Mamma was furious with Marie.

Marie sat in silence as she looked at Mamma, then at me and with a heavy heart, reluctantly gave in. "Alright! Alright! I'll give up the flat."

Mamma smiled with a sigh of relief, as Monica breezed in. "Anyone for coffee?" We all laughed together, something that had been missing for such a long time in our house. While we all sat around the table drinking our coffee, Mamma seemed more relaxed and happy now that Marie was coming home.

The Family Gathering

The blustery winds of March brought scattered April showers and the earth was warming again.

"I've arranged a family gathering here tonight," announced Mamma. She had just got in from morning mass. Normally, she went straight on to her first cleaning job, but today she came home first. She took her shoes off and rested her poor swollen legs on a stool.

"I'll make you a cup of coffee and some toast while you rest, Mamma," I said.

"That would be lovely, Rosina, but I can't get too comfortable here—I still have to go to work. I've called the meeting because I want to see how many people are interested in leaving Oostende. I've also had a word with Uncle Abeel. To my surprise, he's more than willing to help. He's unable to come tonight but I told him I would keep him updated."

"Oh, thank you, thank you, Mamma," exclaimed Marie. "Who's coming?"

"Just the family—it's only to get everyone's opinion. Marie, we need to talk; you do realise what we are asking people to do. We are taking a huge risk, I don't know if I can do it."

"Mamma, I've thought of nothing else for months. What choice do we have?" Marie demanded.

"We do have a choice, Marie." Quietly and calmly, Mamma continued, "We could stay here and sit it out. It may not be as awful as you imagine. If we mind our own business, they should leave us alone. We are no threat to the Nazis."

"Don't bank on that!" Marie retorted as she left the room.

The evening for the family meeting soon arrived and with the tea dishes done and put away, Mamma built up the fire while Marie carried through some chairs from another room and Renata our next door neighbour brought stools from her house. The little ones had been sent to bed but Monica and I were allowed to stay up as we were now involved in matters concerning the war. We sat on the floor in the corner and tried to make ourselves inconspicuous. My sister-in-law, Isabella, was the first to arrive.

"Oh, Isabella, you made it. I didn't think you'd come with only a few days left before the baby's due." Mamma found her a comfortable chair to sit on.

"I thought if I came early enough, I'd get the best seat in the house," she laughed. "How did you manage to carry so many babies, Hanna? This is my first and definitely my last!" Isabella smiled as she tried to make herself comfortable.

"You'll soon forget the discomfort. It's a wonderful experience having a baby so make the most of it. Once this little one is on its feet, you'll be wanting another," Mamma said, laying out the cups ready for coffee, "and I don't mind telling you, I hope it's a boy!" Mamma laughed.

"So do I; that would be perfect," said Isabella.

When everyone had arrived and settled down, Mamma opened the meeting: "Well, I assume you all know why we're here this evening."

Without looking at Marie, she continued, "The suggestion has been made that we leave Oostende while we still can, and try to get across to England. We have the choice of staying here and making the most of it or seriously considering the possibility of leaving. I emphasise, "seriously". It's a soul searching decision."

There was a low buzz as everyone started muttering to the person sitting next to them.

"You will all have the chance to speak in a moment," Mamma said, taking control again. "We have to do what is best for us as a family. I don't want to leave my home so I'm going to have to think long and hard about this."

My Aunt Constance, Mamma's sister, was the first to speak: "I, for one, would rather leave Oostende. My husband, Abeel, and I have spoken about it time and time again. I know my baby would be born in England, but I'd rather that than endure the wrath of a Nazi regime. Abeel is willing to supply the boat."

Ada, my second eldest sister who was twenty-five and was married with two little girls, interrupted, "When would we leave? It needs a lot of planning."

Then someone else spoke: "This is a huge gamble we're taking and where will we go when we arrive in England? What about the children? Will they be allowed to go to school there? None of them speak English."

"That's what I was thinking. Mamma, have you thought this through properly? Do you realise that if we leave our homes now, they may not be here when we get back? We don't know how long this war will last." Ada voiced what many of us were thinking.

Someone else shouted, "Belgium's neutral. We won't be involved."

Then everyone began to speak at once.

Some of my uncles, on Mamma's side of the family, were standing at the back of the room. They were all involved in the fishing industry in one way or another. One of them called for order. It was my Uncle Rob, who we nicknamed "Mighty Rob" because he had strong, broad shoulders, and a thickset neck; his receding hairline exposed a sea tanned, leathery forehead. At the end of both arms were hands that looked like shovels! No one messed with Rob. He was handsome in a rugged kind of way.

"Don't bank on Belgium's neutrality," Rob announced in a deep, composed voice. "Hitler is obsessed with power and he won't stop until the whole of Europe is under his command. The slaughter of innocent people will go on and on! We feel very strongly that we should leave Oostende. I think I speak for all those involved in the fishing trade, when I say that there is no doubt in our minds that Belgium will soon be occupied by the German army and when that happens, which I think will be sooner rather than later, we will not stand by and let the Nazis profit from our hard work."

Everyone clapped and some patted him on his back. Rob continued, "Obviously, there will be boats out at the time of occupation. There's nothing we can do about that."

A sombre mood spread through the house. There were lots of arguments and many were undecided. Mamma told everyone to go home and think it over and to speak to their husbands and wives and she arranged a second meeting two weeks later.

"That will give us time to consider what we want to do and, for those of us who do decide to leave, to start making arrangements. In the meantime, don't talk of this to anyone outside the family," she warned. She thanked everyone for coming and people slowly drifted away in subdued twos and threes.

After everyone had gone, I offered to help Mamma clear the dishes but she refused and told Monica and I to go to bed.

"It's late," she said, "and you both need to be up early for school. Remember what I said: not a word to anyone about this and there's no need to trouble the little ones yet."

Monica had walked one of our cousins to their home. They lived in the next street and I was glad as I needed to be alone with my thoughts. Lying on my bed, the enormity of the situation suddenly hit me. I had no idea of what lay ahead for us. The same dark foreboding I had felt in Zeger's café those five months ago came again. Something pressed heavily on my chest and I struggled to breathe. Sharing a bedroom with the little ones was far from ideal but at least it was my home, my birthplace.

I was thirteen years old; my life was full and I had so much to be thankful for: the gymnasium where I excelled, my school and all my friends, and most of all, my family all around me in my beloved Oostende.

How dare this crazy, insane man they call the Fuhrer threaten to take it all away from me?

Since the meeting, I had many restless nights. The grandfather clock chimed in the hallway. I listened and counted. Was it only five o'clock? I lay on my back, wide awake. My three sisters were still asleep. I crept downstairs where there was a glimmer of light from the embers still aglow near the bottom of the fire.

"Thank goodness," I said to myself as I quickly emptied the tray of ash then added some paper and coal. I put the coffee beans into the grinder then waited for the kettle to boil. The sun was already rising, its watery early-morning rays lighting up the room.

Just as Papa was getting up, I heard the distinctive sound of Mr Nys's horse and cart making such a noise of clattering milk churns as it trundled along our cobbled streets. He was early today but I rushed out before the queue started. "Hello Mr Nys," I said. "We have three jugs to fill today."

As he filled the jugs up, he looked at his watch.

"You're up early today, Rosina," he said.

"Yes, I couldn't sleep," I answered in a subdued tone.

"That's you and the whole of Oostende," he replied. "These are troubled times, my girl. You take care of that family of yours."

"I will, Mr Nys." I patted Jake, the horse, on the nose. I was struggling to carry the three jugs and hoping not to spill any of the milk before Mamma and Papa rose, but I was too late—both were up, sipping their coffees with smiles on their faces and grateful for a warm kitchen. Papa was already fiddling with the knobs on the wireless, trying to find a clear signal.

Suddenly, the broadcaster spoke loud and clear about France.

"The French Premier. Paul Reynaud has just attended his first allied war council meeting in London and he supports Winston Churchill's proposal to mine the Norwegian Leads. The allies hoped it would disrupt the German iron ore traffic." I didn't know what that meant, I just wanted it all to go away.

"I know it's not what we want to hear at the moment but let's hope it works!" Papa stood up to add more coal onto the open fire.

"It looks like Norway and Denmark will soon be under Nazi occupation. The Germans are ignoring all the rules of neutrality. I wonder where that leaves Belgium." Papa had given voice to all our thoughts.

Despite the fear of Nazi invasion, some good news came later that morning. I hadn't seen Mamma so happy in a long time as we had just heard that Isabella had a baby boy in the early hours of the morning.

"A boy! Oh Rosina, I can't tell you how that makes me feel. A boy! A boy! Don't get me wrong. I love my granddaughters dearly but I've longed for a grandson."

"I know that, Mamma. Do you think Isabella will still want to leave Oostende now that she's had her baby?" I asked.

Monica had just walked in to the kitchen and was quick to respond, "It is precisely for that reason, Rosina, that Isabella would go. She has made it clear she doesn't want her little baby brought up under Nazi rule."

Mamma said nothing but agreed with her eyes. I looked at her in surprise. Monica had never really expressed an opinion before, but now I could see that she thought we ought to leave too.

I didn't know what I wanted; I was so confused.

Mamma couldn't wait to tell Papa the good news. "Jakop, you have a grandson!" she shouted as soon as he walked in the door. The horror of the war was temporarily forgotten in the midst of this celebration of new life. Papa didn't say anything but the look in his eyes was one of happiness and a lonely tear fell.

"I must go and see him, Hanna," he said.

Chapter Eight
The Invasion, 10 May

We were all up early. Papa was his usual self, fiddling with the knobs of the wireless set. Mamma was washing the kitchen floor when suddenly, all the spitting and crackling stopped on the wireless; the voice was clear but sombre.

We listened incredulously to the horrifying news that specially trained German paratroopers had broken through Fort Eben-Emael in the early hours of the morning. Everyone had boasted that the Fort was impregnable! The newsreader continued to announce impassively that a small contingent of airborne forces had already seized the bridges at Keldeweadt, Vroenhoven and Kanne while other paratroopers had landed west of the Albert Canal. There was nothing now to stop the German ground troops advancing westwards and southwards.

Mamma screamed, "Oh Lord, help us!" She put her hands over her face.

I tried to calm her. "Mamma please, we all want to listen to what the newsreader is saying." Then Marie began to cry and she quickly became hysterical, screaming and shouting, walking from one end of the room to the other. Little Ellie looked on with fearful eyes; she didn't understand what was happening.

Marie wouldn't stop crying. Mamma caught hold of both her arms and shook her.

She pulled away, looked at Mamma and began to sob pitifully. "Oh Mamma, the newsreader mentioned casualties," Marie spluttered as she tried to regain self-control. "What if Eduard's lying somewhere injured or even dead?"

"Marie, please, the children are listening," Mamma whispered. Marie got up and just made it to the sink where she was violently sick. It was awful to see her so upset. Ellie started to cry and that set the twins off. Mamma was trying to hold herself together and keep everyone calm but within minutes, the house had erupted into chaotic madness. I picked Ellie up and caught hold of Jack's hand while Monica grabbed Louisa and Sara and we took them over the road to the park, but no one was in the mood for playing that day.

Once Mamma had calmed down and was in control again, she shouted from the front door and beckoned Monica and me to come in. She then had us running around to family, friends and neighbours to tell them there was an emergency meeting that night, seven o'clock prompt, due to the morning's devastating news.

Just before seven, the house was bursting at the seams. Mamma wasn't surprised at the number of people that turned up: family, friends and even neighbours who were just passing acquaintances. People stood in the hallway and some pressed into adjoining rooms.

At precisely seven o'clock, Mamma cleared her throat and called everyone to order.

"You will all have heard the devastating news. It will only be a matter of time before the whole of Belgium is occupied. The last meeting revealed strongly divided opinions on the plan put forward to leave Belgium. Now it is urgent that we make a decision one way or the other," Mamma said. There were murmurs of agreement as Mamma paused before continuing, "I think you all know my brother-in-law, Abeel. I managed to track him down and he is with us tonight even though it was short notice. I have asked him to outline the practicalities of our next move."

All heads turned as Abeel stood to his feet. He was a tall, strong man with an open and trustworthy face. Although still quite young, he was wrinkled and weather-beaten after his many years at sea. He could be rough in his speech at times and always spoke his mind, but he had a gentle, kind side to him as well. I loved him dearly.

"Right folks," he started hesitantly. "First of all, I need to know how many of you are seriously considering leaving Oostende. I would imagine that as you've made the effort to come here tonight, at such short notice, it goes without saying that you're mostly eager to leave the country but I need to have a rough idea of how many are coming so that I can plan how to accommodate you all on the boat. I may need to limit numbers but there will be other boats leaving from tomorrow and right up until the German soldiers arrive in Oostende.

"Please be clear about this: once you have left Oostende, I have no way of knowing how or when, or even if, you can return home. For as long as our country is occupied by the German army, there will be no way back. You cannot change your mind. Your decision will be final. I hope I have made myself clear."

A gentleman standing at the back shouted, "Is it possible to leave in the next few days? Hitler's armies could be in Oostende very soon; their soldiers are leaving no stone unturned as they advance through Belgium; they could be here within days."

Almost everyone agreed and Abeel had to shout to be heard, "I need you all to calm down. We are not going to get anywhere if you all carry on like this. The boat I will be using is out at sea and will be back in dock two days before we sail."

"When are we going to sail?" A young boy's voice called from somewhere in one of the other rooms.

"I recognised that voice—it's Jeron Segars," I whispered to Monica. "He has a sister, Carina, who's ten. His Mamma died recently and he is looking after his sister on his own. He must be desperate to leave Oostende with her."

Abeel answered in a confident manner, "I will get to the departure date soon. Now, where was I? Okay, the soldiers will not be in Oostende in a few days."

"How do you know?" the same boy shouted then a few other people joined in.

"Look," Abeel announced. "If some of you feel that you can't wait any longer, as I told you earlier, there will be boats leaving Oostende on a daily basis!" There was quite a bit of fidgeting and shaking of heads as the enormity of what Uncle Abeel had said began to sink in.

"Can I have a show of hands, please? Who definitely wants to leave on my fishing boat?"

Several hands shot up immediately, but others objected that it was too soon for a show of hands.

"Don't you think it's a bit late to be arguing about whether you want to stay or leave the country?" Marie shouted at the top of her voice. I looked at Mamma who was blood red from the neck up.

Everyone stopped talking and turned to look at Marie.

"Well, it's true," she retorted.

Abeel picked up the discussion quickly. "I agree with Marie. We only have a matter of days to organise our escape." He hesitated before continuing, "Whether you decide to stay and suffer at the hands of a dictator or become a refugee in England, you have to be realistic about your decision because it will affect you for the rest of your lives. I can't make it any clearer than that."

Abeel sat down. He looked worn out. Mamma made him another cup of coffee. Everyone began to talk all at once. I couldn't identify where the questions were coming from. Someone near the front door asked, "What will happen when we get to England? Will we all be separated?"

Mrs Zaman who was a very large lady asked, "I have five children ranging from one to nine years old. Will they be able to go to school in England?"

A neighbour who lived on our street voiced her opinion: "I would prefer my children to go to a school in England than grow up under the wrath of Nazi rule."

Uncle Abeel tried his best to answer their questions but even he didn't know all the answers. Finally, he announced, "I've said all I've come to say. The ship will be ready to leave at dawn on the nineteenth of May." There was silence as dread mingled with hope lodged in the hearts of those present.

"The ship will be docked in readiness the evening before, but if you are not there by 6.00 am, I will have to leave without you. Now, a final count of who is going to be on my boat."

Uncle Abeel's eyes clouded over and he lowered his voice, "I just want to wish everyone good luck. We are going to need it. Life as we know it will never be the same again, and the risks are enormous, but what is the alternative?"

Everyone agreed that there wasn't one.

Mamma stood at the door to shake hands with everyone as they left. I think most of the people there that night had already made up their minds to leave but Mamma was still undecided. Aunt Isabella said she was leaving with her new baby son, Sebastian. Marie tried to urge Mamma to leave too and used every means possible to persuade her but Mamma would make up her own mind—as she always did.

Mamma had told Joseph that she was going to stay in Oostende. He was home from sea but couldn't make the meeting because he was working at the docks. He reminded us all, "Just because I'm not at sea doesn't mean I'm not working; I've still got work to do at the docks."

Papa said that whatever everyone else decided, he was staying at home. He would look after the house until we all returned home safely.

Although I would miss him, I was comforted by the fact that our home would still be there for us when we all returned. After tonight's meeting, I knew in my heart that we would be leaving for England, even if Mamma wouldn't admit it.

She would have to face reality sooner or later and there was only a matter of days left. Monica begged to be allowed out with her friends for a little longer but I just wanted to go to bed. As I slowly climbed the stairs to my room, I felt tired and confused.

Chapter Nine
Evacuation

With just a week left before we were leaving Oostende, I decided to get my diary out. I felt I needed to seize the day and capture my thoughts and fears with pen and paper. I tried to think what was more important to me: to leave or stay. My most dreaded fear was having to leave my home, to give up everything I had. It may not have been much but, to me it was my little world. Then I thought if we stay, we would lose our freedom; our choices would be taken away from us; we wouldn't be allowed any opinions of our own; we would be told what we could and couldn't do and would be looking over our shoulder constantly.

We all take life for granted until the day it's snatched away from us. To think this madman, Hitler, could just seize our country and do what he liked with it, forcing people into diabolical situations.

My sullen mood matched the darkness of the bedroom. I tried to picture life in England but, my head was so full of questions that I couldn't answer. I found it difficult to imagine any future at all; more than anything, I just hoped that we would all be together.

How would Papa cope without Mamma? We could be away for years I told myself with tears stinging my eyes. Our future was unknown and that scared me. I must have fallen asleep because I didn't hear Monica coming to bed. I dreamt of boats, water and bombs.

I was walking home the next day after doing some last minute shopping for our journey. I was sad as I walked the streets, seeing my beloved Oostende rapidly preparing for war. Some owners of small businesses deliberately smashed the windows of their shops, before boarding them up again, to protect them from looting by the German soldiers. It was so frightening to witness the preparations for what was expected to come.

Although I didn't want to leave my home, I felt the time had come to leave Belgium. I dragged myself home, tired and despondent.

I opened the kitchen door to hear Monica shouting at the top of her voice, "Mamma, I'm telling you, everyone who's leaving is going the night before and with so many people wanting to leave, there won't be room for everyone!"

"Well," Mamma sat in front of the fire stretching her legs, "if I decide to go, we're not staying on that boat all night. We have a long enough journey ahead of us and I'd like to sleep in my own bed for as long as I'm able to. That's enough, Monica. We'll go in the morning!"

"But Mamma, what if the boat is full and we can't get on it!" Monica was hysterical. I'd never seen her like this.

"Look, Monica, I haven't got time to argue with you anymore," Mamma replied.

Suddenly, the door burst open and in walked Uncle Abeel.

"Monica's right, Hanna," Abeel said. "Hitler is rampaging through every country like there's no tomorrow." Uncle Abeel's eyes were electric. "The scenes of carnage and bloodshed he's leaving behind are apparently horrendous. Sadly for those poor souls, there is no tomorrow. You know how word gets around, Hanna. There's more people than ever before wanting to leave Oostende now. Everyone is fearful that the soldiers are going to be here soon." Uncle Abeel lowered his voice. "We are spending the night before we sail in the basement of the fish market. You are welcome to come with us. Otherwise, try and be on the boat between 8 and 9 the night before."

As Uncle Abeel opened the door to leave, he turned and looked at Mamma. "If you haven't made up your mind yet, I advise you to do it soon, Hanna." The following morning, I woke to the sound of my brother and sisters chatting away; the excitement in their voices was obvious. Seven-year-old Sara was jabbering on about a holiday.

"What holiday are you talking about, Sara?" I interrupted half asleep and they immediately stopped and stared at me.

Sara spoke first, "I heard Mamma and Papa talking. Mamma said we're all going away very soon. I think Mamma is going to take us on holiday but Papa can't come as he's looking after the house."

Monica and I glanced at each other, then jumped out of bed and ran downstairs.

"Is it true, Mamma—have you decided to go the night before?"

Mamma was busy making our breakfast. "I will be honest with you both: I don't want to go but," she said, looking at Monica and me, her eyes shining with tears, "I'd never forgive myself if any harm came to you both. We don't know what those young soldiers are capable of."

"Oh, Mamma, you mustn't worry about us, we can take care of ourselves," I said.

"This is different," she said, glancing at us both. "These soldiers are trained to maim and kill. If it's anything like the last war, they will march into our homes, terrorise us and steal what little we have. They are pure evil. They wouldn't think twice about raping young girls and leaving them on the roadside."

With only a few days left, everyone was rushing around. I came in to the kitchen looking for my purse and Mamma was sitting by the table.

"Have you seen—what's wrong, Mamma?" I asked. Mamma was crying. "What's happened?"

She wiped her eyes then put her handkerchief back in her pinafore pocket. "I told Joseph we weren't going to England. I told him not to worry; I would be here when he comes home from sea! What is he going to think when he arrives home to find we've all sailed off to England." Mamma put both her hands to her face and rocked her body back and forth. "I've lied to my son and I may never see him again. Oh, Rosina, I'm torn between the devil and the deep blue sea. What should I do? Oh, Lord, help me!" She burst into tears and it seemed like her tears would never stop. I led her through to her bedroom so that the younger children wouldn't hear her and sat beside her on the bed.

"Mamma, I think we should still go ahead with the journey. Until the German army arrives in Oostende, there will be lots of boats leaving for England. When Joseph comes home, he may get on one of the other boats and meet us in England. We could even leave him a note with Papa telling him what to do. Uncle Abeel can send a message to the other boats to find out which one he is on. Don't worry, Mamma, we'll soon see him again."

"That's a good idea, Rosina—we'll leave him a note. I'll feel happier if I do that. I think you and Monica should begin to sort out what clothes you'll be taking with you to England. Take a mixture of clothes for all types of weather; we don't know how long this war will last, or where we will end up."

Mamma rubbed her forehead. "I am very worried about Jack travelling all that way on a boat; you know how sickly he can be, and if he's anywhere away

56

from home, he won't eat. Oh, Lord, I hope I'm doing the right thing," Mamma prayed.

When I saw Mamma unhappy and sad, it made me feel low and I questioned myself like Mamma was prone to do. Were we doing the right thing or were we making the biggest mistake of our lives?

I climbed the stairs one at a time. My heart sank as I was preparing to leave my home but I forced a smile for Monica. She had covered the whole bed with all her clothes.

"You can't take all these with you, Monica," I spoke sternly with eyes open wide. She laughed as she held up one of her new dresses in front of the mirror, one that Mamma had made for her.

"I know, we can't take much with us and I've already put a lot of clothing aside," Monica said sorting through her shoes. She lowered her voice as she continued, "It's so difficult to know what to take and what to leave. We have no idea how long we will stay in England."

After Monica had gone downstairs, I sat on the bed and glanced at the dresser where my gymnastics trophies had pride of place. Some were bigger than others so I picked two of my smaller ones and put them at the bottom of my bag. I chose some personal items, face cream and hair grips and one or two pieces of jewellery. There was a small plaque that stood by my trophies, which read: "Wherever you are, Love will follow." I wanted something to remind me of my home in the coming months so I carefully placed it in the bottom of my bag with my other precious things. I sorted through a selection of clothing, mainly warm outfits, and hoped I was making the right choices.

Mamma had gone to do the last day at her cleaning job. She said she needed more time at home to do the jobs that had to be done before we could leave. Money didn't matter anymore.

We had all stopped going to school simply because there was no one there; most of my friends either stayed away, too frightened to attend school or had left the country like my Jewish friends. It was so sad—it felt like the world was coming to an end.

On the seventeenth of May, two days before we were due to sail, we all had to return to school to be fitted with a gas mask even though we were leaving the country. The horror of a small child having their whole face covered by a mask caused the little ones to scream.

"I hope they never have to wear them in reality," I said anxiously.

Uncle Abeel's boat also docked on the seventeenth of May. We all breathed a sigh of relief. We were beginning to worry that the Jackboots, as everyone called them, would capture Oostende before we left. We also heard that the Netherlands had capitulated. There was panic on everyone's face; no one seemed to know what they were doing, but what I did know was that everyone wanted to get away from the horrifying path of destruction the Nazis were creating. Since the invasion of Belgium, the wireless was on constantly. Most of the news was of the German army capturing city after city. We heard that capturing Fort Eben-Emael had been essential for their army's progress. There was nothing or no one to stop the German army sweeping through Belgium.

The night before we were leaving to stay on the boat, Mamma made some beautiful fish pies for Papa to eat when he was on his own.

Uncle Abeel had given Mamma all types of fish from his boat. He told her that he would rather give the fish away to his own people than let the Germans have any. Mamma had agreed to stay on the boat the night before we sailed—much to my relief. There had been a lot of talk in the neighbourhood of people leaving their homes, for fear of the Nazis.

Mamma was worried about Papa and how he would manage to cook meals for himself. "I've spoilt you, Jakop. Over the years, you've hardly ever had to make a meal, now you have no choice—you will have to make something or starve. Are you listening to me, Jakop Callens? I've made extra fish pies for you. You'll be looking like a fish by the time you've eaten them all."

We all laughed at Mamma's joke. Papa had his ear pressed to the wireless as usual. "Are you listening, Jakop?" Mamma asked.

"Yes, yes. Hanna, I heard you. Don't you worry about me. Just make sure you have enough food for you and the children; you have a long journey ahead of you."

Up until now Mamma had been in control; she'd had to be, or the whole family would have fallen apart. She was the one that kept us glued together. But now the tears she desperately tried to hide were visible. She picked up the dishes from the table and put them in the sink to wash. Monica and I dried them and put them away.

Mamma whispered, "I don't think we should be going on this journey. Why should I have to leave my home? It's so unfair."

We tried to comfort her. Monica said what I was thinking. "Mamma, we can't pull out now, all the arrangements have been made and you'll have Aunt

Constance for company. She will need you when the baby arrives. It will be a strange experience for her in another country. Just think, Mamma, we'll all be together."

After Monica and I had finished tidying the kitchen, I crept upstairs to make sure I had everything I wanted to take with me.

Tonight was our last night in our own beds. This time tomorrow night, hopefully, we would have settled down for our first night on the boat. I looked at Jack, snug and warm in his bed, and wondered how he would cope with the big change. He was so vulnerable; he was only six and we were all worried about him.

Monica, excited from the day's rushing around, sat on the bed.

"You'd think we were going on holiday with suitcases and bags all over the house," she chuckled as she sorted through her small travelling bag.

"I just hope we haven't got too much luggage. Monica, have you really thought about the journey? I'm not looking forward to it one bit. The revolting smell of fish will cling to our clothes and settle in our hair forever! We'll never get rid of it!"

Monica laughed. "How can it settle in our hair?"

"Well, you know what I mean, the smell of fish lingers. Where will we sleep, Monica? There won't be room for all of us and another thing is that the German soldiers could be in France already. What about those Stuka planes? I asked Papa what they were and he told me that they dive-bomb to make sure they hit their targets. I don't want to be around when that happens."

"Oh, Rosina, you're looking for obstacles! We won't be here when those nasty soldiers arrive." Monica slipped her nightdress on and got into bed.

I silently wished I could share her optimism but dread had tightened its grip on me.

Chapter Ten
Leaving

The next morning, we were all up at the crack of dawn. Today was the day we were leaving and I felt so tearful. The early morning sun was already shining its rays through a gap in the curtains.

The twins woke first and made sure everyone else was awake. They were so excited, knowing they were going to sleep on a fishing boat that night.

Mamma had gone to her last morning mass and I saw to breakfast while Monica made sure the youngsters were washed and dressed. When they saw the cases in the hallway, little Louisa's sky blue eyes danced with delight. When she saw the suitcases, she sang happily, "Hooray! We're going on holiday today!"

They were so happy and excited that I had to raise my voice to make them listen. "Sit down, the four of you, and don't move until you finish your breakfast," I said as I went to help Monica. "If only they knew the truth," I murmured.

"I don't know how Papa will manage for money," I said to Monica. As usual he sat by the fire, his ear pressed to the wireless, fiddling with the knobs. He then turned the wireless off. The strain of the last few months was visible on his already drawn face and sunken eyes. He seemed unaware of his surroundings. Monica and I looked at each other.

"Papa, what's wrong?" I searched his face.

He didn't answer but lit his cigar then puffed on it a few times. Then he looked at both of us. "I'm so glad you're leaving the country. The situation throughout Europe is horrendous. Holland has been described as desperate. The Dutch army has been forced back to cover the cities of Rotterdam and Amsterdam. Their Airforce, well, they don't have one anymore. Hitler's pouring fear into every human being, reminding us who's boss, and he's heading our way."

Papa looked choked up. He pulled his handkerchief from his pocket and dabbed his cheeks as tears threaten to spill.

"The sooner you're all in England, the more relaxed I'll feel. Just thinking of those soldiers brandishing their machine guns on our streets makes me sick. Everyone thought the last war was the war to end all wars—what a joke that was!" Papa couldn't control his tears any longer and he broke down in front of us. I felt so helpless to think that Hitler could reduce grown men to tears.

"Oh, Papa, why don't you come with us?" Monica and I pleaded with him.

"I can't, someone has to look after the house and be here when Joseph returns from the sea, to give him the note that Mamma wrote for him and explain what has happened. What Joseph's reaction will be when I tell him you've all gone to England, I just don't know."

"Oh, Papa, I wish you were coming with us." I put my arms around his neck and kissed his cheek.

The day passed very quickly. We all seemed to be rushing around making sure we hadn't forgotten anything. Mamma was panicking because she couldn't find her purse. We all hunted high and low.

"Mamma, are you sure it's not in your travelling bag? Let me look."

I rifled through her bag, finally shouting, "Found it!"

Mamma breathed a sigh of relief before moving on to the next thing to be done.

"Right, all of you, upstairs," she said briskly. "There are clean clothes on each bed. Make sure you wash thoroughly. I don't know when you'll get the chance to wash again. I've left warm water in your rooms."

"What would we do without you, Mamma?" I said as we all climbed the stairs. I felt overwhelmed with love for her.

Mamma made us wear our coats, hats, scarves and gloves. "I know it's the middle of May, but it will be cold out on the open sea. You can always take your coat off if you're feeling too warm."

"But Mamma," we all protested. Little good it did us.

She downed the last of her coffee and put the cup in the sink and then applied more red lipstick.

"How long have you been wearing red lipstick, Mamma?" I asked her.

"Long enough, Rosina. I thought you would have noticed by now." We both laughed.

It was seven-thirty in the evening when we finally left the house. Mamma locked the door then made the sign of the cross on her chest before she gave the key to Papa. The evening sun had just gone behind a thin layer of white cloud, which instantly took the warmth away. Both Mamma and I shivered.

"It's still only May," she said and then turning to Papa, she said, "Don't lose this key—it's the only one you've got. Are you listening, Jakop?"

"Yes, I hear you, Hanna," he replied but I could see that he was distracted.

"I have the other one just in case you're not in when we come home."

As we began to walk away from the house, Mamma glanced over her shoulder at the home where she had raised us all and which she loved so dearly. A look of anguish was etched on her face and her eyes were moist. She had had to make a soul-wrenching decision.

"What am I doing, Rosina? I must be out of my mind to leave all this behind." Everyone had gone on ahead except for Mamma. I stayed back with her, hoping she wouldn't change her mind. "I'm leaving all that I cherish so dearly. Everything that Papa and I have worked so hard for. Was it all for nothing?" She looked at me but her thoughts were elsewhere. "Your Papa and I took it for granted that we would spend the rest of our lives here but now who knows what will happen to us. Why should I leave it all behind?"

She kept repeating herself and looked so forlorn. Her tears fell unchecked.

"Oh, Rosina, I hope I'm doing the right thing."

Part of me wanted to tell her, "No, Mamma, we're not doing the right thing. We should stay and stick it out," but I said nothing.

She wiped her eyes. "It's so unfair," she whispered. I felt sorry for her and annoyed with my sister Marie she was the one who really wanted to go.

"Well, I don't think this war is going to last long so we'll soon be home, you wait and see," I said as I tried to make light of the serious situation we found ourselves in. I don't think Mamma believed a word I said.

Papa came with us to help carry the luggage. Marie and Ellie had been ready to leave hours ago. Marie had written a long letter to Eduard just in case he came home on leave as she had no way of letting him know that she was leaving for England. She left the letter on the kitchen table.

Ada, my married sister and my two nieces were leaving in the morning as they didn't want to stay on the boat all night. Isabella, my sister-in-law, and her new baby son were meeting us on the boat. The note that Mamma had left had become a long letter for Joseph, explaining why she had changed her mind.

On the walk down to the harbour no one spoke, not even Sara and the twins who were usually so noisy. I too felt sad at leaving my home but I just knew I'd be back.

The little ones were usually tucked up in their beds by now so they were tired already. What had been a warm gentle breeze throughout the day had now changed into gusts of cold, swirling wind around our faces. I shivered as unsettling thoughts crept into my mind. Would I ever again see the sun setting here or walk this road that I'd walked so many times? My mind was in turmoil. "I just hope this war ends soon," I muttered under my breath.

We made our way past the shop of Mr Smet the butcher. Mamma whispered, "I will miss him. He was such a nice man, always pleasant; and Mr Zeger, the cobbler—I often called in if one of you needed your shoes repaired and he would do them on the spot. All such lovely people, I'm missing my beloved Oostende already."

Marie tucked her arm under Mamma's. "Well, at least we won't be here when the enemy arrives. I can't wait to be on the other side of the English Channel. We'll be safe there, Mamma."

"I hope you're right, Marie; we're taking a huge risk." Mamma sounded tired and she had slowed down considerably. As we turned the corner onto the road down to the docks, I felt an overwhelming sense of fear churning inside me. We were passing the boarded up gymnasium when two of the boards on the windows suddenly fell down leaving the windows bare. We all jumped! I happened to look over and felt the colour drain from my face as the two windows were like glass eyes staring back at me. Were they trying to tell me something? I couldn't take my eyes off them. I felt a sudden chill.

"Why did the boards fall just as we were passing? Is this another warning?" I whispered. I could still feel those glass eyes penetrating my back even though we were well past the gym.

Monica came over and gave me a hug as we carried on walking down to the boat. "Hey, you never know—there may be a great gymnasium in England," she said.

"I know you're trying to cheer me up, but it's not working Monica. Let's get there first before making plans," I replied, not even trying to keep the bitterness out of my voice.

By the time we reached the docks, we were all exhausted. Papa walked up the ramp first with the twins close behind. They were nervously hanging onto

Papa's coat when they realised there was water underneath them. I was the last to board. I thought there'd be an unpleasant smell of fish but to my relief there wasn't. I just didn't want to be there—it felt so wrong and there were already quite a lot of people on the boat. As Mamma walked over the gangway on to the deck, there were children running about chasing each other and they almost knocked her over. I shouted at them, "Calm down or there's going to be an accident!"

I turned to look at Mamma; she was trembling and tears ran down her cheeks. I thought she was going to faint. Monica quickly found a box and we sat her down.

"Are you all right, Mamma?" I asked anxiously.

"No, Rosina, I'm not! The boat is still in the dock and I'm being knocked about by unruly children. I want to go back home."

"What do we do now, Rosina?" Monica asked.

"I don't know, Monica," I replied. "How do we convince Mamma to stay?"

Monica seemed agitated. "Well, I'm not going home! I won't go home!" she retorted.

Papa had been talking to Uncle Abeel. I called them both over and I explained to them what Mamma had said. Papa went and sat down beside her.

"Hanna, you must go to England. You don't want to be here when the soldiers arrive," Papa begged.

Uncle Abeel went to get her a strong cup of coffee.

"Drink this, Hanna. I've told the parents that they're responsible for their own children; any more running about and they'll be put off the boat." The look on Mamma's face told me Abeel's comforting words did nothing to help.

She finished her coffee, wiped her mouth then glanced up at Uncle Abeel. I couldn't believe what she said next. "Maybe Jack, Louisa and I should stay home and the rest of you go on to England."

"No, Mamma, we can't go without you! It will be too dangerous for you to stay here—especially for Jack and Louisa. Please, Mamma, don't do this!" I pleaded.

Uncle Abeel caught hold of Mamma's arm. "You need to rest, Hanna." He took us down a narrow flight of stairs to our lodgings and his cabin.

"It will be quieter down here. I've made some adjustments which I hope will suit most of you. Isabella, you have that bunk bed over there for you and the baby. It has cot-sides. Hanna, I thought this one would be more suitable for you as it's lower." Mamma didn't say a word. She hobbled over to the bed and patted it with both hands. She forced a smile, then lay down and closed her eyes. My heart was breaking. I felt so guilty.

Then Uncle Abeel turned to the children: "There is one bed left. It's up against this wall." He showed us how to pull it down. "I thought you two younger girls could sleep on it if you top and tail."

"We're used to sleeping like that in the house," Sara said.

Mamma opened her eyes and suggested Jack sleep with her so that he wouldn't feel left out.

Uncle Abeel then turned to Monica and me. "I'm afraid you two older girls will have to make do with the floor. There are some sleeping bags under the bunk beds." He showed us where they were.

"For you, Marie, there's a bed in the next room—it's small but I thought it would suit you and Ellie."

"That will do us fine," Marie said following him through to the other room.

Then Abeel lowered his voice, "There's going to be about a hundred and fifty people on board by the morning. That's why I brought you down here now so that you'll have a bit of peace. Constance and the rest of the family are staying in the basement of the fish market tonight. I will be leaving shortly but will be back at five o'clock in the morning and we sail at six prompt.

"One more thing, some of my men are staying on the boat tonight, so if you need anything, just look for Rufus or Marcus. They're brothers, two of my best men. They will see to all your needs. I've also arranged with the milkman to deliver ten churns of milk in the morning, so at least the children will have something to drink." As he was about to leave, he turned to look at us. "Try and get some rest. It will be a long day tomorrow. Goodnight all."

"Goodnight Uncle Abeel!" we all said with what little cheerfulness we could muster.

Monica and I took the children up to the top deck so that Mamma and Papa could be alone. The children thought it was great to be up at such a late hour.

"The separation must be tearing Mamma and Papa apart. Not knowing if they'll ever see each other again must be horrendous for both of them," I said in hushed tones.

"Oh, Rosina, what a mess all this is," said Monica who was near to tears.

"Don't cry, Monica. There's thousands like us. Do you know I can't express the hatred I feel towards this evil man, Hitler. How can he cause so much misery and hardship to so many people? I've never hated anyone in my life but I do now!" I realised that I was shouting.

Monica didn't know whether to laugh or cry. We had to try and think of the positive reasons why we were leaving our home.

Chapter Eleven
Departure, May 1940

At five o'clock in the morning, Uncle Abeel woke us.

"Good morning all. I hope you were able to get some rest." When Uncle Abeel reached the top of the stairs, he shouted down, "The milk has arrived, so if one of you would like to come and fill up the jugs."

We didn't tell Uncle Abeel but none of us had slept much, we were all shattered and the little ones were hungry. The washing facilities were inadequate: just a small boiler on one of the walls and already, I felt dirty—and we hadn't left Oostende yet.

"Will someone go upstairs and fetch the milk so we can all have our breakfast?" Mamma asked.

"We'll go," Monica and I said quickly. We couldn't wait to breathe in some fresh air because it felt so unhealthy and sickly down there. As we climbed the stairs, I could hear someone behind me. I glanced around and realised it was Mamma.

"Have you forgotten something?" I asked.

"Yes, it's suddenly dawned on me that Ada and her girls are not here. I hope she won't miss the boat." Mamma looked worried. Our Aunt Constance, who was heavily pregnant, and all my cousins had arrived but still there was no sign of my sister, Ada, and her little girls. Uncle Abeel brought down a folding bed for his wife, Constance. He managed to lay it out in the only walking space we had. The rest of their family had to sleep on the upper deck. It was just as well Monica and I were staying upstairs too.

"Look how many are on this boat?" I said, nudging Monica. "We won't all be able to sleep down there tonight even if we wanted to!"

We found some jugs and quickly filled them with milk. Before taking the jugs downstairs, Monica turned to me and said, "I'd rather stay up here tonight

67

than be overcrowded down there. I don't care how cold it is. We have our coats and scarfs with us."

"But we'll have to wait until Mamma and everyone else is asleep. I don't think she would let us stay up here otherwise," I replied.

"You're right about that," Monica agreed.

At six o'clock, the engine clunked reluctantly once or twice then seemed to take heart and settled into a steady throbbing.

"Mamma, come quickly. Papa's here, look, he's waving at us," I shouted. "I wish you were with us, Papa. I'm really going to miss you!" I called to him.

We stood on the top deck crying, shouting and waving all at once. The misery and pain mixed with an overwhelming sadness took my breath away. I just couldn't stand there and stare at Papa's lonely figure growing smaller and smaller until he eventually disappeared into the buildings. Not knowing if I'd ever see him again was too much so I walked away and slumped onto one of the boxes.

Ada and my nieces hadn't turned up and Mamma was frantic.

"Someone find Abeel! He's got to stop the boat! We must turn back!" She went looking for him but only found the skipper's mate.

"Please turn the boat around. My daughter and her two children should be here. Please turn back!" She pleaded.

"I'm sorry, madam, but we have a tight schedule to keep. There will be many more boats leaving Oostende today so she may get on one of them."

As the ropes and fenders were thrown aboard, our boat—the "Independence II"—dipped her way towards the open sea.

We left Mamma alone with her troubled thoughts. I couldn't begin to imagine what was going through her mind. Suddenly, she turned and said, "I can't bear the thought of Papa alone in the house. It's breaking my heart." She dried her eyes then slowly walked down the stairs. Halfway down, she stopped and turned to look at me.

"It may be a blessing in disguise, Rosina, that Ada hasn't turned up." These were my thoughts exactly, but I kept silent.

Once we were out of the defensive arm of the harbour, the wind stirred the sea and picked up the spray to scatter along the decks.

Marcus, one of the fishermen, shouted to Monica and me, "You better move from there. You're sure to get a soaking from the spray."

"We don't mind getting wet," we both laughed. It seemed like an adventure to us. As the propeller churned the wake into a white, tumbling froth we gazed in silence at the receding coastline of our beloved homeland. In the slowly appearing daylight, we began to notice other boats moving out of the harbour. Most people had fear in their hearts and a dread of the unknown future.

Captain Abeel Lokermans shouted above the noise of the engines, "Get the little ones down below! It's going to get stormy and I don't want any small children up on deck."

Monica and I didn't want to go below but we took the four younger children down and found some toys they had brought with them and some pencils and colouring books. After finding them a quiet corner, we left them there to play.

Mamma had fallen asleep on her bed so we both sneaked back upstairs and found some boxes to sit on near the stern of the boat. We wrapped our coats tightly around our bodies as the wind rocked the boat to and fro. "I'm so glad Mamma made us take our coats with us—it's freezing," I said.

"I know we couldn't have stayed on the deck without them," Monica replied.

We could hear people vomiting and children crying. Sara came back up to find us later as she wanted us to play with one of her games.

"I wish we had stayed at home. I don't like this boat!" she said.

I was caught by surprise as she had never mentioned anything about not wanting to go to England.

"Sara, look at me. Sara!" I spoke firmly.

She lifted her head slowly and she looked so sad. I could tell she was scared! I caught hold of her hands, "Look, once we get to England, things will be different—you wait and see. You'll be glad you left Oostende. Now, come on, let's play this game of yours." A fleeting smile swept over her face and I knew Sara would cope.

We stayed near the coast so it didn't look as if we were fleeing refugees. The day was cold and grey, with low rain-filled clouds which were as heavy as our hearts. It was difficult to relax and be positive with the fearful thoughts churning in my head. The younger children laughed and played. They thought it was fun to be going on holiday in a fishing boat. They weren't aware of the gravity of the situation, which was just as well. Once we were in England we would all be safe; at least that's what I kept telling myself.

I felt cold so I made my way down the stairs to the cabins to fetch a jumper to put under my coat but I stopped dead halfway down. I could hear Mamma; she must have woken up and she was talking to her sister Constance.

"I wish I hadn't agreed to do this. If Marie hadn't been so persuasive, I would never have left Oostende."

"Oh come now, Hanna. You must stay positive. You don't want the children to see you upset. Would you rather live under the Nazis? Because that's what will happen, there's no doubt about that?" Constance replied.

"No. of course not." Mamma lowered her voice, "I just can't see us settling in England and I don't feel well; my legs are so painfully swollen. I just don't want to be here. I'm missing Jakop already and the comforts of home." I could hear Mamma sniffling. I was sure she had been crying and I felt awful knowing how unhappy she was.

I climbed back up the stairs and said nothing.

Later Marie joined us on the top deck.

"How are you coping with the rough sea?" she smiled. I hadn't seen Marie this happy for a long, long time. It made me really angry with her.

"Well, at least someone is happy, Marie," I said looking at her sternly, "because Mamma isn't. I've just heard her crying to Aunt Constance, saying she is sorry she came and she wants to go home."

Marie thought for a moment. "Well, I'm not sorry and I don't think Mamma will be once we arrive in England," she retorted and walked back downstairs.

"Marie is only thinking of herself," I told Monica. By late afternoon we were all fed up. Monica and I were feeling bored; it felt like we had been on the boat for days! The rain had stopped and the clouds cleared to give some warmth from the early evening sun. At least that was something, I thought to myself.

We were all hungry. Mamma had made lots of sandwiches but they were dwindling fast. She opened some tins of meat and we devoured our food in seconds.

"My goodness, what's wrong with you children? The sea air must be giving you enormous appetites," Mamma laughed as she handed out apples and bananas. "We need to keep the rest of the sandwiches for tonight," she announced. I felt more relaxed, seeing her happier but Jack refused to eat anything.

When the Independence II neared Dieppe at about nine o'clock in the evening, the roar of sirens wailed and a German reconnaissance plane flew low across the town as darkness descended. We were all terrified that bombs were going to fall on us.

"Don't worry, there's no need to be afraid," Uncle Abeel shouted from the stern. "Alarms are sounding here all the time but nothing ever happens. Dieppe is a hospital harbour. There's never any bombing here."

Arrival in Dieppe

When the boat docked in Dieppe, we were all exhausted, physically and mentally. The little ones were fretful and hungry. Sara, Louisa and little Ellie wouldn't stop crying!

"I want to go home," Sara shouted.

"So do we!" the others shrieked. Jack just sat by Mamma. He was speechless and fear masked his little face. None of them understood why they were here.

With too little space and too many bodies, the stench mingled with the heat from the engine room made a disgusting smell. It was foul and I couldn't wait to go upstairs even though it was pitch black and there was no light anywhere.

Quite a few people left the boat and fled to the hills to sleep for the night. That meant we had more room for us. Mamma shuffled herself off the bed and started to organise our sleeping arrangements, which were pretty much the same as the night before.

"I can make room for Louisa to sleep in here," Marie called from the next room.

"No, Marie, leave the sleeping arrangements as they are," Mamma instructed.

Facilities were limited on the boat which was equipped solely for use as a fishing vessel but with Mamma in charge she soon made it comfy enough for us all to bed down for the night. Monica and I glanced at each other, knowing that we would sneak upstairs later as we'd planned, but first we needed to eat.

The following morning we all woke stiff and tired. No one expected to remain in Dieppe that day, but we did. That meant we had to leave the boat to find a café, even though we were instructed by the Port authorities to stay on board until the boat left for England. We weren't sure what the delay was but I knew we just couldn't stay on the boat all day. So we planned to leave the boat and tread French soil in two's and four's, trying all the time not to be too conspicuous.

71

"Mamma, we must go into town to find a café so we can have a hot meal," I insisted.

Everyone agreed to go except Mamma. She called Marie from the next room. "Marie, you, Monica and Rosina take the children and make sure they eat something warm. I'm not able to come with you as my ankles are too swollen—I need to rest them."

As we were leaving, Mamma called me back. "Rosina, try and make sure Jack eats something. He hasn't eaten since yesterday morning."

"I know, Mamma. We'll make sure he does. I'll also bring you something warm back."

"Don't worry about me," she said.

Marie was the first to leave. She took Ellie and Sara, and ran down the road; five minutes later Monica and I took the twins, Louisa and Jack. We ran as fast as we could. We noticed other people were doing the same as us.

I was worried for Jack as he was so timid and susceptible to illnesses and he was only six.

"We must make sure Jack has breakfast," I told my sisters. Marie and Monica agreed.

As we neared the town, we had all caught up with each other. People were staring at us. Someone shouted at us in French; we couldn't understand what they said but then we heard the word "German".

We found a café not very far from the harbour. It was empty so we all dived in and almost filled it. Marie made a point of telling the owner that we were from Belgium and not Germans and he seemed to be satisfied with that. We ordered lots of hot waffles with syrup which were delicious. Even Jack ate all his breakfast!

We left the café the same way as we left the boat. When we got back Mamma was happy to see us all fed and more like ourselves again.

We had brought some waffles and hot coffee in a paper cup for Mamma.

After lunch she went for a short walk with her sister Constance. She seemed to have difficulty walking but she had to get her legs moving as they were still swollen. This was our first day away and it worried me to see her like this already. She was going to try and make arrangements for all of us to go home, except for Marie, of course.

"I'm not going back to Oostende, Mamma!" Marie was adamant.

"We've come this far and I think the worst is over now. Living like this isn't ideal I know, but it's not for long. Tomorrow we'll be on our way to England. Surely you can stick it out until then?" Marie demanded.

Mamma was so annoyed with her. "No, Marie, I can't. The children are unhappy and Jack's not eating. I must have been out of my mind listening to you." Mamma's eyes were glazed and I could tell she was really upset. The situation was dreadful to say the least, with cramped conditions, no hot running water and the toilet facilities were of a very primitive kind. Little Jack had an upset tummy and had us constantly running to the nearest toilet with him.

About mid-afternoon, we could hear Mamma's raised voice, "Surely there is someone who could take us back to Oostende, Abeel? We can't stay on this boat any longer. You didn't tell us that we had to stay on the boat for this length of time. It's not fair to the children."

"Listen to me, Hanna. I don't think it's a good idea to go back to Oostende. The situation must be critical by now. There will be German soldiers everywhere. Do you want the children living amongst those soldiers?"

I crept halfway up the stairs to see what was going on.

"Hanna." Uncle Abeel lowered his voice and entwined his large weather beaten hands gently with Mamma's. "It won't be long before we'll be on our way to England and I'll organise a place of safety for you and the family. Try to persevere." As he was about to walk away, he turned to Mamma. "Hanna, I don't think you'll find anyone that will take you back to Oostende, not now."

Chapter Twelve
Disaster at Dieppe

We had another restless night. We ached all over and felt irritable. We were constantly woken by planes flying at low altitudes causing the little ones to scream and as soon as we settled them another plane would fly over. It was horrendous and very frightening. We all wanted to go home.

There was still no sign of the boat leaving so Mamma told us to go into town again and have a good breakfast. We planned to do the same routine as yesterday.

"There's not much food to go around and I'm afraid you'll all have to stay in the same clothes again today. We've used up all the clothes I put in the overnight bags and I can't get hold of the cases until we get to England," she said wearily.

I knew Mamma was upset at seeing her children so dishevelled. She had always prided herself in making sure we were well-dressed, clean and tidy. She sounded and looked worn out; I was so worried about her. I felt that, not only Marie, but Monica and I had also had a hand in forcing her to do something she really didn't want to do, which was to leave her own home.

On the way back from the café a reconnaissance plane flew over very low. We were really frightened and ran all the way back to the boat spilling the coffee we had brought for Mamma. We did manage to bring her something to eat. She was grateful for anything and she smiled as we gave her half a cup of coffee.

All through the day we noticed more and more ships arriving at Dieppe harbour. Not only fishing boats but state ships, Tilbury ships and packet boats, one of which was painted with the Red Cross and which was loaded with wounded people all waiting to leave for England.

Mamma felt uneasy seeing all these boats docked near ours.

"I don't like this one bit," she gasped, fearing the worst. "Why are there so many boats? Surely all these can't be waiting to go to England. What have I done?" Despair was evident in her fragile voice as she put her hands over her face and broke down sobbing. She turned away exhausted and stumbled back down to the lodgings. I'd never seen Mamma so upset; she was a wreck. We all followed her downstairs.

"This is a nightmare I'm so sorry for putting you through such a horrendous experience." She glanced up at each one of us.

"I should have listened to my heart not my head. I knew this was wrong." She started to cry again and shake her head back and forth. I looked at the little ones; their faces all had the same expression: fear! Their sad little eyes moist, their bodies trembling; I didn't know what to do first: try to reassure the children that everything would be alright or rush to Mamma's side.

I decided to try and comfort Mamma. With the situation becoming increasingly terrifying for us all, we needed her strength. We all relied on her to take charge and lead us out of this horrendous, chaotic situation. If she fell apart so would we!

"It's not your fault, Mamma. We're not alone; almost all of Oostende was living in fear and wanted to escape from the Nazis." I rounded up the children and motioned to Monica. "We'll take the children for a walk while we still have daylight. Why don't you lie down and try to rest, Mamma—you look worn out," I said.

Marie pulled me aside. "We can't all go together," she whispered.

"No, we can't. We'll do what we did this morning," I muttered.

As we put coats and wellies on the children, we could hear someone shouting at Uncle Abeel. I recognised the voice—it was Mr Henri. His children had been in the same school as me.

"Abeel, we assumed we would only be on this boat for one night. It's not fair to the children. What is keeping us in Dieppe? Two of my boys have been sick since we arrived here; they can't keep anything down. The sanitation on this boat is not suitable for children. It's disgraceful! Be honest, Abeel. When are we likely to be leaving for England? If you cannot give me a straight answer right now, I am taking my family off this boat and some way or other, I will try and find my way back to Oostende. I think I speak for everyone that has children on this boat."

"Yes, we are all fed up," someone shouted from the back. "There is no food on this boat and my children are starving, and in dirty clothes that they've been wearing for three days now. What is the hold-up, Abeel?"

About three or four voices from the back of the ship echoed these complaints.

Uncle Abeel sounded apologetic but firm with his answer: "Mr Henri, I apologise for the inconvenience this has caused you but, I did say that the journey wouldn't be easy. After all, this is a fishing boat not a ferry equipped for passengers. I was led to believe that my brother would have been here waiting for us yesterday. I don't know why he hasn't turned up. Please! I beg you, Mr Henri, do not leave the boat. Don't try to make your way back to Oostende, especially with the children. There will be German soldiers along every road from France to Belgium. It would be too dangerous. I promise you, we will be leaving for England tomorrow whether my brother is here or not."

Mr Henri had calmed down. "Do I have your word, Abeel?" Mr Henri begged.

"Yes, you do. I'm unable to wait any longer. We will be leaving on Tuesday, I promise."

"Okay, we will stay." Abeel shook Mr Henri's hand.

As he walked away, Abeel shouted, "We will be on our way to England this time tomorrow afternoon."

Everyone shouted, "Hooray!"

I continued to get the children ready. "Have you all got your coats and wellingtons on? There are some caves in the nearby cliffs. Would you like to see the caves?" I called to the younger ones.

"Yes please, Rosina," they all shouted, but Mamma was worried about us going that far.

"I don't think you should take the children to the caves, Rosina. It's too far," Mamma stressed.

"We'll be fine, Mamma, the children can't stay on the boat all day with nothing to do." And for an hour or two, we forgot about all our troubles.

We woke again the next morning feeling as if we hadn't slept all night. We were miserable and worn-out and felt as if we hadn't eaten for days, but at least we knew we were leaving for England that day. We had worn the same clothes for three days now. Monica and I felt really dirty and had no clean underwear. We knew all this was upsetting Mamma so we didn't complain.

We all went to the café again in twos and fours. Even though we were leaving that day, we didn't want to upset the French authorities. The little ones looked forward to the waffles and syrup. On the way back to the boat, we saw many more low-flying planes than usual. We grabbed the hands of the little ones and rushed back to the boat all together. We didn't care if we were told off by the authorities—we were leaving soon.

I felt very uneasy; that familiar dread I had experienced so often threatened to overwhelm me but I tried to keep strong and not say anything for the children's sake.

Mamma loved the hot steaming coffee we had bought her but wouldn't eat anything. She heaved herself up on to the bed and drank the coffee. A little later, about midday, we noticed many cannons and machine guns were being manned, on the forecastle of the larger ships and also on a few rooftops.

Mamma was frantic. "Look at that!" she exclaimed. "They've actually put a machine gun on the bow of that French fishing vessel right behind us. It looks like they're expecting something. Abeel shouldn't wait until four o'clock—we should leave right now."

Suddenly, a voice came over the loudspeaker: "We, the Port authority, prohibit the departure of any boat that is bound for England today. There are a multitude of magnetic mines that have just been deployed in the Channel. We order you not to leave."

Our boat lay near the front of the dock, ready to depart for England.

Right after we heard the message, Uncle Abeel stood on the bow and spoke to us all: "I know we've just been told not to try and leave but I'm going anyway. I'm just waiting for one of my engineers. He's gone into town to get more supplies for the journey to England. He shouldn't be too long."

We all went downstairs to the lodgings. It was almost four o'clock and we were expecting to hear the roar of the engine any minute. Mamma used up the last of the bread and jam and there was just a little bit of milk for each of us to drink.

"Rosina, will you go and look for Louisa's jumper, she's cold?" Mamma asked. "I think she left it on the upper deck."

I could hear the roar of planes above us but didn't think too much of it as we were all used to it by now.

As I reached the top of the ladder and stepped onto the deck, there was an almighty bang; it was a huge explosion and the whole boat shuddered. I was transfixed with horror. I couldn't think, but realised quickly that our boat had received a direct hit from a bomb dropped from one of the low-flying German planes. There was metal and wood flying everywhere! I had to cower down to stop myself from being hit.

I looked down the stairway I had just climbed and saw to my horror that the lodgings were completely flooded. I screamed uncontrollably and tried to make my way back to where Mamma and my brother and sisters all were but it was impossible.

The water was rising rapidly. The boat had almost split in half and the fore-part sank immediately. A fire had started on the other side of the boat.

I screamed and screamed, "Mamma! Mamma! Where are you, Mamma?" I tried to grab hold of the handrail which was attached to the ladder that connected the lodgings to the cookhouse, but the ladder collapsed with the force of the water.

I couldn't see any of my family.

The other half of the boat was still afloat but listing badly with flames reaching out. I crawled on my hands and knees to reach the top of the deck, grabbing anything I could hold on to, but it was almost impossible as the deck was so wet and slippery. All the boats around us were on fire and belching out thick black smoke. In no time at all the harbour was alight with red and orange flames spouting fearlessly to the skies. I was terrified that I was going to be burned to death.

I lay flat on my stomach and waited to die.

Suddenly, there was an abrupt jerk and I was thrown into the icy waters. I wanted to scream like a madwoman, but the water was so cold I lost my breath completely. I was gripped by a degree of horror I had never known or imagined. The water around me had turned black with oil and I could see bodies on fire.

It was an image of hell. I knew I was dying and everyone else with me. I screamed, "Mamma! Mamma! Where are you, Mamma? Help me!"

Over the chaos I could hear the shrill piercing screams of babies and children above the roar of the planes. I saw some women I recognised from the boat trying to keep their heads above the water. They had young children on their shoulders and were desperately trying to save them. I helped one of the women who was trying to keep her baby above the water but it was difficult to hold him up as the baby was struggling and hysterical.

We were all absolutely terrified and in the chaos, I don't know what happened to the baby. I was aware of someone beneath me; whoever it was grabbed hold of my legs with tiny hands, desperately trying to pull themselves up above the water, but by doing so they were pulling me down, deeper and deeper, until my head was below the water. My mouth tasted of salt and my throat burned. I thought I was going to die. I kicked and kicked to free myself from the hands that were undoubtedly pulling me down to my death!

Then I thought of my little sisters, Louisa, Sara or even my niece Ellie; did the hands belong to one of them? Had I kicked my sister to her death? I dived back under the water looking for them then I swam to the surface hoping to see them. I kept calling their names again and again, screaming as loud as I could.

"Oh, God, no!" It could have been little Jack's hands! I shouted his name over and over. I dived under again but there was no one I could see. The water was so filthy I found it difficult to see anything even as I swam to the surface.

Suddenly, I could hear an even more deafening noise. I wasn't sure what it was but as I struggled to lift my head up through the smoke filled skies I saw planes; they were diving towards us, dropping more bombs and firing their machine guns at the survivors floundering in the water.

I froze in complete horror! And waited to die. I did not know this level of evil and savagery existed. Only the mothers screaming, trying to protect their children, urged me to move to help a woman with a little girl who was screaming in terror and agony. I tried to lift the little girl onto her mother's back and wrap her arms around her mother's neck but I had no strength left and the effort was beyond me.

The planes were flying deliberately low hoping to kill everyone that still lived in the water. I dived under the water again and almost bumped into someone that I thought was Mamma. I tried to call out to her but I could make no sound. I kept diving under the water but every time I tried to grab hold of her she kept slipping away.

It was hopeless.

I dived under the water again. I saw Mamma again but her face was distorted and deathly white. She was lifeless, and her beautiful, long hair was flowing loosely all around her head and face. She looked wild, then suddenly, she was gone.

I swam to the surface to get air. Breathless, I tried to call out, "Don't leave me, Mamma, please, please, don't leave me!"

The oil had blurred my vision and my ears felt as if they were blocked and deafened. I reached out to death and waited to die. I couldn't stay afloat any longer; then I felt something touch my arm. I tried opening my eyes but they were hurting and stinging and I couldn't see. I spread my arms out to feel, and realised it was a long piece of wood. I grabbed it and threw the top half of my body over it. I don't know how long I held on. I was drifting in and out of consciousness. My body kept slipping off the wood and only my arms held me above the water. I could hear voices calling but couldn't make out where they were coming from. I kept trying to open my eyes but the pain was too severe. I stretched out one arm to feel my way. There were lifeless bodies floating everywhere and I became totally disorientated. I could no longer kick my legs or hold on to the wood. I was going under as once again I waited to die.

Then, something hit me on the head. It was a rope which I automatically grabbed hold of. I heard someone shouting, "Put the rope over your head." I couldn't see who it was, but the voice kept shouting to me: "Put the rope over your head and lift your arms. I've made a loop. Hold onto the rope."

He kept shouting at me and I somehow found the strength to lift my arms and put the rope around my waist, but by doing so, the wood floated away. I grabbed hold of the rope tightly as my life depended on it. I was dragged through the polluted water. I tried to keep my eyes and mouth closed but I still felt I was choking. Finally, I was being hauled up out of the water and on to the harbour's edge.

Chapter Thirteen
Confusion

I couldn't stand. My legs were so weak, I lay on the ground but I couldn't stop my body from shaking. I had never felt so cold.

Someone took the rope from me and started to dry my face. I noticed that I was wrapped in a blanket. Bombs were still falling all around and I felt the vibration of them. Terrified because my vision was still blurred, I called out, "Mamma, is that you? I thought you were dead. Oh, Mamma, Mamma! I'm so glad you're alive!"

"I'm not your Mamma! What boat were you on?" The voice was stern and unrecognisable. She kept asking me where I was from but I just burst out crying.

"Where is my Mamma and my family? Please, please, find them!"

The person spoke again, "What boat were you on?"

I tried to think but in all my confusion I screamed at her, "I don't know, I can't remember!"

Someone picked me up and put me on the back of an open lorry.

"Where are you taking me?" I screamed.

"To a clinic in the town," said the lorry driver.

"But I can't leave! My family is still in the harbour! I need to look for them." I tried to wriggle free and get off the lorry, but one of the soldiers held me down, there were a lot of other people on the lorry screaming wanting to get off.

"You must stay on lorry." His voice was harsh.

On the way to the clinic, my eye-sight improved slightly and my memory became clearer. I sobbed uncontrollably and through my tears I tried to explain. "I was on the Independence II. Please take me back to the harbour—my family are there," I begged but the soldier just shrugged his shoulders.

"It's too late. You must go to clinic. Someone will speak to you there. All boats, in harbour, been bombed."

I was hysterical as they took me into the clinic. I started to kick and tried to break loose from the strangers who were holding me down. And then I felt a sudden sting in my arm. I fought to keep awake but my eyelids grew heavy; I was spinning into a drug induced blackness.

Chapter Fourteen
The Clinic

For a moment, after I woke up as the effect of the drugs wore off, I thought I was at home in my own bed and it had all been a scary dream.

Then I saw someone standing over me, she introduced herself, "Bonjour, ma petite, je m'appelle Nurse Raphael. Comment allez-vous?"

I shouted at her, "I'm not French, I'm from Belgium."

She looked at me then put both her arms up in the air, shrugged her shoulders and walked away.

Later, when I felt a little stronger, I realised there was someone on the bottom of my bed but she was asleep. I slipped out of the bed hoping not to wake her. I couldn't believe how many people were in this one ward. The windows were draped in heavy dark blankets touching the floor. There were two to three people on every bed. It was difficult to see if any of my family had been admitted to the clinic. The only way I could find out was by walking around each bed in the hope of seeing a familiar face amongst the crowds.

It was absolutely horrendous: people were sobbing, some were vomiting, babies were crying in cots where no one seemed to be attending to them. As I came to the last bed, before the large main doors, there was a little girl lying on her side. She was crying pitifully. I couldn't see her face but I recognised the cry. She was sobbing into her pillow. I ran to the side of her bed and gently turned her over.

"Oh Sara, thank God, you're alive!" I cried. I held her in my arms. She was so distressed and was shaking and incoherent.

"I've hurt my shoulder, Rosina. I can't move it. It's so sore. I want Mamma, Rosina. Have you seen her?"

"No, not yet but try not to worry. Lie back down, Sara."

"The doctor said I am to stay in bed. Rosina, if you ask the doctor, maybe he will let us go to look for Mamma and the rest of our family."

"No Sara, we can't go looking for Mamma right now. Look at you, you're in no fit state to go looking for anyone."

"I'm okay, I just want to look for Mamma," she sobbed. I was trying to comfort her, when a doctor came to the bed.

"Do you know this child?" he asked.

"Yes, she's my sister. We were on the same boat when it was bombed, and we can't find any of our family."

"Well, your sister can't leave hospital just yet. She has dislocated her shoulder and I've had to put it back into place for her. She will be in great pain for a while. She has had a pain relief injection which will hopefully help her settle for the night. I'm Doctor Marc Mathias."

He shook my hand and he started to walk away but I called after him, "Doctor, is it possible for my sister and I to have some dry clothing. Our own clothes are wet and full of oil."

"Of course, I'll get one of the nurses to find something for you and your sister."

I cradled Sara in my arms and within minutes, she was asleep. I gently laid her down and covered her with a blanket. Then I went to look for more of my family.

I walked through some large wooden doors and down a long wide corridor to the other wards. There were so many injured people but I spotted the Doctor talking to a nurse.

When the nurse left, I walked over to him; "I'm sorry to bother you, Doctor, but I'm looking for my family. We were all on the same boat—" I started to tell him, but he raised his hand.

"Look, you're clearly very upset and the need to find your family is of utmost importance to you but as you can see for yourself, we've had many casualties today. It's impossible to know who's who. The only thing I can tell you to do, if you're feeling well enough, is to go round each ward and see if you recognise anyone, then come and find me." I thanked him but I could see he was rushed off his feet.

Sara and I stayed in the clinic for two days and during that time I searched every ward to see if I recognised a face, a voice, a cry.

When I came to the last ward, I noticed a little girl about Louisa's age and she had similar colouring. She was lying on her side. I could hear her whimpering. I ran over to her bed, hoping with all my heart it was Louisa. I gently turned the little girl on her back.

"Oh, I'm so sorry I thought you were someone else," I apologised.

She looked up at me. I'll never forget her little red eyes as she pleaded for me to find her Mamma.

"Have you seen my Mamma? I can't find her?" she said. I held her small little hands.

"No, I haven't, and I'm looking for my Mamma too," I replied. She began to cry. I stayed and held her little hands until a nurse came with one of her relatives but I don't think it was her Mamma.

I walked away, despondent and exhausted. My body ached and I longed for Mamma and the rest of my family.

"Where can they all be, surely all of them can't be dead," I muttered, but there were no answers to my questions. The nurses didn't have much patience or bedside manner with foreigners and I knew if I became hysterical, they would just inject me again so I kept as calm as I possibly could and answered their questions.

I couldn't eat or sleep, I just wanted to go back to the harbour to look for Mamma, but now I had Sara to consider.

The following morning, Sara and I were given a parcel of second-hand clothes, which didn't fit, and a dirty old coat each, then we were put on an open lorry, not knowing where we were going until a French soldier shouted to the driver, "This lorry is bound for Oostende. If you see a German patrol, drop them off and return."

Chapter Fifteen
The Return

We were with complete strangers. It was raining and cold. We found a space in a corner of the lorry. Sara laid her head on my lap and cried. An elderly lady came over and she put her hand on my shoulder.

"Are you two girls alright?" she asked.

"No, we're not. We have lost all our family!" I answered her. She looked frail and her eyes told many stories. She must have seen it all in the Great War and thought, *Not again*.

I tried to hold back my tears. I hadn't cried since finding Sara. I felt I had to be strong for her but now my tears fell unchecked. I couldn't tell her our horror. She put her arm around me and stayed by my side all the way back to Oostende. Neither of us spoke. I couldn't understand how we were the only ones who had survived. I kept going over it in my head.

"What about the little ones? Surely they weren't all dead and what about Mamma? Oh, Mamma, where are you?" I cried to myself.

We were stopped at a checkpoint on the Belgium border. The driver was told his lorry would be confiscated once he arrived at the docks and he would not be allowed to return to France. He pleaded with the German officer to allow him to return home but it was in vain. He was told to move on and we travelled slowly until we arrived at Oostende late in the evening.

I said my goodbyes to the kind stranger that held me through our nightmare journey. She was a gentle, elderly soul and I was so grateful for her quiet kindness to us.

"I hope this war won't be as bad as the last one." I said as I thanked her and squeezed her hand.

I began to walk away but she caught my hand and looked at me quizzically. "This may not be what you want to hear, my dear, but, if you should suffer a great loss through this pointless war, you will survive. There will be times when you will feel you cannot go on, when everyone is leaning on your strong shoulders and looking to you for guidance. Remember my words. You were saved for a purpose. I bid you goodbye and urge you to take care."

I kissed her on the cheek then walked away.

I looked up and, to my immense relief, I could see Papa and my sister Ada running towards us.

"Oh, Rosina, Sara, you are safe! Where's Mamma and your brother and sisters?" Papa held us both tight.

"I don't know," I cried. "I was separated from them and I couldn't find anyone. I don't know where they are, Papa. When the bomb hit the boat, I was on the top deck fetching Louisa's jumper!"

"Did a bomb actually hit the boat?"

"Yes, it was a direct hit and the boat split in half instantly. The next thing, I was thrown into the water. Oh, Papa, it was horrific. I thought I was going to die. I hate those Germans. Why did they do this to us, Papa? It's not fair. We've done nothing to them."

"Life isn't fair, Rosina," was all Papa could say.

For the first time since I found Sara in the hospital, she wanted to talk about the bombing. She looked at Papa, then me, and as her tears mingled with the falling rain which had just started, she spoke quietly: "I can't remember much but, what I do remember is the boat filling up quickly with water and Monica pulling me out. Because my shoulder was hurt I was taken to hospital in the town." Sara began to sob. "I couldn't see Mamma anywhere. What has happened to her, Rosina? I want her."

I wiped the tears from her cheeks. "I know you do, but we'll find her soon, I'm sure of it, Sara. Do you remember what happened to Monica? Did she manage to get off the boat herself?" I asked urgently.

"I don't know. I didn't see her after that. I was on my own and my shoulder was really hurting, it was awful."

Papa hugged her and said, "You don't have to say any more, Sara."

"Yes, Papa, we do," I interrupted. "We need to tell you everything, so that when you go to the authorities you'll know exactly what to tell them." I was close to tears but held them back.

"Let's get you both home out of the rain. I'm afraid we will have to walk home as there are no taxis anywhere; the German army has confiscated them all.

I came down to the harbour last night hoping to get some news, any news. I'm surprised you were allowed back in the country."

Papa crossed the road and we followed, walking back up the road we had walked so many times before but this time it felt so strange; nothing seemed real. I was walking in someone else's shoes. The clothes on my back were two sizes too big and the second-hand coat was so small with the sleeves only coming to my elbows. I tried to piece together the last few days, but with so much going on in my head I couldn't deal with it.

Maybe when I'm home, I will feel more relaxed, I told myself.

Poor Sara—her clothes were much too big for her; the coat was dragging on the ground which was now wet from the falling rain.

We walked past the gymnasium where the boards were still lying where they had fallen as we walked past on our way to the doomed boat. The two windows still looked like eyes and seemed to mock me as they followed me up the road, as if to say, "I warned you not to go." Everything seemed so unreal.

"We can talk in the morning when you've had a good night's sleep," Papa said.

"I don't want to sleep. I can't sleep, Papa. I haven't slept since it happened, only when they gave me a horrible injection. I need to stay awake, Papa." I knew if I closed my eyes I would relive the horror of it all.

"Don't you have any luggage?" Ada asked.

"No, we have nothing, only the clothes we're standing up in and even they are not ours and they're filthy! We've lost everything," I cried.

Ada wrapped her arms around me and said, "We'll find you both some clothes—don't you worry about that. Let's just get you home."

I dreaded going into the house.

"I'll put the coffee on and make you a sandwich," Ada said. She unlocked the door and went inside. Sara followed quickly behind her and went straight upstairs to be with her toys. We arrived home just in time as the rain was getting heavier and the night was closing in. I stepped into the kitchen and everything was just as we had left it: Mamma's cardigan was still lying over the back of her chair, her slippers were neatly sitting by the fire-place, waiting for her return.

Even the cup from which Mamma drained the last dregs of coffee was still in the sink with red lipstick smudged on the brim. I remember us both laughing over the colour of the red lipstick. I picked the cup up and put it in a paper bag that I had been given in France.

I will never wash this cup, I thought, realising I was acting as if Mamma was dead. I felt that we had been gone for months but in fact it was less than a week. So much had happened in that short time.

"Oh Papa, this is awful! Everywhere I look, I see something of Mamma's," I cried.

"Rosina, you're talking as if your poor Mamma is dead. Don't jump to conclusions, come and have a drink and something to eat," Papa said.

"I'll have a cup of coffee but I can't eat as I feel sick all the time. I can't put into words what it was like, Papa. I will never forget that day," I told him.

"Oostende has changed, Rosina. In the short time you have been away, a curfew has been put in place."

Papa explained that the curfew meant no one was allowed out after dark; the curtains were to be closed tightly so that no light was showing.

He went on to warn me, "You'll have to be very careful if you decide to go out in the evening, Rosina. In the short time the soldiers have been here, they've changed the time of the curfew three times without putting any notices up telling you of the changes. If they see you out, they can take you down to headquarters for disobeying orders. What they do down there I wouldn't like to say. The Germans have been here less than a week and life is not what it was." Papa rubbed his forehead with the back of his hand.

"Why must there be no light showing?" I asked.

"Because of air raids; any light showing increases the risk of bombing. We must make sure no light can ever be seen from any part of the house," Papa explained.

Mamma's sweet-smelling fragrance suddenly caught in my throat and I flopped on to her chair and buried my head in her cushion and cried until I could cry no more. My body ached, my hair smelled of oil and my eyes were blood-shot. I needed a bath but I couldn't care less—I was exhausted; it could wait until morning. I just wanted my family back home where they belonged.

I knew Papa was under tremendous pressure, he was hurting too but I had to ask, "Papa, can't you do something? Please Papa, try!" I saw he was sweating and he wiped his brow again.

"Rosina, you must calm down. When I heard on the wireless about the bombing all around that area, I hoped with all my heart that you were all in England by then, as you should have been. The following day, I went straight to the authorities to ask if they had any news of survivors in Dieppe. They told me it had nothing to do with them, as Dieppe was in France. I couldn't get any information.

"The civil servants were still in place at the municipal building but when I called yesterday it was closed. We can only hope it will re-open but it could very well be the army in charge as they've taken over everything else." He paused then sat down on the chair opposite me.

"Oh, Rosina, you won't recognise the place. Everyone is too frightened to say anything as there are German soldiers everywhere. I'll try again tomorrow when I go out to get some food for us. It's difficult to get certain food so I have to take whatever I can find. I think there will be rationing soon as there is talk of it already." He cradled his head in his hands and I could see he was worried about Mamma and my brother and sisters.

I tried to reassure him. "Maybe someone from Dieppe will contact us about the rest of the family Papa. They could be in different hospitals. It all depends if they have any injuries and if they're well enough to travel," I said, looking at Papa's sad face.

"I don't think so, Rosina. The Germans don't care if our family is alive or dead. No one will be allowed in or out of the country and while we're under occupation there will be soldiers at every border, watching who enters and who leaves."

"Well, how are we going to find out where they are Papa?" I said.

"We'll just have to be patient and hope and pray they are alive somewhere."

He got up to fetch coal from the bunker outside. It was then I noticed how hunched over he had become. So much had happened and he seemed to have aged ten years in such a short space of time.

He came back into the kitchen and put a small amount of coal on the fire. Then he said, "If I'm not here, don't use too much coal, especially during the day as we only have enough for a few days. I've only been lighting the fire in the late afternoon so that I had enough heating to cook some food and take the chill away in the evening. With you and Sara home now I'll light it earlier in the day. We have the summer months ahead so hopefully, we won't need to light it for so long. I haven't seen the coalman since the occupation."

I didn't know anything about rationing—only what Papa had told me from the last war. Papa explained that supplies were scarce so rationing had become stringent even at the start of the war.

"Oh, Papa, I wish we were all in England; we would be safe there."

It was very late when we finally fell into bed. Sara was out like a light and I thought I'd be able to sleep but I couldn't because I was afraid to close my eyes. Every time I tried, I saw Mamma's pallid face under the water, her staring eyes fixed, her hair flowing. It was awful. I tossed and turned all night, eventually falling asleep about six o'clock.

Sara woke me at seven. She went downstairs but I lay there thinking, wondering where they all were. And Marie! What had happened to her? She was the one that had wanted to leave Oostende. And Monica, what about her?

Sara had told us that she had pulled her out of the boat. Where was she now? Had the little ones survived? Hopefully, they were in a clinic somewhere, or in England.

I dragged myself out of bed, got dressed and went downstairs. Sara was sitting quietly in Mamma's chair with a faraway look in her eyes. Papa had made some coffee and I made sure Sara ate what was left of the bread. I still couldn't stomach anything.

Chapter Sixteen
Devastating News

We had only been home three days when there was a knock on our front door. Papa was dozing in the chair and Sara had been upstairs but was now in the kitchen.

"Maybe it's about Mamma?" she smiled.

"Hopefully it will be, Sara," I said and I squeezed her hand as Papa got up and went through to answer the door. I ran to the front window and I saw two men standing there. Papa opened the door and I immediately recognised their voices.

I went through to the hallway and said, "I know you two—we were on the same boat, weren't we? It's Marcus and Rufus, isn't it?"

Both nodded but there was trepidation behind their smiles.

Papa spoke first, "When did you boys get back?"

"Yesterday. We managed to get through at the Belgian border only because we work for the fishing industry and as luck had it we didn't lose our fishing license or our identity cards. It's just as well because we had no other way of proving who we were. We lost everything else. It would have made life very difficult for us if we hadn't had our papers."

I sensed some awkwardness between them as they glanced at one another.

Finally, Marcus said, "I am so sorry but we have come with some very sad news. There were casualties from the bombing in Dieppe." Marcus looked at Sara and me. "Your Mamma is dead. Only Monica, Jack and little Ellie survived."

I had lost Marie and little Louisa, baby Sebastian and his Mamma, Gabriella also. In fact, 21 members of my family perished on that dreadful day.

The tears were falling unchecked down Marcus' cheeks. We were stunned into silence. I didn't know if I had heard him correctly. My brain wouldn't couldn't—accept what we had just been told. We were just staring at him.

Then Sara began to scream, "No! No! It can't be true! Mamma's alive! She is, she is!"

I went to hug her but she pushed me away. She then stared at me.

"Rosina, you told me we would find Mamma alive and I believed you." She ran from the room screaming and sobbing.

Rufus then took up the conversation. He hesitated before saying,

"Casualties ran into thousands that day! I've never known anything like it. More than half the men from the fishing fleet lost their lives." He paused before continuing, "I have more news that may upset you more, Rosina." The strain in his voice matched the surge of sympathy in his eyes and it frightened me.

"What else, Rufus, could possibly be worse than what you've just told us?" I exclaimed. He caught hold of my hands across the table and squeezed them.

"Well, because of the situation, victims of war are buried as soon as possible. Your Mamma and sisters were buried the day after the bombing in the Municipal cemetery in Dieppe."

I gasped. The pounding in my heart was unbearable; my breathing came in short gasps; my arms felt heavy; I had pins and needles in my hands and I had no control of my body. I pulled away from Rufus and I felt so weak. The tears were running down my face.

Papa sat staring, not saying a word. Words weren't adequate to express the grief he felt.

I began to scream and scream, "How can I live with myself, knowing that I was actually in the clinic in Dieppe when Mamma and my sisters were dead and buried? The cemetery couldn't have been that far away surely? If only—"

Papa held his hand up. "You weren't to know, Rosina. There must have been hundreds buried that day."

"But at least I could have paid my respects, Papa, and said my goodbyes to Mamma. Now there's nothing, nothing at all—she was buried alone."

"No, Rosina your sisters would have been buried alongside her," Marcus whispered softly. He placed a glass of water into my trembling hands. Papa hadn't said much at all but he sat there nodding his head, agreeing with everything that was said.

Marcus continued but in hushed tones, "When the bomb hit the boat, Rufus and I were down in the engine room waiting for the order from Abeel. The water rose so quickly in the lodgings we could only manage to pull some children out. I don't know who they were."

I put my hands over my ears, crying, "This is too awful! I can't cope, it's too much to take in, too much to believe." I didn't want to hear anymore. Marcus came around to my side and held me. I was so confused, nothing made sense.

"There is some good news," Rufus almost whispered. "Monica, Jack and little Ellie sailed that same night to England with Abeel and Constance. They were all hoping to stay in London for a few days but after that, I don't know. The majority of people on the Independence II died, most of our friends are dead and the war has barely even started." Rufus shook his head in sorrow.

"Well, at least we know they are safe in England," I said in hushed tones. I was worried about Papa and how he would cope with losing his wife and children.

Rufus said to us, "Ada will have to be told soon. It's a mercy she missed the boat. She will be a tower of strength in the coming months."

"I'll go over and see Ada later," I told them.

I felt my strength returning and my hands had stopped trembling. I made Papa a strong cup of coffee and put quite a lot of whisky in it. I let the boys pour themselves a cup. I put both my arms around Papa's shoulders but said nothing— there was no point in talking; at this moment in time I just wanted to be near him.

"Drink it up, Papa, it will help you," I gently said. He glanced up at me, not really seeing me. His eyes were glazed, his face distorted with shock and disbelief.

"The enormity of the horrific events we've learned about today will stay with us for the rest of our lives. I don't think I will ever be able to rid myself of it," Papa said soberly.

I was worried about Sara and I was just about to go and see how she was, when Rufus said, "There is something else we need to discuss with you both."

I thought, *What else could there possibly be?*

"You know that Joseph is at sea and still doesn't know anything?"

"Oh no! In all the confusion, I had forgotten about Joseph. He will be expecting Mamma to be here as that was the last thing she said to him," I replied.

"His boat is due to dock in about two days, depending on the weather. We thought it would be better if he was in his own familiar surroundings, and we also thought it would be kinder for you to break the news to him," Rufus said.

"He will be so upset to think that Mamma went back on her word. I'm going to dread telling him, Papa!" I said as more tears fell down my cheeks.

Papa put his arm around me and spoke gently: "You leave Joseph to me, Rosina. I will tell him."

"We'll do it together, Papa."

Thoughts of that dreadful day began to fill my mind. Step by step my memory took me back to the moments before the bombing. I stared at each one of them sitting around the kitchen table. "Everything is suddenly clear. I was just at the top of the ladder. Mamma had asked me to get Louisa's jumper and that's when the bomb hit the boat. I didn't see anyone after that. Then there was the huge jolt and I was thrown into the water. If Mamma hadn't asked me to do that, I would have most probably died. Oh, this is too much to bear!" I cried. "I must go and see to Sara. Thank you for taking the time to call. It can't have been easy for you both to do this."

"No, it wasn't but we wanted to be the first to let you know. We didn't want you hearing it from strangers."

Both men agreed to stay with Papa while I went to check on Sara.

As I climbed the stairs to Sara's room, I could hear her muffled sobs. I sat on the bed and pulled her up on to my lap, taking great care of her painful shoulder.

"Why did Mamma have to die, Rosina?" she wept. Her little face was red and her eyes were swollen with sobbing.

"I can't answer you, Sara. Who knows why. I didn't expect this. I thought they would have been in a hospital somewhere in France but I do have some good news. Rufus has just told us that Monica, Jack and Ellie sailed that same night to England. That's good, isn't it?"

"I wish we could go to England, Rosina!" She looked so vulnerable and lost.

"It's too late for us, Sara. We wouldn't be allowed to leave the country, not while the German army is here. Sara, you must always remember I'm not going anywhere—just keep that in mind. I will also need your help to look after Papa. He's not only lost his wife but also his children. He's going to need our help and I can't do it on my own. Why don't you come downstairs and I'll make you something to eat?"

"Not yet, I don't feel like anything," she answered wearily.

I left Sara and slowly walked up to the attic. I could hear Marcus and Rufus talking to Papa. I needed to be on my own, to digest the full horror of what had happened. I now knew that I hadn't kicked Jack away to drown but, I thought of little Louisa. What had I done? That must have been her in the water. To think I kicked her away. I wanted to scream but I knew Sara would hear.

I tried to think back to when I was in the water, to the feel of little hands holding tight around my legs. For me to be able to free myself so quickly it must have been a child!

"Oh, Lord, forgive me. I didn't mean to kill anyone. I should have stayed below the water longer, searched harder. Sara, Ellie and Jack were saved. It must have been Louisa."

I pounded the pillow with my fists. I wanted to scream and shout.

How could I live with the memory of my little sister, knowing I might have killed her? I asked for God's forgiveness again and again for I knew I would never be able to forgive myself. "I am so sorry, Louisa," I whispered into the silence.

I must have fallen asleep because, when I woke the room was dark and for a moment I didn't know where I was. I jumped out of bed and ran to Sara's room to find it empty. I bolted down the stairs where Sara was sitting by Papa—both were asleep. I left them alone as they looked so peaceful, in our otherwise turbulent world.

I decided to go to Ada's and on my way, I realised I shouldn't be out in the dark.

This is going to take a great deal of getting used to, I told myself.

Ada was devastated to hear the sad news and my nieces were inconsolable; they both loved their Meme dearly.

In just a few days without Mamma, we found ourselves in such disorganised chaos that I didn't know where to start. I soon realised how efficient Mamma had been. If I should ever marry, I hoped I could be half the person she was.

My sister Ada called round every day and she was very supportive. I had never cooked a hot meal so Ada gave me some tips on the amount of food to cook, and how to put any leftovers we had in the pantry which was the coolest part of the house.

The most drastic change to my life, apart from the grieving, was making decisions and hoping they were the right ones. The running and organising of the home, practically and financially, was so daunting. I dreaded asking Papa for money to buy food and I hoped he would deal with that side of it.

I had to make sure Sara had adequate clothing as she had lost most of her own clothes during the bombing. I kept a watchful eye on Papa as I didn't want to overwhelm him because he had enough to cope with. I wanted him to know that my shoulder was there for him to lean on if the need should arise, and he was grateful for that.

"I can already see Mamma in you," Papa sighed.

When he went out to the shops, and Sara was upstairs, I took the opportunity to check every room to make sure there wasn't anything that needed sorting. I had no clue how Mamma ran the house.

The silence was unbearable. I saw visions of the little ones playing with their toys. Their laughter could be heard as it echoed throughout the house. One of Jack's toys, a sports car, was lying in a lonely corner.

"I'm going to leave this toy here, Rosina. Not because I don't like it but because I'm afraid I may lose it," Jack had whispered in my ear before we left to go to the boat.

Tears stung my eyes.

"How will he survive with a different language and only strangers to care for him? I'm so relieved Monica is with him and Ellie; at least they're alive," I told myself.

I picked Louisa's slippers up and held them against my chest. She had forgotten to take them with her and she was quite upset about it. I remember telling her, "Once we've settled in England, we will look for a shop that sells slippers."

She had looked up at me with one of her silly faces and said, "Do they sell slippers in England?"

I remember picking her up and laughing with her. "Of course, they do, slippers are sold throughout the world."

I will miss her dreadfully, I murmured to myself.

"Oh Lord, why did she have to die?" I would be asking myself that question until the day I died.

I dreaded going into Mamma's and Papa's room. I had purposely avoided their bedroom since I came back home.

As I opened the door, the first thing I noticed was the hollow dent in Mamma's pillow. I slowly climbed on to the bed and buried my head in it; my tears mingled with Mamma's scent; I was so overcome with grief.

I got up and left the hollow in the pillow. I thought maybe Papa would prefer to leave it as it was. As I left the room, I noticed a letter in an envelope addressed to Papa on the side of his bed. It looked as if it hadn't been opened. It was from Mamma. I left it where it was.

I made myself a cup of coffee and wondered how we were going to tell Joseph. He should be home any day now, weather permitting. Papa had only mentioned yesterday that he was dreading telling Joseph.

After arriving home from Dieppe, the thought of going out anywhere on my own terrified me; I was so frightened of the soldiers. Papa was doing the shopping at the moment but I would eventually have to pluck up the courage and do it myself.

One particular day, when Papa came back from the shops, he had a worried look on his face and I wondered what was wrong.

"I've just been to three of the shops that Mamma always went to. I had the shock of my life—there was hardly any food left because people are stocking up on everything. Already some of the shops are closed and boarded up. One of the shopkeepers told me that he had a supply of goods in today but he's not sure when he'll get any more deliveries. And the war has only just begun!" Papa said in despair.

He continued, "It's very worrying, Rosina. I hope this war won't last as long as the last one. Another thing—we must not light the fire in the morning, it will have to be lit late afternoon so that we have some heat to cook the food and have warmth for the evening. I have no idea when the coalman will call again."

The next day, Papa, Sara and I went to one of the Municipal buildings to register for identity cards with a photo attached, and for ration books. Renata, our next door neighbour, told us we should get them as soon as possible. I was dreading it—the thought of seeing German soldiers was frightening, but at least I had Papa and Sara with me. I tried hard not to show Sara how afraid I really was.

They asked us lots of questions about everyone in the house, even those no longer living there. They wanted to know who had died, how and when they died. We were in there for over an hour. We all had to have our photos taken. Sara was fed up and wanted to go home.

"You'll have to be patient, Sara. We must get this all done today," I told her.

After the lady had finished, she told us to call the next day to collect the identity cards, pouch and string.

"Tomorrow? That's quick," Papa said.

"Yes," the lady replied, "the local police are now under the control of the German forces and have been instructed to issue everyone with identity cards as a matter of urgency." The lady beckoned us to come closer and whispered, "Make sure you wear them at all times. If you don't, the soldiers could take you down to Gestapo headquarters for questioning and who knows where you could end up. Many people have gone missing since the invasion." She then told us that we would have to wait longer before being issued with ration cards.

Chapter Seventeen
Joseph's Homecoming

We had just sat down to our evening meal when the door burst open and in walked Joseph. We had been expecting him home any day, but now that he was here our hearts nearly stopped.

"I hope Mamma has some leftovers for me because I'm ravenous," he laughed as he flung his sack on to the chair.

I was so happy to see him but knew our happiness would be short-lived. Without saying a word, Papa jumped off his chair and held him so tightly I thought Joseph would burst.

"Oh, son! It's so good to see you. We weren't sure when to expect you because the weather has been so rough," Papa said.

Ignoring Papa, Joseph asked, "Where is everyone?" There was no reply from Papa. He just kept hugging him until finally he sat down and pushed his half eaten meal aside.

"Sit down, Joseph, I have something to tell you and it's very upsetting news." Papa cleared his throat. "I'm not sure, Son, if you heard about the heavy bombing in Dieppe," he said.

"Yes, we did. There was a message to get back to Oostende as soon as possible. I'm so glad Mamma didn't go. What about the rest of the family? Did they manage to escape to England?" Joseph pinched a piece of fish from Papa's plate. "I hope they're alright. Where's Mamma? Is she still at work?"

Papa was sweating. He wiped his brow with his handkerchief and I knew that he didn't know how to begin to tell Joseph the terrible truth. We all knew that in Joseph's eyes there was no one quite like Mamma; he worshipped the ground she walked on.

Finally, Papa spoke: "As I just said, I have some terrible news to tell you, son. There was heavy bombing in Dieppe." Papa hesitated then took a deep breath. "Your Mamma changed her mind at the last minute and decided to go to England with the rest of the family. She left a letter for you asking you to follow on if you were able to. There was a direct hit on the boat they were in, while it was docked in Dieppe harbour and a lot of people died."

I watched in horror as my happy-go-lucky brother's face was gripped by fear.

"Your Mamma, Marie and Louisa were all killed during the bombing," Papa choked.

Joseph turned deathly white and I thought he was going to keel over.

Suddenly, he ran out of the back door and began to vomit outside. I got to him as quickly as I could. He was trying to talk and heaving at the same time. It was awful seeing him like that. I kept wiping his forehead with a wet flannel. He came back into the kitchen but wouldn't sit down; he just kept walking and mumbling to himself,

"It can't be Mamma, it can't be!" He kept saying it over and over again and then he dropped down on to the chair. "She promised me she wouldn't go. Why did she change her mind?" he cried.

"Joseph, we all persuaded Mamma to go and she didn't want the younger children to go without her. That's why she went, "Papa said gently. "Mamma left you a letter to explain why she changed her mind."

Papa knelt down by his side and put his arm around his son's shoulder. He was sweating profusely. "Joseph, a lot of people died that day; twenty-one of our own relatives lost their lives during the bombing. It's been awful here this last week."

Joseph wiped his eyes with the back of his hand. "I remember seeing a lot of planes going over but I never thought anything of it at the time."

Papa sat back down on his chair.

"Joseph. Mamma and you're brother and sisters: sailed on the eighteenth, you would never have made it back in time. She felt very guilty that she was changing what she had told you but she couldn't let the little ones go to England without her; she had to put their wellbeing first."

Joseph was barely listening to us. He got to his feet and said, "I must go to Dieppe and see for myself. You could be wrong. She may be in a hospital somewhere in France."

Papa sat him back down on his chair. "Listen to me, Joseph. Mamma and your sisters were buried in the Municipal cemetery in Dieppe the day after the bombing. Gabriel and her baby son were buried there too. Please, please, Joseph, do not try and go to Dieppe. It's a crazy idea. You'll never make it," Papa pleaded.

"But you could be wrong, Papa. You didn't witness the burial so how can you say that?" Joseph cried.

"He has a point, Papa," I whispered but I could see he was annoyed with me.

There was no talking to Joseph any more. He just wouldn't believe us; his mind was made up. He kept shaking his head in disbelief and you could see his heart was broken as he sobbed for Mamma.

Papa made him a cup of hot cocoa and added some brandy.

"There, drink this, son." I think Papa was hoping it would make him sleepy as Joseph wasn't used to alcohol. Slowly, his eyelids grew heavier and heavier with the sheer exhaustion of just having received such devastating news. Finally his chin rested on his chest. He kept mumbling and calling for Mamma. Papa and I almost carried him into the bedroom where we laid him on the bed and covered him with a blanket.

"I hope he'll sleep all night, Papa, but I dread to think how he'll be in the morning," I whispered.

"We'll deal with that when morning comes." Papa was so matter of fact and sensible but Sara was very upset at seeing her brother so distraught.

"Will he be alright tomorrow, Rosina? I don't like seeing my brother upset. I hope he won't try and go to Dieppe. There's not many of us left now." She was near to tears herself.

"Oh, you poor thing," I said as I gave her a big hug. "Try not to worry too much about Joseph. I'm sure by the morning he will have had a change of heart."

The following morning I woke to the sound of someone banging on our back door. I jumped out of bed, my heart pounding. The knocking got louder and louder. I looked at the time and saw it was only six-o-clock. Who on earth could be knocking so early? I wrapped my dressing gown around me and ran down the stairs just as Papa was coming down from the attic.

"Don't you answer it Rosina. It could be the soldiers."

As Papa went to unlock the door, Renata, our next door neighbour, pushed it open and stumbled into the kitchen.

"I'm so sorry for disturbing you but is Joseph home from sea?" Renata asked.

"Yes he is," Papa said looking annoyed. "You've woken us up just to know if Joseph is home? He's in bed. He came home last night."

She glanced at us both then said, "Joseph is not in bed—at least I don't think he is."

"What do you mean he's not in bed? Where else would he be?" Papa asked, irritated by Renata.

I didn't like the way this was going. I ran to the room that Joseph was sleeping in. It was pitch dark; the curtains were tightly shut and a dark blanket was draped over them. I switched on the light and there on the bed, instead of Joseph, was a letter. I screamed for Papa: "Come quickly! Joseph isn't here; he's left you a note!"

Papa came running into the bedroom with Renata following behind. I handed him the letter and we read it together:

Dear Papa,

I'm sorry to do this to you but I must go to Dieppe to see for myself if Mamma is alive. I cannot believe she is dead. Papa, I've borrowed your bike. I promise to bring it back in one piece.

Love to you all,
Joseph.

Papa ran his fingers through his hair. "What a foolish boy! How did he think he could cycle to Dieppe? There are soldiers everywhere in the cities and towns. There will be patrols on all the country lanes and roads." Papa sat down and buried his head in his hands. I felt terribly sorry for him, so much had happened to our family.

"Joseph is being very selfish. I'm so annoyed with him, Papa," I said.

"Don't be, Rosina, He's had a terrible shock hearing of his Mamma's death. You know how close he was to Mamma."

"Well, we all were, Papa. Look what Sara and I have gone through. It's just as bad for us."

Renata went to sit on one of the chairs. She was pale and her hands were shaking. I thought she was going to collapse. Something told me this was only the beginning and there was worse to come. Papa had built the fire up and I put the coffee to percolate on top of it.

"Are you alright, Renata?" I asked, but she ignored me.

Then she stood up again and said, "I have something to show you both; it's outside."

Papa and I glanced at one another. He opened the door and instantly his colour drained and he leaned against the wall. I went to look.

"Oh no! This is your bike, Papa, but where is Joseph? Look at the state it's in!" I exclaimed.

"Where did you find the bike, Renata?" Papa asked in a stony voice. I knew that he was desperately trying not to fall apart.

"I was on my way to morning mass when I found the bike on the footpath. It looked like something heavy had run over it. I didn't think much of it until I found this near the bike." She handed Papa a small white card from the fishing industry with Joseph's name on it. Papa leaned back against the wall, his face grey with shock and worry.

"He must have lost it while trying to get away from the soldiers. They must have him, Papa!" I cried.

"We don't know that yet, Rosina," Papa replied.

"How can you say that? We more or less have the proof." I was exasperated by Papa because I wanted to go and look for Joseph immediately. "He could still be up in the fields hiding. Why don't we go and look, Papa?"

"Calm down, Rosina. We are not going to get anywhere if you carry on like you are," he said.

"I don't know how you can be so calm," I shouted.

"Well, one of us has to be," Papa answered.

"What other reasons could there be? The soldiers must have been chasing him and ran over his bike. I hope he's not lying somewhere injured," I said with a rising panic in my voice.

Renata wrapped her hands around the cup of coffee I had just given her. She looked awful.

"I looked around the fields but I didn't see anything else of Joseph's. I couldn't go to morning mass after seeing your bike twisted and mangled. I had to come home," Renata said, expressing her anxiety.

She had been there when Joseph was born. She had held him first while the nurse saw to Mamma and because of this she had always felt close to Joseph.

"What are we going to do? Who can help us, Papa?" I realised there in the light of day, there was no one to turn to, no one that could help us. It was the same feeling of helplessness I had before we knew that Mamma and my sisters had died.

We couldn't seek advice. We couldn't go to the police; they were now working under direct control of the German Commandant so it would be a waste of time going to them.

"It's only now I'm beginning to realise how isolated we are, Papa, and I feel so vulnerable. We are on our own. How can you be so calm, Papa?" I said, raising my voice in annoyance.

"I'm anything but calm, Rosina, but we must think where they could have taken him," Papa said puffing on his pipe. "When the bombing happened in Dieppe, I went into the Municipal Offices to see if there was any news about missing persons. As I told you before, they just said because it happened in France there was nothing they could do."

"Well, Papa, this has happened in our own country, so maybe they will be able to help." I knew I was clutching at straws.

Papa put his shoes and coat on. "I'm going to walk up to the playing fields now. The grass has been overgrown since the invasion and Joseph could be hiding somewhere up there."

"Be careful, Papa. If the soldiers see you looking around, they may take you away. I'll come with you."

"No—I'd rather you stay here for when Sara wakes but don't say anything about Joseph yet. Sara can stay with Ada while we go down to the offices." He continued, "Thank you, Renata, for your quick response to Joseph's disappearance. We're sorry for any abruptness that occurred earlier," Papa said.

"No need to apologise. It's very understandable that you are so upset," Renata replied.

Papa and I hugged her before she left and promised we would tell her as soon as we had any information about Joseph.

Papa looked weary and tired and the fresh lines of worry across his forehead accentuated his already deeply scarred brow.

"We don't know what's happened to him, Rosina, or where they've taken him. I have a bad feeling about this. He's a young, healthy boy; he could have been captured and then sent anywhere: to do their dirty work," Papa stressed.

Papa left to search the fields, but when he returned he had no news.

Sara kept asking for Joseph. "Where is he? And why is Papa whispering to you?" she asked with fear in her voice.

"Joseph has gone for a walk to clear his head," I told her.

"Why has Joseph got to clear his head?" she said.

"Because of the brandy Papa gave him last night," I lied.

Sara had always been inquisitive and I loved her for it, but not today. I persuaded her to stay with Ada as I didn't want her to witness what we had to do today. We would have to tell her eventually but not yet.

I told Ada that we were trying to find out where Joseph was and that I would let her know of any new developments but, not to tell Sara. I would tell them both everything when I got back.

As we set off for the Municipal Offices, I hung on to Papa's arm and said, "I'm worried that the soldiers will stop and search us, Papa.

"Don't worry, Rosina. We have nothing to hide. Stay close. You're not alone."

I could tell he was very anxious about Joseph. "I'm not expecting much information from this office," he said with a grim look. As we got nearer to the building, we saw two military policemen with guns strapped to their shoulders, they stood either side of two wooden doors, on one of the doors there was a notice which read. CLOSED.

"It looks like the office is closed, Papa, shall we go now." I felt so nervous, as I held on to him:

"Don't be afraid, Rosina, just stay by my side.

"The police are not like our police?" I murmured.

"No, they are not." Papa replied.

"Is this building closed?" Papa asked one of the Military police.

Ignoring Papa's question, the policeman said: "You have identification papers?" Papa went to take the papers out of his inside jacket pocket but the policeman forcibly pulled Papa's hand away and he took the identity papers out himself. He looked at us both then at the photos and handed them back to Papa.

Papa asked again. "Is this building closed?"

The other policeman came right up to Papa's face. I began to shake, my teeth were chattering, I hoped he couldn't hear me. "Can't you read, old man? Yes, it's closed, on your way, you pathetic old fool!"

"Oh Papa, that was scary, I thought he was going to hit you." I said, alarmed at Papa's calmness.

"Well, if I don't ask, I won't know. There's nowhere else I can think of where we can seek help or advice." He sounded so disheartened.

"Where do we begin to look for Joseph?" I asked anxiously.

"Rosina, you leave the searching for Joseph to me. I think I'll take a stroll around some of the streets now that I'm down in the town. Some of the cafés may have word on young boys being snatched off the road."

"Is that what you think, Papa? Joseph has been snatched by the soldiers?" I said, trying to hide my fear.

"Yes, with regret I do believe that. But you never know; someone may have seen him. Anyway, you have enough to do in the house," Papa announced.

"Well, that's put me in my place," I said to try and lighten the mood. "If I wasn't in Mamma's shoes before, I certainly am now."

Papa offered to walk me home before renewing his efforts to find Joseph. But just before he left, I reminded him that I needed some money to buy food.

"Of course, I keep forgetting the financial responsibility lies with me, sorry Rosina."

When Papa left, I did feel slightly vulnerable and nervous walking up the road; this was the first time I had ventured out on my own. I called in to Mr Oscar at the butcher's shop to see if he had some veal for our tea. Papa said that was the cheapest meat to buy.

"How are you, Rosina? I'm so sorry to hear of your dreadful loss," he whispered.

"Thank you, Mr Oscar," I replied. I asked for some veal. He went into the back of the shop and brought out a small bag of food.

"Look, I've put some butter, eggs, meat and three potatoes in this bag, and as I'm selling milk now, I've put a small container in as well. Mr Nys has finished with the milk round as he is too old now."

"But, Mr Oscar, I can't pay you for all this. I just came in to see if you had some cheap veal."

"I don't want any money. Your Mamma was one of my best customers. If she couldn't pay on the day then I knew that by the end of the week my money was safe. I'll miss her too, Rosina. She was a lovely woman and honest to the core."

I couldn't hold back the tears as I blurted out, "Oh, Mr Oscar, something terrible has happened to Joseph as well! We think the soldiers grabbed him this morning and have taken him to the labour camps in Germany." I wiped my eyes with the back of my hand as I continued, "We may never see him again." The thought of never seeing Joseph again made me weep even more.

"You must have faith, Rosina. I know of some boys that went missing and were found a few days later, safe and well. Let's hope the same will happen to Joseph." Mr Oscar gave me a hug. "Mind how you go now and hold on to that food."

"I will and thank you, Mr Oscar, for everything." I gave him a peck on the cheek. Then I made my way home, holding my food parcel tightly inside my coat. I was hoping I wouldn't see any soldiers but as I turned the corner into our street, I was horrified to see three soldiers abusing a young girl who was in the middle of them; they had ripped her coat off and she was hysterical.

One of the soldiers grabbed her hair and pulled her head right back, shouting at her in German.

Suddenly, I recognised her. It was Colet, an acquaintance from the gymnasium.

"Colet, are you alright?" I shouted. "Leave her alone!" As I ran across the road, the one that was holding her hair let go and turned towards me.

"Rosina, you go!" Colet shouted. "I'm alright. Please go, Rosina!"

"I'm not leaving you with these hooligans who are nothing but school kids disguised as soldiers!" I screamed. I had had enough of Nazis for one day. I knew I had said too much but I didn't care.

The soldier pushed Colet away as he came towards me. He must have been over six-foot tall with a face you'd never forget. He was terrifying and I was shaking from head to foot. He stood in front of me with his hands on his rifle and shouted, "Was hast du gesagt?"

I didn't understand a word, and I was determined not to let my fear show, even though I didn't come up to his shoulders. Another of the soldiers shouted, "He asked you what you said!"

I shouted, "Why are you picking on young girls? You are all cowards. Isn't it enough you have our country!"

I thought he was going to strike me but instead, he ripped the buttons off my jacket. I jumped and all the food fell to the ground. His eyes widened as he looked at me then waved to the other soldiers to come. I deliberately stood on the eggs and managed to kick the rest of the food away before he pushed me aside.

"Where did all this food come from?" he said with menace in his voice. I didn't answer. "I will ask you again. Where did all this food come from?" he screeched.

I jumped again with fright. I tried to hold back the tears as I wasn't going to give him the satisfaction of seeing me cry.

"The butcher gave it to me as we have no food," I replied.

"You lie, I don't believe you! You stole this food. I will take this food or I will take you to Gestapo headquarters."

I had heard of the Gestapo; they used brutal force and I wasn't about to let them use it on me.

"Take the food! Take all of it," I cried and I tried to kick the rest of the food further away but he stood in front of me.

With contempt in his voice, he sneered, "If I catch you stealing food again, I will take you to Gestapo headquarters and beat you myself. Do you understand?"

"I understand but I didn't steal any food," I shouted.

They picked up what was left of the food and scornfully laughed as they raised their arms and shouted, "Heil Hitler!"

Colet and I leaned against the wall and breathed a shaky sigh of relief. "Thank goodness they're gone. Are you alright, Colet?" I asked as I helped her put her jacket back on. Her hair was dishevelled and she was deathly white.

"We'll stay here for a few minutes, to make sure they've gone out of sight. You don't want your Mamma to see you so upset," I told her.

"I know she will never let me out of her sight again. She doesn't trust the soldiers and some of them look very young," Colet said.

"That's what Papa said too," I answered.

"I thought they were going to strip search me, Rosina. I was so frightened. I don't know what would have happened if you hadn't come then. They kept shouting at me for more food. I only had one small loaf of bread. I'm sorry to get you involved, but I am so grateful that you turned up at the right time. Thank you, Rosina. I do feel awful that you've lost all your food," she said.

"Yes, that was all the food we had in the world. I didn't think life could get any worse." My tears fell fast and furious. There on the main road, I cried for Mamma, my sisters and now my brother. I explained to Colet, briefly, what had happened to Joseph.

"Oh come here. You've had such an ordeal." Colet hugged me tight. "Come back to our house and we'll share our food with you. It's the least I can do. Then Mamma and I will take you home. We haven't heard anything about where my Papa is either and we don't know if he is alive or a prisoner of war."

"I understand what you're going through. This wretched war is tearing at the hearts of all of us. It must be torturous for you, not knowing if your Papa is alive or dead," I sympathised.

"It is," Colet confided. "I often hear Mamma crying in her bedroom and there's nothing I can do to help."

"I know that feeling," I replied.

As we walked up the street to Colet's house, she confessed, "I'm sorry about what happened in the gymnasium. Sophie was always jealous of you."

"Past differences are gone and buried, Colet. A lot has happened since then. I try not to dwell on the past," I replied.

"Neither do I," Colet agreed.

When we arrived at Colet's house, she told her mother a watered-down version of what had happened to us but she couldn't hold back the tears and that started me off. Her Mamma reached out and held us both.

"Rosina, I'm so sorry about your family. It must be very difficult for you having to cope with everything and this awful war. Anytime you need a chat, Colet and I are here; just remember that."

They gave me some butter, bread and cheese. I was grateful for the little amount I was given and thanked them before they walked me back home.

"Rosina, why don't we meet up sometime. Maybe we could go to the picture house if it reopens again," Colet said, seeming eager to be my friend.

"Yes, maybe—I'll be in touch." I turned the key in the lock and said my goodbyes.

Arriving home, I couldn't wait to close the door on the world. I slid down on to the floor and sobbed and sobbed; I thought I'd never stop. Eventually, I picked myself up and put the food in the pantry, then tried to wash away any evidence of the horrible day and the fear of what lay ahead for us.

Suddenly, the back door swung open and in walked Ada and Sara.

"Where have you been, Rosina, I've been waiting for you?" Sara said. She seemed very agitated. I then realised I should have picked her up from Ada's.

I sat her down on the chair and then put the coffee on for Ada and me. "I have something to tell you both. This morning, Sara, when I told you Joseph had gone for a walk, that wasn't exactly true."

"So you lied to me, Rosina," Sara said crossly.

"Yes, but I will explain everything to you both—just bear with me." I poured Ada and myself a cup of coffee.

"Where's Papa?" Sara asked.

"Just wait a minute, Sara. Don't be so impatient. During the night, Joseph left the house. He took Papa's bike and thought he could cycle to Dieppe."

Ada gasped, then made the sign of the cross. "Oh Lord, what a silly boy," she said.

I told them how Renata had been the one to alert us that Joseph was missing and that Papa was in the process of trying to find him.

"Why did Joseph think he could cycle all the way to Dieppe?" Ada shook her head in disbelief.

"Joseph couldn't believe that Mamma was dead. He wanted to go to Dieppe last night to see for himself. It's only because Papa put some brandy in his cocoa, that he fell asleep and didn't leave last night. You know what he's like when he gets something in his head he cannot let it go," I answered.

"There was no one like Mamma to Joseph," Ada said.

"I hope Papa finds him, Rosina. There's only you and me now," said Sara, her lips quivering.

"Oh, Sara, my darling, don't expect too much. It's war time; life is nothing like it used to be," I warned her.

"Well, what can we do, Rosina?" Her voice was barely a whisper.

"We'll keep looking for Joseph. That's all we can do, Sara," I replied, trying to sound confident.

When Sara went upstairs to her bedroom, I shut the door and said to Ada, "I didn't want to say too much in front of Sara. But Papa seems to think young boys are being snatched off the streets and taken to the labour camps in Germany. We may never see him again.

"Oh Lord!" Ada said putting both hands over her face to silence her sobs. "He's just a young lad; only sixteen years old!" Ada broke down and cried.

"I don't think he could survive in those camps," I whispered.

After Ada left, I climbed the stairs to the attic bedroom, hoping I could relax and close my eyes just for a while, but every time I did, the horror of Dieppe flashed before me. I must have dropped off because, the next thing I knew, Papa was waking me up.

"Rosina, are you ill? It's not like you to go to bed in the middle of the day." I could hear the anxiety in his voice.

"No, Papa, I'm not ill—just very tired. I didn't think I'd fall asleep but I must have. I'll come down now. Have you heard any news about Joseph?"

He looked weary and he could hardly walk. He was really suffering; the anguished look on his face showed his distress. He shook his head. He didn't offer any information and I didn't ask any more.

"I don't feel like anything to eat, Rosina. I think I'll have an early night," Papa said.

"Shall I make you some hot cocoa?" I asked.

"No, not just yet. Maybe later. I feel so helpless, Rosina."

I decided not to tell Papa about what had happened to me on my way home from the butchers; there was no point in burdening him with more heartache. I couldn't accept that I would never see Joseph again, even though all the evidence pointed to that. *I must be positive*, I told myself. The thought of the soldiers beating him was unbearable. If Mamma was here, she would have gone crazy with worry. He was just an innocent young lad who loved the sea.

Chapter Eighteen
The Occupation

At the beginning of the invasion, everyone was ordered to hand in their wireless sets. Papa handed in the larger of the two we had and hid the smaller one down in the basement, but we had to keep the volume turned down very low, for fear of the soldiers hearing it. We all looked forward to listening to Big Ben in London every hour. We were trying to keep believing that soon the war would be over and there would be peace on this side of the Channel. Our English, that we had learned at school, was really tested but improved as time went on.

Sara was growing out of the clothes that she had left behind when we set off for England. She had insisted on taking her two new dresses that Mamma had made for her. It upset her to think they were now at the bottom of the ocean. We had no money to buy clothes so I sifted through Mamma's, Marie's and little Louisa's remaining clothing, hoping to salvage what I could and turn rags to riches.

Mamma had taught me to sew at a young age but, I had never cut out patterns for skirts and dresses. I wanted to make something special for Sara but without her knowing. I thought it would keep me busy which would be good therapy for me. As I began to cut through one of Mamma's skirts, I had this incredible longing to see Mamma just one more time, to tell her that although I was struggling, I would do my very best to look after Papa and Sara.

When I thought of the future, it was without her in it. If I should marry and have a baby, it would be without her there to help me. A future without Mamma broke my heart.

Since the occupation, whatever was broken, smashed or ripped had to be repaired time and time again and if it couldn't be repaired then it was thrown out with no hope of a replacement. In a matter of weeks my life was moving in directions I wasn't familiar with. I was literally thrown into being a responsible grown up.

The newspapers had started publishing again but there was little of interest for the Belgian people, only information about coupon exchange. Colet and I often met up to go for a walk or, if I could scrape some money together, we would go to the picture house. Because the curfew varied from day to day, we had to be extra cautious when out in the evenings. It was when we were out one evening that we hatched our plan to look for work. We had heard rumours that some of the hotels near the beach had vacancies. They were looking for cleaners and waitresses. Colet and I had interviews for cleaning jobs and we were both accepted.

"I dread to think how Papa will react," I told Colet.

"He was hoping I would go to college in October to do dressmaking. I most probably would have if Mamma was alive. But the gymnasium was my first passion; if it hadn't closed, I would have worked really hard at becoming a first-class gymnast."

"You were very good too, Rosina," Colet smiled.

"Well, it's all in the past now and that's where it has to stay."

"I agree," Colet murmured.

When I got home, I announced, "Papa, I've found a job." I thought I might as well come straight out with it.

"You've what?" he shouted.

"Don't be annoyed, Papa, be happy for me. We need the money," I answered him.

"How on earth did you find a job with a war going on and more to the point, where is this job?" His look of suspicion told me this wasn't going to be easy.

"It's in a hotel down by the beach," I said.

His look was enough. "No daughter of mine is going to work in a hotel where the Nazi soldiers stay. Do you hear me, Rosina?"

"Stop raising your voice, Papa," I pleaded.

"I'll stop shouting when you go back down to this hotel and tell the manager you can't work for him. What about college in October? You told Mamma you wanted to become a dressmaker?"

"Oh, Papa! Life is not the same now as it was when Mamma was alive. I may have gone to college but the war has changed everything. We have no money and I'm fourteen now and quite able to work.

"Anyway, you know Mamma taught me how to sew when I was only six, I don't need to go to college for that. Colet is starting with me so I won't be on my own. You forget, Papa, Sara and I lost almost all our clothing in Dieppe and Sara's growing fast. We have no money left over each week and it's better that I go out to work than you, as there is more work available for me. Please don't spoil this for me now. I've made up my mind."

My determination seemed to silence Papa into a reluctant acceptance that I had entered adulthood; it was earlier than either of us would have wanted but I knew it was necessary if I wanted to support my family.

We were one step away from Winter of 1940 and already the coal situation was worrying me. If we didn't light the fire, we couldn't have a hot meal. We were trying to save as much coal as we could for the winter months but there were days when the house was really cold and we had to light a small fire late afternoon.

"Papa, if we're feeling the cold now, I dread to think what the winter months are going to be like," I said.

"Well, I was thinking the same thing, Rosina," he replied. Papa was standing in front of the fire, deep in thought. "If I keep the ash in the shed instead of throwing it out onto the wet ground, then we will only need to use a small amount of coal each day. And when I'm out and about, I could pick up some wood that's lying on the ground. It is not ideal, but we have to think of ways to keep warm. Don't worry, Rosina, we will survive."

The food rationing had begun to bite and we were constantly hungry. I had to plan how much we could eat each day. Papa often went down to the harbour to get some fish hoping that he would see Marcus or Rufus. They always gave us extra and charged less and we were very grateful. Sara was always hungry.

"Rosina, why can't I have more than one slice? I used to have lots of bread when Mamma was alive. It's not fair," she complained.

"Oh, sweet darling Sara, life isn't fair. Our lives are not how they used to be. Because of the war there isn't much food to go round. Everyone is hungry. I'll cut half a slice again so then you'll have one and a half slices and a small glass of milk. That will have to last you until we have our evening meal," I told her. Our last meal of the day was now pushed later into the evening so that we wouldn't go to bed feeling hungry.

"Where's the butter?" Sara snapped.

"There isn't any; use the jam—there's some in the pantry."

"What! No butter either? When is this war going to finish?" Sara cried.

"I don't know. Nobody knows but soon I hope," I retorted.

How was I meant to explain to a seven-year-old that our lives were now restricted and governed by the military police. Our main problems were empty shops and empty tables. I was struggling to come to terms with it myself.

"I don't like this war, Rosina. I want it to go away," Sara grumbled.

"Look, tomorrow I'll try my best to look for some butter and bread; otherwise it's jam but it's better than nothing," I said, trying to cheer her up. It seemed to work as she turned and skipped off with a mouthful of bread.

Everyday Papa walked the streets of Oostende in the hope of finding Joseph. A whisper or any kind of clue to his whereabouts would have given Papa some hope, but there was nothing.

As winter approached, daylight hours became shorter and shorter; with black, bleak nights, very few would venture out except for Papa. He continued to go out searching day and night in the pouring rain and high winds. Even when hailstones stung his face, it didn't deter him from scouring the streets.

I begged him to stay at home some days. "Papa, you are not going to survive this winter if you carry on like this. You have to face facts—Joseph is most probably in Germany."

"Oh, please don't say that, Rosina. I couldn't stand it if he was. The thought of him doing forced labour in that country is unthinkable. What I miss, Rosina, is when Joseph was home on leave, we had long chats well into the night. The stories he told you wouldn't believe! I used to laugh at his loud chuckle. And how he loved the sea," Papa smiled fondly at the memories.

"I know you used to wake me up laughing so loudly," I replied with an affectionate smile.

"Now my beautiful boy has been taken by those monsters. God only knows where he is!" he said giving vent to his feelings.

I tried to comfort him, by reminding him of the memories he had locked away but he looked a weary broken man.

"Some days the grief is so overwhelming I wonder what is the point of all this?" Papa threw both arms up in the air.

"Oh Papa please don't talk like that. What would Sara and I do if you weren't here?" I pleaded.

"My darling Rosina, you are doing a brilliant job on your own."

"I still depend on you, Papa."

"What I find so difficult is trying to come to terms with such a massive loss of life in one day. I can remember begging for peace and quiet when we were all home together. But now I would give my right arm to fill our house with noisy, screaming children. I can't stand the silence, Rosina.

"When I wake each day, my first thought is of Mamma and my lost children, I didn't think life could get any worse but now, to have Joseph taken from right under our noses is nothing short of diabolical. It's hard to face each day, knowing we'll never see them again, and that's not mentioning those of our family who escaped to England. We might never see them again either.

"Even those alive, I still sorely miss. Tell me Rosina, how are we to pick up the pieces and continue as if nothing has happened," and then Papa wept.

"Our lives will never be the same again," I replied with sadness. "But we must look to the future even though there is a war raging here. For Mamma's sake, we must. She would do it for us, Papa."

"I know she would, Rosina," Papa said and he put his arms around me and we both squeezed each other tight.

I didn't know how much more pain and heartache one person could handle in a lifetime? I felt helpless not knowing what to say or do for him.

Chapter Nineteen
A New Job

On the Sunday before I was to start work, I tried to make some soup for the following day. I had two potatoes and a small piece of mutton. It didn't go well. I felt so frustrated that I started to cry.

"I can't make soup, it tastes horrible," I wailed.

Papa came over and tried some himself. "You're right, Rosina, it is awful. Have you added any salt? And I'm sure we have some stock left from the bit of veal we had a few days ago." Papa brought a small block of salt and a bowl from the pantry.

"What is stock?" I asked in bewilderment. I felt overwhelmed by the responsibility of housekeeping that had been thrust upon me. Papa explained how to make stock and how I could use it to flavour soup; the simplicity of this culinary lesson allowed me to grow confidence in my new responsibility.

Although Papa knew that I was to start work on the Monday, I thought I had better remind him.

"Papa, you do realise I'm starting work in the morning?" I said.

"Rosina, surely you could find work somewhere else? What about the butcher's shop, maybe he could give you some hours."

"I'm not going to work in a butcher's shop. I could never cut up animals even though they are dead. What sort of person do you think I am, Papa? Anyway it's all arranged now. I'm meeting Colet at the corner of our street just after seven. I'm fourteen now and lots of girls work at my age. I have to try this, I may not like it but just give me a chance," I replied.

"The thought of those Nazis manhandling you horrifies me. You know what they're like."

"Oh, Papa, nobody is going to manhandle me. I won't allow it. Don't you trust me, Papa? Please don't be so serious. For the first time since Mamma died,

I actually feel happy I'm doing something with my life, so please don't spoil it for me."

The following morning I was up at the crack of dawn, even before Papa woke. I left the tray of ash and added some paper and wood, just enough to put the coffee on to warm.

It wasn't long before I heard Papa enter the room.

"I wanted to see you before you start your shift, Rosina. Any nonsense and you finish, do you hear me?" he said.

"Yes, yes, Papa, I hear you. I must go now—Colet will be waiting for me. Goodbye," I said as I gave him a peck on the cheek.

As we both nervously walked down the long road to the Hotel, Colet said, "The soldiers are out in force today."

"They've most probably been out all night," I replied.

"I hope they don't stop us, Rosina, I couldn't bear it if I was searched again."

"Try not to look too worried, Colet. If we're stopped, we just tell them we're going to work."

Our first day went better than expected. We were given brown overalls which really left a lot to be desired and we were also given scarves to wear as turbans on our head. We couldn't stop laughing at them as we weren't sure how to fit them so we ended up doing each other's.

We were both given our duties; the hotel was huge and we had two floors each to cover but for our first day, we worked together. We were both very grateful.

Hugo Boon, our boss, was okay. He worked us hard but we didn't mind; having a pay packet at the end of each week and being a little bit independent was worth it. The following week, we were taught how to lay the tables which was a bit tricky, but we learned.

This was just in case there was a shortage of waitresses—then Hugo could rely on us to help out. I loved being a waitress, but Colet didn't.

"I don't like being amongst the soldiers; I'd rather be upstairs out of the way," she explained.

About a month into our jobs, Hugo approached me and asked me to follow him into his office. My mouth went dry and I wondered nervously what I had done wrong and if he was going to sack me.

"Sit down, Rosina. I've called you in because I have something to ask you. Are you happy with your job?"

"Oh, yes, Sir, I love my job. I'm really happy here; it's given me my confidence back and everybody is so nice."

"Yes," he replied, "I've noticed you seem to get along with all the staff."

I quickly nodded in agreement. He hesitated before speaking and I was still convinced he was going to sack me.

"Rosina, there's an opening here in the hotel for a full-time waitress. I would like to offer you the position. How do you feel about that?"

I was amazed and speechless.

"Me! A waitress?" I eventually gasped.

"Yes. Why not you?" Hugo commented.

"Well, I had heard some of the girls talking about the position when I was in the locker room but didn't take much notice," I replied.

"You will be in charge of the shift rota. Do you think you could handle that?"

"Well, I'll certainly try," I replied. "As long as I'm shown what to do, I should manage the rotas."

"Right, I'll get someone to show you today. The sooner I have the rotas up and running, the sooner life will be back to normal," Hugo said as he looked at me with a distracted frown. "Well, as normal as we possibly can be under these circumstances."

"I'll do my very best," I smiled at Hugo.

"I know you will," he assured me. "I also have two waiters starting next week. So go home and talk it through with your family. There will obviously be a pay rise."

"My answer is yes! I will speak to Papa but I will accept the job. I thought you were going to give me the sack," I said.

"Good heavens! Why did you think that? You're one of the most conscientious workers I've had the privilege to know."

"Well, you looked so serious when you called me into your office, I thought I had done something wrong."

He laughed. "And one more thing, Rosina, please don't call me Sir; I'm Hugo to all my staff."

"Okay, Hugo," I said smiling as I closed the door behind me. I couldn't wait to tell Papa.

As soon as I got home, I burst out my news: "You'll never guess what, Papa! I've had a promotion. Hugo asked me if I would like to be a full-time waitress with extra hours and extra pay and I said yes."

120

To my relief, Papa congratulated me and seemed pleased that despite being there only a short time, I had impressed my boss. Papa came over and kissed my forehead and hugged me.

"I still don't like you working there, Rosina, waiting hand and foot on those Nazis, but if you're happy then who am I to stop you? I am very proud of you."

"Thank you, Papa it means, so much to me to hear you say that. It will mean extra money which we so desperately need." For the first time in a long while, I felt happy and relaxed.

Everything was going well until the day Colet and I walked through the main doors of the hotel and I accidentally bumped into one of the soldiers. He came so close that he brushed against my shoulder. I started to apologise then he turned around to face me. I stopped in my tracks and turned my face away.

Colet gasped in horror as we recognised him as one of the soldiers who had stolen our food and threatened to beat me.

He glanced at Colet then me, eyeing us suspiciously. My heart was racing and I hid my hands behind my back so that he couldn't see them shaking. I thought he was going to question us but he was with some other soldiers and they were laughing. As they left the hotel, he was the last to leave. I looked over my shoulder to make sure they had gone. His sinister smile sent shivers down my back as he sneered, "I know who you are."

I wasn't sure if Colet had seen what I saw and I wasn't about to tell her. We couldn't get downstairs to our locker rooms fast enough as we were so frightened.

"I wonder if those soldiers are staying in our hotel," Colet said.

"I hope not," I replied. As I glanced at Colet, she burst into tears.

"Oh Colet," I said, "don't let them win."

"But what if I'm on my own upstairs? I could be trapped in one of the bedrooms; nobody would hear my cries for help and we've already suffered the wrath of this lunatic! He's capable of anything. I don't know if I can work here now, Rosina," she said, trembling.

"Of course, you can still work here. Don't let those Nazis stop you earning a little bit of money. Look how independent you've become," I said, helping her with her turban and squeezing her hand.

"I'm going to tell Hugo," I continued. "It's wrong that we have to work under such pressure and are constantly looking over our shoulder."

"I'm glad we're on the same shift. I wish I was as tough as you, Rosina," Colet sighed.

"Life has made me tough. I'll let you know what Hugo says and in the meantime try not to worry," I said.

I told my boss everything about them stealing our food and what had happened here in the hotel and he was very annoyed.

"I can't do anything about the food they stole from you but when it's in my hotel and it affects my staff, I will not tolerate it. I'll have a word with his superior. Leave it with me," Hugo said and then hesitated before adding, "Rosina, I have to be truthful—nothing may be done about it. They simply don't care how they treat us, especially you young girls. Thank goodness, they only come in for their breakfast." Hugo sighed.

All bank holidays had been cancelled since the invasion. School times had been reduced to half a day. Nine-forty-five to twelve-fifteen was all the schools were open for because of the night air raids, which caused the children to lose a lot of sleep. Sara was quite pleased with a lie-in every morning, but Papa couldn't wait for her to be back at school.

After her first day back, she told me that the infants were now mixed with the juniors.

"Are you pleased with that, Sara?" I asked her.

"Umm, I suppose so. We were looking after the little ones who were upset and missing their Mammas," she replied.

"That's good of you, Sara. They must be very frightened on their first day at school. I'm very proud of you." I gave her a massive hug.

Living in such dangerous times brought our nation closer. It united us, from the very young to the very old.

One day, when I was about to finish my shift in the hotel one of our neighbours from the street, Mrs Delee, who was a cleaner in the hotel, approached me with her concerns about Papa.

"Rosina, I thought you should know that last week, your Papa was strip-searched on the road for all to see. The weather was atrocious, but that didn't stop the soldiers. They ripped his coat off and threw it on the wet ground. He had to take his shoes and socks off and he was standing there in bare feet in the pouring rain. I thought, what had he done for them to be so cruel to him?

"He was shivering and I felt so sorry for him. He had to put his hands on top of his head while they searched him from head to foot but it was in vain—he was not carrying any food. It was really awful. After they left, I ran over to him. The humiliation of the search had reduced him to tears. He looked so lost and he was wet through. His coat was wet and dirty and his socks were too wet to put on but I helped him with his shoes then I walked home with him. I wanted to make sure he got there safely. I thought I had better tell you."

"Oh, Mrs Delee, how frightened Papa must have been. Thank you for helping him. It is so worrying I've heard stories regarding the elderly being cruelly searched on the open roads. These soldiers obviously have no respect for the older generation which is a disgrace," I said bitterly.

I thanked her and made my way home. I expected Papa to be in the house when I arrived but he wasn't—he obviously hadn't been put off by that episode. It was well after six o'clock in the evening when he came home, his clothes soaked through to the skin.

"Where have you been, Papa? I've been so worried?" I cried. "Look at the state of you! Why do you punish yourself like this? I know you're concerned about Joseph but this is not the way, Papa. Mrs Delee, from across the road, told me how the Nazis strip-searched you the other day."

"Who?" Papa asked irritably.

"She's a neighbour of ours who lives in our street. She works in the hotel and she was very concerned about you."

"I can't remember what the soldiers did," he replied.

This concerned me but I decided it was best to change the subject. "Have you had something to eat?" I asked him.

"I don't feel like eating," he said, looking so sad.

"Come, Papa, sit by the fire," I said gently. "You look frozen." His face was red from the icy wind. "You can't go on like this. I know I'm repeating myself but Sara and I are very worried that you will be picked up and taken to God only knows where. What are you hoping to prove, Papa?"

"I don't know, Rosina, but what I do know is if I stay in all day it's endless, the time goes so slowly. When I walk down to the town I walk with hope in my heart that maybe there will be a whisper, a tiny clue to Joseph's whereabouts. I have to keep searching, Rosina."

He stood up and hobbled over to the sink with his empty coffee cup. He had aged so much in such a short time.

"I'm going to bed," he announced.

The war had only just begun but for Papa, it felt it had been forever and a day.

The following morning he seemed to be back to his old self. He greeted Sara and me with a big hug.

"I must stop searching for Joseph. You're right, Rosina, if these soldiers are nasty enough to pick on an old man like me, they'll just as easy whisk me off to the labour camps."

"Oh, Papa! I'm so relieved you're seeing sense at last." I started laughing. Papa and Sara looked at me as if I'd gone mad.

"It feels like the roles are reversed. I'm Mamma and you are the little boy," I said as we all laughed together. It was a brief moment of relief in the midst of deep anxiety.

Chapter Twenty
Winter Shortages

The shortage of food became so severe that Sara woke one night screaming, "My tummy hurts, Rosina, I feel sick."

I knew it was lack of food. "Lie back down, Sara. I'll see if there's any bread left."

Thankfully, there was a little bit wrapped in brown paper so I cut one thin slice and spread a little butter carefully. I needed to keep the rest of the bread and butter for breakfast. I was lucky that day, as I had managed to buy a small amount of butter and some milk from the butcher's. She ate the bread and washed it down with a tiny drop of milk.

"Take your time, Sara," I chided.

"But I'm hungry, Rosina. Can I have some more?" she begged.

"I'm sorry, Sara but we have to keep the rest for tomorrow. There's a glass of water on the side of the bed—drink some of that," I said, cradling her in my arms until the early hours of the morning when she finally fell asleep, exhausted from crying.

A worrying thought crept into my mind that we were only a few months into the war. *How will we cope if this war drags on for years?* I asked myself. The amount of food we were allowed was a pittance. We were now receiving ration stamps for 225 grams of bread and only 35 grams of butter. If we wanted any kind of meat, we had to queue outside the butcher's for hours to get as little as 90 grams of meat, which included bones. I worried how we were going to manage as the war dragged on because of the alarming speed with which the food rationing had come into force and how severe it was. It made life very difficult and frightening to us.

One fortunate thing was that after finishing our shifts in the hotel, Hugo didn't have to ask us girls twice if we would like a small portion of food to eat.

If it was possible, I would keep some of my lunch for Sara and Papa. It wasn't much but whatever it was, it was better than nothing.

1940 was our first Christmas without our family and I was dreading it. St Nicholas day arrived just like every other dismal day. There was nothing to celebrate.

Papa sat in his chair for most of the day drinking whisky. Sara was out on her roller-skates. I had managed to find a second-hand pair for her. Papa cleaned them up and oiled the wheels.

I thought back to our last St Nicholas day together. I was sad but also grateful to have those memories locked away in my heart. Mamma had worked so hard to make St Nicholas day the best we had ever had as if she knew it was her last with us.

"Oh, Mamma, life is so hard without you. Every day is a struggle," I whispered.

I had booked the day off work which I was beginning to regret; the loneliness was unbearable.

On New Year's Day of 1941, we all went to morning mass. Ada and her two daughters came and even Papa blessed us with his presence to give thanks for guidance through a difficult time. I was surprised that Papa came because he had stayed a Protestant while Mamma and all of her children were Catholics.

The arctic weather lived up to its wintery name and we braced ourselves for a very cold January, with blizzard conditions, treacherous walk-ways and icicles hanging from window ledges. Darkness engulfed our pitiful land and Jack Frost paid us long visits.

Our coats never left our bodies; the windows were frozen on the inside as well as the outside and the house was bitterly cold. Even Papa kept his coat on. It was horrible knowing you were coming home from a hard day's work to a freezing cold house. We had no coal, only little bits of wood and there was hardly any food in the pantry. I just wanted to hide away, somewhere, anywhere, from the misery Hitler was causing us.

Sara was sitting on one of the easy chairs shivering even with Mamma's coat wrapped around her and a blanket to keep her feet warm. She watched the last of the flames withering to ash. We had used the last of the coal and there were just some twigs of wood left to burn.

We were living in horrendous conditions, but no matter what life threw at us, we embraced it and continued the fight for survival. There was nothing else we could do.

One day Papa had gone to pick up our food rations and when he returned home, he also had some wood tucked under his arm. It was wet and we had to dry it before we could burn it, but it gave me an idea although I wasn't sure if Papa would go along with it.

"Where did you get that wood from, Papa?" I asked.

"I found it in the playing fields under the overgrown grass behind the church. Some of the trees have been cut down. You can't blame people; you've got to have heat to survive."

"Papa, how would you feel if we cut up some of the old furniture we no longer use? I'm sure we have some cupboards in the basement. I remember Mamma didn't want to throw them out when you made the new ones for the kitchen."

Papa looked at me in surprise but then surprised me with his answer,

"Well, I suppose desperate times call for desperate measures. I could cut the wood quite thick so it will last longer and light it in the late afternoon; that way the fire will stay in longer so that we can have heat for cooking and warmth for the evening and we wouldn't have to go to bed so early just to keep warm. Good idea, Rosina—why didn't I think of that?"

Papa cut up all the old furniture that he could find and piled it in the corner of the basement. It gave him the incentive to clean up the basement and make it cosy enough just in case there was bombing and we had to take shelter there. Every time he went out he came back with some wood, not much, but every little bit helped; he'd then dry it and stack it in the corner of the basement with the rest of the wood.

It was so comforting to come home from work knowing that there was a fire waiting for me. The warmth brought back memories of Mamma's cosy kitchens.

Colet and I were walking home from work late one afternoon. We were both shattered as we had had a very busy day, running around at the mercy of the Nazis. As the sun dipped behind some dark grey clouds, the icy winds stirred the waves into a frantic rage; even our coats couldn't protect us as the waves crashed with such force against the promenade wall, causing swirls of spray to fly along the pavements.

We had just turned the corner into our street when we saw a group of people running towards us. They kept looking over their shoulder and some of the women were crying—they looked petrified.

I shouted to one of them, "What's wrong? Why are you all running?" One of the women stopped to catch her breath, her hands were shaking. She leaned up against a wall and bent over to put her hands on her knees; she wasn't that young.

"There are soldiers on this road frightening the life out of people. They used their fists and boots to beat an old man. It was awful!" she cried. The woman paused for breath. "They are shooting anyone who gets in their way. I saw a woman fall and I don't know if she's dead. I just ran for my life! The soldiers looked like young boys just out of school." She glanced at us both. "You two are young girls. I wouldn't go up that road even if you live there; you don't know what these soldiers are capable of." Colet and I looked at each other. "Go back the way you came," the stranger warned us.

A moment later she whispered, "Someone said they're looking for a gang of boys who killed one of their soldiers. That's all I know but it seems to me they're out to get revenge." She wiped tears from her eyes with the back of her hand. Fear was etched on her face.

"God help us all! Take care," She said then ran off to catch up with the others.

"I am so glad you're here, Rosina! I don't know what I would have done if I was on my own!" Colet cried.

"We need some sort of plan in place so that if anything like this happens and we're on our own, we'll know what to do. God forbid it will never happen," I said.

"What sort of plan do you mean, Rosina?" Colet replied.

I thought quickly, grappling for some sort of strategy that would ease Colet's distress.

"Well, I suppose if we are really desperate then the first house we come to, we would have to try to find shelter there. I'm sure the people living there would understand. That would be the best thing to do but if not make your way back to the hotel if you're on your own, especially if they are the really nasty soldiers. The way that woman described them they are capable of anything so you need to take precautions even if you're almost home.

"I don't want to scare you, Colet, but it sounds like those particular soldiers are the ones that seem to pick on us. Come on, we better make our way back to the hotel." I sounded more confident than I felt. I caught hold of her hand as we ran back down the road.

"I'm worried, Rosina, how are we going to get home? Mamma will be frantic, wondering what's happened," Colet voiced what I was thinking.

"I'll ask Hugo if there's anyone to accompany us home. I'll explain what's happened and we'll go the long way around."

As we neared the hotel, we saw a bunch of soldiers congregating near the entrance. It was now dark and there were no streetlights on because there could be bombing at any time.

After the invasion, the Nazis always toured around our streets announcing through a loudspeaker that no one must venture out after dark but it was now pitch dark and we were still out. We linked arms to keep together.

Suddenly, Colet stopped. "I can't go in there, Rosina, I can't pass those soldiers," she said, shaking like a leaf.

I tried to reassure her, saying, "I don't think they're the same soldiers. Come on, this is the only way we're going to get home." I practically dragged her along the path.

As we got to the steps, some of the soldiers whistled and laughed when I said, "Excuse me, boys, could you let us through please?" I was both relieved and surprised when they parted and let us through. As we shut the large foyer door behind us, we both breathed a sigh of relief.

"I wouldn't like to go through that again," Colet whispered. I squeezed her trembling hand in agreement.

Hugo looked surprised to see us back. "What are you girls doing back here? I didn't realise you loved your jobs that much," he joked. His smile turned to anger when I told him what had happened.

"Hugo, is there someone that could walk home with us? We're afraid, with the roads being so dark and soldiers threatening everyone," I begged.

Hugo immediately called the receptionist over and asked him to find Johan Mattis, the head porter.

"Don't worry, girls. Johan will walk you home; he's a big, strapping boy and he won't take any nonsense."

Hugo wasn't exaggerating! Johan was over six-foot tall with wide strong shoulders and great big hands. He was handsome in a rough sort of way with dark brown eyes and dark wavy hair.

"How come we haven't noticed him before?" I whispered to Colet.

"I've seen him," she replied, her face turning scarlet when Johan looked at her. I felt sorry for Colet: she was very pretty, tall and thin with blonde hair and pale blue eyes—just the type that Hitler was looking for.

"Right girls, I'll just put my coat on and we'll be off," Johan said. I felt better knowing we were in safe hands, but as he stretched to put his arm through his coat sleeve I saw a handgun in one of the inside pockets of his coat. I didn't mention it to Colet but I was a little nervous walking with him by our side. If we were stopped by a German patrol, would he use his gun on them? Thankfully, the streets were now more or less empty, with just a couple of soldiers on the opposite side of the road. However, as we neared our street, we heard some shots fired. I instinctively grabbed Johan's arm.

"Girls, you are nearly home. Run as fast as you can!" he whispered urgently.

"What about you, Johan? Do you want to come to one of our houses?" I asked.

"No, no, I don't live far from here. You go now," he answered, and he urged us again to move quickly.

Papa and Colet's Mamma had been out in the streets looking for us and were frantic with worry by the time we made it home. Papa was angry too—they had taken a risk being out after curfew; if they had been caught, they could have been flogged or even worse. I had never seen Papa so angry and even though it wasn't my fault, he banned me from going out other than to go to work and back.

"You are still only fourteen years old. If I had my way, you wouldn't be working at all. After everything we've gone through, I can do without this!" His voice was raised and he slammed his fist on the kitchen table.

Then all of a sudden, he sat down and put his hands over his face and began to cry. I was beside him in an instant, overcome with pity at his vulnerability.

"Oh, Papa, please don't cry!" I begged. "What happened today is unlikely to happen again," I continued, desperately trying to reassure him. I didn't want to remind him that I was the only one bringing money in so I said no more.

"I hate the fact that it is you out earning money, Rosina. It should be me," he said.

"Papa, we discussed this when I started working. In most houses the youngsters are the breadwinners and the parents stay at home—it's a way of life now."

"Since when did you become the adult?" Papa said but his smile told me that he had calmed down.

Chapter Twenty-One
The Air Raids

The first time I heard the air-raid siren, Sara was in school and I was at work. It was very loud and I was worried about Sara. I knew there was no shelter in the school and I wondered what the teachers would do and where they would all go. I knew Sara would want to be at home with Papa and me, so I tried to leave work.

I told Hugo, "I can get to the school, pick Sara up and be home before any bombing starts." But he wouldn't let me go. He locked the main doors of the hotel.

"No, Rosina, you can't go now. Any minute now there'll be bombing. I don't think you realise how close we are to the docks—we're sitting ducks. The British Airforce will be trying to immobilise all that area. You could be killed! Think of your family, Rosina," he said.

Reluctantly, I obeyed but fear clung to my heart as I thought of Sara's frightened little face.

Hugo clapped his hands together and called, "Right, everybody, down to the cellar!"

Suddenly, there was an almighty explosion and the hotel shook! Then a powerful flash seemed to light up the world for a split second. It rooted me to the ground, then unwittingly, I jumped into Hugo's arms. Realising what I had done, I immediately moved away, feeling very embarrassed.

He looked at me with a grin but spoke gently when he said, "This is just the beginning, Rosina."

We all hurried down to the cellar but we could still hear the bombs as they rained down for what seemed like hours. I tried to take my mind off the noise by concentrating on what was in the cellar. I'd never been down there before. It was dark but our boss had managed to install a small electric light on the wall which we were grateful for as there were no windows to give us any light.

The cellar was quite wide and it was on two levels with a few steps down to the lower level. One side of the wall was taken up with shelves on which were stacked bottles of wine, gin, whisky, and other kinds of alcohol. On the opposite wall were large barrels of beer all in a row. Hugo had managed to make the cellar comfortable for us, there were old settees and broken wooden chairs which I thought would be very handy for our fire at home. There was an oil heater on one of the walls but it didn't give out much heat, so all of us girls huddled together to keep warm although we were all still shaking with fear.

We could hear the drone of the engines above us and someone said: "What if they hit the hotel? We'll all be buried alive!"

We all shouted together, "Shut up!"

After what seemed like hours, the all clear sounded and as we all emerged out of the dark cellar, I made my way home as quickly as I could.

I scooped Sara up in a hug that took her by surprise, I was so glad to know she was safe. She was taken aback and was more interested in telling us about her day. She was so excited with the innocence of youth.

"Papa, when the bombing started, we were very frightened and some of the children were crying, but I wasn't," she said pointing a finger at her chest.

"You were very brave not to cry, my good girl," I said and gave her a peck on the cheek.

"I would rather have been at home, Rosina, but Mrs Boone, our teacher, told us we couldn't leave the school. We were told to go in pairs and stay under our desks until it was over. My friend Katlyn and I stayed together."

When she finally stopped for breath, she skipped over to the pantry and poured herself a tiny drop of milk and a very thin slice of bread. I marvelled at her awareness of our situation and how we had all been forced into a strict routine about the amount of food that passed our lips. Sara, still only nine years old, realised our predicament and out of habit, ate very little. I felt very proud of her.

After she finished, she put her hands on her hips, turned her head to one side and continued, "Do you know, Rosina, it felt like we were under the table for hours and hours." She lowered her voice. "I wanted to go to the toilet, and I was worried I wouldn't be able to hold it for much longer but I did."

I couldn't help but laugh at her and marvel how much she had grown up in the past year.

I eventually got used to the sound of the planes but I was very frightened and wondered where the bombs would fall. Papa told us that if we were out anywhere on our own, not that Sara ever would be, we were to find the nearest assigned public shelter and stay there until it was safe to leave.

It was nearing the end of March when I woke to the sound of birds tweeting and singing their hearts out. The sun's rays burst through a gap in the curtains which formed a golden glow in the bedroom. It was most unusual to hear the birds. For so long it felt as if they had abandoned us in our hour of need. It had been a long hard winter, but now I welcomed the birdsong, feeling I could look forward to summer.

There was a lot of bombing over Oostende by the British Airforce and the German Luftwaffe would take to the air to challenge them. Papa called them "dog-fights". Along the streets, trucks and jeeps paraded, the soldiers in them chanting "SIEG HEIL", which was like a victory chant. Nazi flags flew high on municipal buildings, reminding us of their superiority. On the wireless in the evenings we looked forward to listening to the BBC, hoping for some encouraging news but, more often than not there was nothing of interest to us in Belgium. Morale was low, our future looked grim.

The lengths people went to, to find a morsel of food was freakish to say the least. I had heard that cats and dogs had been plucked off the roads and ended up on tables filling empty stomachs. I felt quite anxious whenever I called in at the butcher's, wondering if he would tell me if he was selling such products. We were desperate people living in desperate times—so hungry we would eat anything, even if it was something we disliked in our past life. Now I wouldn't leave a crumb on my plate. We were constantly drinking water to try and ease the hunger pains.

Some days it got so bad, and our energy levels fell so low, that I felt like I wouldn't survive the day. Since the invasion, our freedom had been taken away. The day to day suffering we endured left us so despondent that life became meaningless. I lived simply because my heart kept beating.

The summer sun with all its warmth was welcomed by me with open arms. The warmer months brought fresh fruit and vegetables and there was a little more food around to buy, but even though I was working, I could only afford certain things.

The curfew hours of darkness became shorter, it was like heaven to me. Not that I wanted to go out in the evenings, but it was great to laze around the house with the heat of the day lingering well into the evening. I sometimes sat on the bench in the garden for hours making clothes for Sara and myself.

Chapter Twenty-Two
New Horror

Whilst living under a harsh brutal regime, our lives were governed by fear of this dictatorship. We could not assume that whatever had happened in the past would stay in the past. Never more so than one evening in September of 1941:

I had invited our neighbour, Renata, around for supper with us as she was feeling lonely; her husband had dropped dead just weeks before the invasion and her only son had been killed whilst trying to protect his country. We had just finished our meal and were relaxing with a cup of coffee that Papa had just made for us. I was only just able to talk about Mamma without shedding tears. We were talking of past times and lost loved ones.

Suddenly, there was a loud frantic knocking at the front and back doors almost simultaneously.

"Who on earth is that?" I said as I jumped off the chair in fright.

"You stay here, Rosina," Papa said sternly. "I'll answer the front door. Renata, you open the back door."

"Okay," she answered nervously.

I heard scuffling in the hallway then the door burst open and in walked two tall officers dressed in black uniforms. I ran to Renata, who by this time had let in a young soldier who couldn't have been more than sixteen years old. My heart nearly stopped when I saw who he was; I recognised him as one of the soldiers who had stolen my food on the roadside all that time ago.

"Can I help you, Officer?" Papa asked in a seemingly calm tone. They ignored him. One of the officers pushed Papa aside to get to a large cupboard in the kitchen. They completely emptied it.

"How many people live in this house?" the officer shouted.

"Just me and my two daughters, the youngest is staying the night at her friend's house. I do have a son but he has been missing for over a year. He's a fisherman," Papa explained.

"Is your name Jakop Callens?" the officer asked sternly.

"Yes, it is," Papa replied, somehow managing to keep any fear out of his voice.

The officer's eyes widened and he shouted again. "You are a liar! You have more than three children!"

"Yes, I do have more than three children but some were killed in the bombing and some escaped to England. There is no one else living in this house!" Papa answered, his calm veneer starting to slip.

The officer then turned to look at Renata. "And where do you live?" he asked aggressively.

Renata began to shake. "I live next door, on my own," she answered quickly.

They opened drawers and cupboards and all our personal belongings were scattered all over the floor. I began to tremble as a sickening thought crept into my head: "We could all be murdered in our own home that night". They were so vicious. No one would know if we were left for dead. They seemed to know all about us but I didn't know how that could be.

I could see Papa gearing himself up to talk to the officer. My heart was thumping loudly.

"Do you mind telling me why you are here, Officer? Whatever it is you are looking for? I may be able to help you." Papa braved an anxious smile.

The younger soldier shouted, "Sit and shut up! Speak when you're spoken to, old man." The soldier glared at Papa. I was by his side in an instant.

"Leave him alone," I shouted to the soldier. He looked at me with bloodshot eyes.

"Who told you to speak! Sit and keep your mouth shut!" He bellowed.

Before I could sit down, he grabbed my arm and pulled me close to his face, his breath was disgusting and his evil eyes bore down on me, as he hissed, "I know who you are and now I know where you live."

He pushed me back onto the chair. Claws of terror gripped my heart.

The officer then pointed to Renata and yelled, "Sit!"

The soldier in charge stopped what he was doing and focused his eyes on Papa. My blood went cold as I could see the revulsion on the officer's face. It was so intense that I feared for Papa.

The officer raised his voice as he stood over Papa. "I don't need a reason to search this house or any other house," he screeched.

"You have a son—Joseph Callens?" he continued.

"Yes, I do. Have you found him, Officer?" Papa tried to speak in a calm, collected way, but his questions fell on deaf ears. The officer took his gloves off and peak cap and placed them neatly on the table.

"Do you have a photograph and identity papers for him?"

"Yes, I do," Papa replied. "Joseph has been missing for over a year; we have had no contact with him," he stressed.

"You are lying," the soldier snarled. "Two other boys were admitted to the hospital with your son. They also had no identification on them. Unfortunately, they died or they would have been marched down to Gestapo headquarters and severely beaten for having no identification on them!"

"I don't know of any other boys. I only know my son is missing. Is he in hospital, Officer?" Papa asked anxiously. "The only papers I have are for my son. They're in the bedroom. May I go and get them?"

The officer nodded his reply and told the other soldier to follow Papa. Within seconds, Papa returned and handed the papers to the officer who carefully surveyed Joseph's documents. He then told the same soldier to go back into the bedroom and pull everything apart.

"If you find any kind of documents, bring them to me and be quick about it!"

"May I speak?" Papa asked again. Taking no notice of Papa's request, the officer grabbed Papa's shirt and hauled him out of his chair. Papa began to tremble as the officer fixed his murderous eyes on him.

"See these documents I have here?" he yelled and almost rammed the papers down Papa's throat.

"Stop it! Please! You're choking him!" I shouted, but to no avail.

The Nazi continued, "They should be with your son! Not in the bedroom!" the officer was screaming at Papa. I was terrified he was going to kill him.

By this time the other soldier had come back from searching the bedroom, he shook his head to the Commandant who was losing his patience with Papa.

"What parent lets their son out with no identification on him! You were warned at the beginning of occupation! Everyone is to carry on their person photographic identification papers at all times. Your son was admitted to hospital with no documents on him and no photograph! How are we to know who is who?

You should be whipped for being an irresponsible parent who has no control over his children."

He tightened his grip on Papa's shirt and I shouted again at the officer, "Let him go! Please, let him go! You're hurting him. Look at him—he can hardly breathe. I'm begging you, please let him sit down, he can answer your questions better if he is sitting down."

He totally ignored me and continued his ranting rage on Papa.

The hatred in the officer's eyes was terrifying and I thought he was going to kill him. He then shrieked at him, "You will speak when I tell you to. Is that clear?" Papa couldn't get any words out. "Answer me, you pathetic old fool."

"Yes, yes, Officer, I hear you," Papa finally managed to croak, before he started coughing and spluttering. I couldn't sit any longer and watch this crazy brute, who called himself a human being, torture my Papa any more.

I jumped up and kicked the officer on the legs but he had high boots on and felt nothing. I tried to prise open the officer's hands from Papa's throat but the other two soldiers pulled me away from him. I was screaming, shouting and kicking at the soldiers, I just didn't care.

"Do something, Renata! He's going to kill Papa!" I cried in desperation. Then I saw the soldier's hand rise and felt the sting of his sharp hand across my face.

"What is it going to take to get you to shut up—another slap?" the soldier yelled.

"Oh, Lord, help us!" Renata shouted. "What can I do, Rosina? He's not going to listen to me."

Suddenly, the officer was nose to nose with Papa; his hypnotic stare was terrifying as he shouted, "I will be watching you!"

He pushed Papa with such force that he hit his head on the back of the wooden chair. Papa screamed out as he was violently jerked back and forwards. I struggled free from the other soldiers by kicking one and biting the other on his hand.

"Let me go!" I screamed. "Look at him! He's in pain!" I scrambled to Papa's side and cradled his head in my arms. He was desperately trying to be brave.

The younger soldier shouted at me as he came to grab me away from Papa. "You will respect the commandant at all times!" He looked like a crazed animal. The commandant beckoned to the soldier to let me go.

I knew I had to calm down as I was making a terrifying situation worse. I glared at the soldier but said nothing.

I could still feel the sting of his hand on my face. The hatred I felt for these Nazis brought such revulsion that, if I had the chance at that moment in time, I could kill. I became so overwhelmed with guilt for such horrific thoughts that the tears I so desperately tried to hide slid down my face. I had never experienced such deep dark emotions in all of my young life.

As I held Papa's head to me I checked my hand; it felt wet and sticky then I saw it was covered in blood; it had also seeped down on to the collar of Papa's shirt. I looked at the back of Papa's head; there was a gash almost an inch long where his head had struck the wood on the back of the chair. Papa's hair was thin on the top so you could see the wound clearly.

"Look what you've done! His head is bleeding! Let me bathe the gash on my father's head," I begged frantically. There was no response from any of them as they ransacked our home.

Quietly, Renata and I attempted to stop Papa's bleeding with towels and warm water.

The officer turned his evil eyes back to Papa again. "If your son wasn't in hospital, he would have been severely beaten for having no proof of identity on him. He was caught by the night patrol trying to flee the country. If he had his papers he would still be with you today, and we would have been able to inform you of his whereabouts months ago. See! We are trying to help you!" He let out a crazed laugh which frightened me even more.

"He thought he could get away by escaping through the fields but, as you Belgian people are learning the hard way, we have eyes everywhere. There is nowhere to run and nowhere to hide. We will find you in the end. It doesn't matter how long it takes—we will win." The officer spat out his words, then turned his cold eyes on each one of us. "You have all been warned!" he shrieked at us.

Papa tried to stand but his legs gave way and he flopped back down onto the chair. I sensed he was trying to build up the courage to speak. "Officer, where has my son been all this time?"

"That is not my concern. You as a father should know where your son is at all times," was the heartless reply.

I hoped Papa would let it rest but he wouldn't.

"I begged my son not to leave the house, Officer, but he left while we were asleep. He wanted to go to Dieppe to find…"

But Papa's words fell on deaf ears again. The officer put his arm up.

"Enough! I don't want to hear your feeble excuses! You have no control over your family!" The officer accused Papa again. "You must have control! This country needs control!" he bellowed as he punched the table with his fist.

I jumped, frightened of the officer's rage. I desperately wanted to see my brother. I knew I was pushing it but I had to ask.

"Are we allowed go to the hospital tonight to see my brother? Please—we haven't seen him for over a year?" I begged the officer.

"No, you cannot go to the hospital. It's too late so you will be in breach of curfew laws," he said, smiling maliciously.

The officer put his peak cap back on his head, spread his fingers into his black leather gloves then he straightened his body and, along with the other two soldiers, put his arms up and shouted, "Heil Hitler!"

We all turned our faces away, refusing to acknowledge such misplaced reverence.

Before leaving, the officer looked at us one by one and said, "Let me make myself clear: if you disobey my order and go to the hospital tonight, you will all be put in the guardhouse for an indefinite period. Do you all understand?"

Chapter Twenty-Three
Heartache Again

When the front door slammed behind them, I breathed a sigh of relief. My tears: tumbled down my cheeks again. I cried and cried for all those I had loved and lost. I sat on the stairs for a few minutes, as I didn't want Papa to see me like this. I took comfort in the fact that Joseph had been found. This should be a happy time for us so I dried my eyes then walked back into the kitchen. Papa had tried to stand again but his legs were too weak.

"What do you want, Papa?" I asked, feeling helpless.

"Will you get my bottle of whisky from the pantry? It's down on the floor behind the rubber boots. All the glasses we have are smashed but there's some cups in the sink. They will need to be washed first. At least they didn't take my whisky." He smiled half-heartedly.

"Are you alright, Papa? You sound breathless." I glanced at him.

"Don't worry, Rosina—a couple of glasses of my medicine will do the trick," he said as he held up his cup for another.

"Can I have some, Papa? I don't think I'm going to sleep tonight."

To my surprise, Papa agreed.

The traumatic events that had happened that night showed the sheer hatred and disrespect for us and our home that these men had. That really frightened me.

"How can they be allowed to walk into people's homes and rip them apart, breaking, and smashing the little that we own?" I declared bitterly.

"Listen, Rosina—they don't care," Papa answered.

"They rule our country and we have to abide by it. The same happened in the last war but, then we had to leave the house, while they rummaged through our home. Mamma was so very upset she wanted to clean everything they had put

142

their grubby hands on. It took days for us to clear everything up." Papa looked worn out as he recounted previous traumas.

A horrifying thought suddenly crossed my mind: the fact that the soldier knew where I lived was very frightening. I hoped Papa didn't hear the threats the soldier had made.

"That was terrifying," Papa muttered as he downed his third cup of whisky. "But it was worth it to know that Joseph has been found alive."

"I hope for both your sakes that it hasn't been too long since Joseph was first admitted to hospital," Renata said, and both Papa and I silently agreed.

Suddenly, I shivered. "They could have killed us here in this room tonight. Sara could have walked in and found a bloodbath here," I uttered in horror. "I will be constantly looking over my shoulder from now on," I continued, but when I saw the anxiety furrowed on Papa's brow, I changed tack. "But at least you don't have to walk the streets anymore. Soon Joseph will be home safe and sound," I said trying to sound more reassuring as I smiled affectionately at Papa.

"Yes, I can't tell you how happy I am to know my son is alive," he responded with a measure of relief.

"A toast to Joseph!"

We all shouted "Joseph!" And raised our cups, despite them now being empty. I had to try and put tonight's episode to the back of my mind. Now that Joseph had been found, he was our main priority. We had to get him home as soon as possible. I felt my head was bursting with questions that I couldn't answer.

I looked over to Papa but, his head had suddenly dropped onto his chin and he had fallen asleep. I whispered to Renata, "Will you help me to take him through to the bedroom? I think those soldiers upset him more than he's letting on."

"When that officer grabbed your Papa out of his chair, I feared for his life," Renata said quietly, there was no mistaking the fear in her voice. "What vile soldiers, and what that officer said about this country not being ours anymore is not true! It's not!" Renata tried desperately to hold back the tears as I held her in my arms.

"I don't know how we would have coped if you hadn't been living next door, Renata. You have been a power of strength since Mamma died and I'm very grateful," I said as I hugged her. Between us we carried Papa into his room and helped him into bed.

Renata was a sweet lady who was thoughtful and understanding of our grief. She excelled in kindness and this reminded me of Mamma. She held me at arms-length. "I've told you, Rosina—I will always be there for you." She squeezed my hand.

Later that night, I checked on Papa and was relieved to find his wound had stopped bleeding. I made a start in clearing up some of the mess the Nazis had made. As I picked up broken picture frames and smashed crockery, the thought of their grubby hands contaminating everything we owned made me feel physically sick, and I just made it to the sink in time. It would take me a long time to get over this.

It was very late when I finally fell into bed but I just couldn't sleep. I tossed and turned all night. Step by step I tried again to analyse what had happened that night. We were at the soldiers' mercy, and who or what was to stop them barging into our home again? The way they had treated Papa showed a chilling hatred of the elderly.

I began to wonder who the other boys were who had been captured with Joseph. It gave me a small measure of comfort to realise that at least he wasn't on his own.

The following morning Papa and I were up at the crack of dawn.

I was thankful that Sara had stayed at Ada's the previous night and had not had to witness the traumatic scene that had taken place in our home.

Papa was obviously thinking the same thing as he suddenly said, "Sara must never hear of what took place last night."

Renata had decided the night before she would come with us to the hospital and we were so grateful to have her company as we didn't know what to expect at the hospital.

We called into Ada's on our way to the hospital and I explained briefly to her what had happened, and said I would let her know once we had some information ourselves.

We waited and waited for the tram and when it finally arrived it had standing room only. The smell of body odour and other disgusting human stench was so overwhelming that I felt sick. I put my hand over my mouth and couldn't wait to get off.

"Why is it so crowded?" I whispered to Papa.

"The soldiers have seized all the buses to transport their troops so the only transport the people of Oostende have left is the trams," he explained.

144

I hadn't felt brave enough to travel on my own anywhere since the invasion and as the tram left the station, I was shocked and saddened to see how rundown and overgrown the gardens were: toys were left out and pushchairs were turned on their sides as if the occupants had been in a hurry to leave their homes. But what saddened me the most, was the houses that were empty, with all their windows smashed and all their furniture lying broken on the lawn. I felt like my nation had crumbled.

"Not far now, just one more stop," Papa whispered.

"I think the soldiers are stopping the tram," Renata said.

As Papa leaned over to look out of the window, the tram came to a sudden halt. Everyone who was standing was flung forwards and then we heard shouting and we were all told to get off. Papa whispered urgently, "Don't say anything to these soldiers. They are the Gestapo that came to our house last night. Hopefully, he'll realise we are on our way to the hospital and will let us get on our way."

We all had to line up and put our hands above our heads. Every one of us was going to be searched. Those with food and forbidden goods were either taken away to be interrogated or set free but without their goods. I was shaking as we stood there in the line-up.

When it came to my turn, I only then realised it was the nasty soldier that had previously stolen my food.

I just couldn't get rid of him. He put his hands on my head, then down my arms, then down my body, never taking his eyes off me. When he had finished, he gave me a vile smirk. An icy fear coursed through my veins.

When it came to Papa's turn, the officer stared at him with suspicious eyes.

"You look familiar, I've seen you somewhere before?" he said in a nasty tone.

"Yes, officer, you came to our house last night and told me that my son is in hospital. That's where we are going now, to see him," Papa bravely replied.

There was no reply from the officer other than a look of contempt.

When the soldiers had finished searching all the people, they ushered us back onto the tram. Some people had their hands tied behind their backs and were then marched off to a waiting lorry. I felt sick as I wondered what would become of them.

"Thank the lord they've let us go," Papa whispered as he made his way to one of the seats.

When we arrived at the hospital, we looked for the ward number which the officer had the decency to give us. We found it straight away but there was only one bed with curtains around it. Papa and I looked at each other with great concern as we could hear people talking on the other side of the curtain.

Renata squeezed my hand trying to reassure me. "He may not be in this ward or they could be getting him up to wash him. Don't worry until you have to," she told me.

Papa popped his head through one of the curtains but he couldn't see anything before a nurse pushed him out.

"Who are you? You're not allowed in here at this hour," she said crossly. She was a nun with a long stern face and searching eyes.

Papa spoke first, "We were told that my son is in this hospital. His name is Joseph Callens."

Her eyes widened when his name was mentioned.

"A German officer told us he was in this hospital. Could you please help us to find him?" Papa stressed.

The nurse frowned as she stepped back behind the curtain. There was a whispered conversation and then a doctor came out and introduced himself as Doctor Van Hoost.

"Your son is Joseph Callens?" he asked.

"Yes, do you know where he is?" Papa asked anxiously.

The doctor hesitated before he spoke again.

"Follow me please," he said as he opened a door to his office then called one of the nurses to fetch two more chairs. He avoided our eyes until we were all seated. Again he asked, "Your son is Joseph Callens?"

"Yes, he is," Papa repeated. "Is there anything wrong with Joseph, Doctor?"

Out of nowhere, a darkness seemed to enter my heart as the doctor spoke again: "I'm sorry to tell you, but your son died in the early hours of this morning."

I gasped, unable to take in what I had just heard.

Papa turned grey, a look of disbelief clouding his lined face; a lonely tear trickled down his cheek. I knew that he was desperately trying to hold it together and he just managed to gasp: "It can't be my Joseph; he's a young fit boy."

There was a heavy silence before Papa eventually said, "What happened to my son, Doctor? How long was he in this hospital?" Papa wanted answers. He pulled his handkerchief from his pocket and blew his nose. The doctor unlocked

146

a filing cabinet and pulled out a thin file; he glanced at Papa before he spoke. There were deep dark circles beneath empty, sad eyes that told of many sleepless nights. There was no emotion in the doctor's voice in fact it felt quite cold and well-rehearsed. How many more families did he have to repeat the same words to, over and over again, because of this senseless war?

"Your son has been here for eight days," the doctor told us.

"What? Why has it taken so long to contact us?" Papa's raised voiced trembled.

"Well, at first we had no idea who he was until he was recognised by a nurse who lives on the same street as you," the doctor explained. He quickly went to another drawer and pulled out some other forms. "These are the admission forms. Bear with me and I'll try and find out where he came from."

After several minutes, the doctor was able to tell us that Joseph had been sent from a labour camp somewhere in Germany. I gasped as I pictured my kind, thoughtful brother having to do slave labour. The thought of him there alone and frightened caused tears to trickle down my face. I felt an arm around me and looked into Renata's gentle face as she handed me her handkerchief.

The doctor continued: "Wherever he was taken to, it looks like he was there for over a year."

Papa tried to explain to the doctor when he was snatched from us but he broke down and couldn't continue.

The doctor turned to me. "Do you know what happened to your brother?"

"I can only tell you what you already know: he has been missing for over a year and this is the first time we've had any news of him and…and…now he's dead," I choked through my sobs.

"I'm so sorry it's taken so long for you to know of his whereabouts," Dr Von Hoost said compassionately. "But this war is cruel and the situation is grim. Your brother was admitted here with a large gash on his head and he had contracted typhus, which suggests that the wound had been there for a long time already. We tried everything in our power to save him but the typhus was too far gone, he was in and out of consciousness the whole time that he was here. With a shortage of medication, it's almost impossible to treat patients effectively."

With a heavy heart, Papa looked up at the doctor. "So you're telling me, Doctor, that my son may have lived if he had been brought here earlier?"

The Doctor nodded his head in agreement. Papa burst into tears again and he covered his face with his hands. I put my arms around him helplessly, trying to console him.

The doctor glanced at the three of us. "Joseph wouldn't eat anything at all. We tried in vain to get him to eat, even just a few mouthfuls of soup but he wouldn't. He kept shouting for his Mamma. Is she still alive?"

"No, she's not," I told the doctor. "Most of our family were murdered, a few escaped to Britain as refugees. There is no one left except us. This news is almost too much to bear. Joseph might have lived if we could have come to see him every day and encouraged him to eat and given him a reason to live. If only he had remembered to take his identity card and photograph of himself." I was distraught thinking about how we had been unable to help.

"I can understand your anguish," the Doctor said, closing the file. "I'll go and ask if he's ready for you to see him. Once again I'm truly sorry." He shuddered as he went on, "The Gestapo comes here every day and they decide who stays and who's put out because they want the beds for their own troops and they have eyes everywhere."

"You don't have to tell me that, Doctor," Papa said. He had managed to control his tears. "I would like to know who were the other boys that were admitted the same day as my son? We know nothing of these boys but, the Gestapo seems to think we are harbouring young boys with no identification on them and it's not true." Papa stood up and straightened his suit.

Dr Von Hoost was only able to tell us that both the boys had also died and no-one knew who they were or where they came from.

Before the doctor left his office he turned to Papa. "Your son will be ready for release tomorrow afternoon, but you can see him now."

The three of us followed the doctor along the corridor.

Dread filled my heart as the doctor pulled the curtain aside. I didn't know what to expect; I had never seen a dead body before. I clung to Renata and Papa. When I saw him I just couldn't believe the transformation of my handsome young brother. I gasped, horrified at his unrecognisable appearance. Papa looked drawn and shocked too.

"He's so small and thin, Papa! He doesn't look like my brother—he looks as if he's been starved!" I cried aloud.

"He probably was," Papa replied bitterly.

"Poor Joseph—he's been on his own all this time. He must have been wondering why we never came to see him, lying in that bed day after day alone and frightened," I sobbed into Papa's shoulders. "I was so looking forward to him coming home. I would have looked after him like Mamma did."

I just wanted to take him home and keep him there forever. The whole of Joseph's head was bandaged but what really jumped out at me was the torment and torture portrayed on his young deathly white, face. Only he didn't look young any more, his face told many stories. He must have suffered terrible torment to have aged so much in such a short time. I stood at the bottom of the bed. His eyes were half open and he looked as if he was staring at me. I shuddered. My blonde, beautiful brother had gone forever.

Papa touched his face with his fingers.

"Only seventeen years old, look at him. He looks like an old man. What have they done to you, my son!" Papa wailed.

After several minutes punctuated only by our sobs, Papa spoke again: "My only consolation is that he's with his Mamma and his sisters. Oh Lord, I don't know how much more this old body of mine can take."

Papa leant over and hugged and kissed the son he thought he was going to see again. Weakened by his heartache, he could hardly stand. I asked the nurse for a chair. Papa sat down and put his head on the bed. He held Joseph's lifeless hand. Renata made the sign of the cross then kissed Joseph on the forehead.

Before we left I went around to the other side of the bed. I caught hold of his other hand then whispered in his ear, "Good-bye my brave, handsome brother. You are with Mamma now. Rest in Peace." I kissed him on the cheek.

Renata and I left the ward and waited for Papa outside, giving him some time alone with his beloved son. I felt it was pointless and too painful to stay any longer—it wasn't my brother lying there. Joseph was now in heaven with Mamma, I told myself; this was my only consolation. We thanked the doctor and then left.

On the tram home, it was a repeat performance of the morning where we all had to get off the train and stand in a row with our hands above our heads. I hoped Papa wouldn't say anything to the soldiers as I knew he was in shock and not thinking straight. Thankfully the journey passed without any major incident.

As we walked home, Papa shook his head in disbelief. "Do you know, Rosina, in my heart I really thought I would see my boy again. That's why I walked the streets so much, hoping one day I'd see his face amongst the crowd. Now there's nothing." He began to sob again.

"Oh, Papa, you still have us. I'll come with you to the undertakers and we'll arrange the funeral together."

"You will, Rosina?" he sighed gratefully.

I turned to Renata. "I couldn't have coped without you there today. Thank you for all that you've done," I said, as I kissed and embraced her. Renata then put her arms around Papa.

"Keep strong," she told him. Then turning to look at me she caught hold of both my hands. "Rosina, I'm only next door if you need anything. This war has cost the lives of so many. I've lost one son and that was bad enough but you have lost almost all your entire family. I can't begin to imagine what you're going through," Renata said.

Papa and I made our way to the only undertaker we knew. Mr Von Doon. Papa explained about Joseph, how he had died and arranged for the undertaker to pick Joseph's body up from the hospital the following day. The funeral was arranged for two days later.

I was dreading having to tell Sara as she was very close to Joseph. When we arrived at Ada's house I took Sara aside and told her gently what had happened to Joseph, while Papa told his eldest daughter.

Sara sobbed in my arms. "Our family is disappearing so quickly, Rosina. I hope you and Papa won't die too then I'll be all on my own."

"No, you won't—you'll still have me," Ada said as she squeezed Sara's hand, "and anyway Papa and Rosina are not going to die."

Joseph was buried in the municipal cemetery in Oostende. It was a small funeral, just the family and a few of his friends from the fishing industry. They came to pay their respects, which was comforting for Papa, but it was a hideously bleak occasion.

Night after night I sat on the floor outside Papa's bedroom, listening to him cry himself to sleep and only then did I sleep.

Chapter Twenty-Four
Another Winter

Soon it was St Nicholas day 1941. It was as bleak as it had been last year. I managed to bring some food home from the hotel for our meal but the house was freezing as we only had a small bit of coal and a few sticks left. We kept our coats on for most of the day, then Papa lit a small fire late in the afternoon, so that I could warm up the food for our evening meal, and we could stay up a little longer. Some days we went to bed early with our coats on. I knew Hitler would have somewhere warm to stay after a hard day's work killing people.

1942 proved to be another bitterly cold winter. Wood was thin on the ground and trees were disappearing on a daily basis. If you were caught cutting even a branch from a tree, punishment was harsh. We found out that some men had been shot just for doing that, trying to keep warm through the winter months.

Since the death of Joseph, Papa hardly ever went out but, on the odd occasion that he did, I begged him not to bring any wood home even though we were freezing.

"If I find any wood lying about, Rosina, I will bring it home," he said stubbornly. "We need fuel to cook and to keep us warm. We won't survive a winter like this one without it. Be practical, Rosina."

"But Papa!" I shouted.

He cut me short by putting his hand up. "Enough Rosina!" he barked.

As the war dragged on, the night air-raids were much more frequent and on one particular night it was really terrifying. A bomb hit one of the houses three doors down from ours and it literally shook our house from top to bottom. I wanted to run out into the middle of the road, as I was so afraid of the house falling down on top of us.

"You can't go outside, Rosina!" Papa shouted, over the noise of the aircraft. "The all-clear siren hasn't sounded yet; it's not safe out there."

That night it was horrendous; it went on for hours and hours, and then suddenly there was a brilliant flash and another explosion which shook the house violently again. I peeped through the side of the curtain only to see smoke and beams of orange light filling the sky. I shut the curtain quickly. Sara was screaming and all I could think about was the house crumbling on top of us and being buried alive.

Finally, the all clear siren wailed and we could all get out and I breathed a sigh of relief. Everyone wanted to see what damage had been done. Nearly every house, including our own, had shattered windows which couldn't be replaced. Some roofs were blown off and you could see people's personal belongings. It was horrific, but we considered ourselves very lucky because just a few doors away the house that caught the bomb was totally flattened.

We had heard terrifying rumours of beatings and tortures by the Gestapo, so once the streets were in darkness I wouldn't dare go out. I became very nervous, even during daylight hours, walking to work or to the shops. I was constantly looking over my shoulder, wondering if that soldier was watching me. I hadn't felt safe since that vicious soldier had come to our house. Every step I took outside, was a step into danger. My confidence had hit rock-bottom and I was annoyed with myself for feeling this way.

This day Papa came with me for company. We picked up our rations and bought some scanty food. There was nothing much in the shops. Normally, we'd go straight home but that morning the streets were quiet and empty, just the odd bunch of soldiers on street corners.

I said to Papa, "Why don't we walk over to the docks and see if there's any fish available? Ada told me some of our relatives who survived the Dieppe bombing have returned to their old jobs and are now taking their boats out whenever they can in the hope of catching some fish in between the bombing."

"What a good idea, Rosina."

"Oh Papa," I hesitated. "I forgot you haven't been down to the docks since Joseph died. Will this upset you?"

"I have to do it; I can't let those Nazis win." I was so relieved to hear the determination in his voice again. I squeezed his hand as we walked down to the harbour.

As we neared the docks, we could see a scuffle going on and we stopped dead.

"Oh Papa, what are those soldiers doing to that man on the boat?" I cried.

"I don't know but it doesn't look good," he answered.

Suddenly, more soldiers approached the man and they pulled him off the boat and threw him to the ground where they searched him and tied his hands behind his back. A lorry pulled up and the soldiers picked him up and threw him on to the lorry.

"That's the last we'll see of him," Papa said shaking his head.

"Oh, no—I hope that's not one of our uncles," I murmured.

Papa wanted to go down to see what had happened but I protested, saying we could get fish another day. However, Papa was determined. "You stay here, Rosina. I'll just stroll over and see if I can find out who the man was."

"Be careful," I said as he hurried away.

Once the soldiers had gone, I saw Papa talking to one of the men who worked on the boats. I could just about see it was Maurice, one of my uncles, giving Papa a small parcel which he put into his inside pocket. Painful memories flashed before my eyes of soldiers stealing my food and threatening me. If Papa was caught, I dreaded to think what they would do to him, especially considering that they had no respect for the older generation. I couldn't wait to get home but I was curious to know what had happened down on the docks.

"Did you find out anything, Papa?" I asked.

"Yes. I didn't know the man, but he was caught sneaking some fish into his coat pocket; that's all it was. The poor man will most probably be beaten to death just because he wanted to feed his family," Papa replied.

"Oh, Papa, I wish this war would end! These soldiers are capable of anything. I don't think Oostende will ever be the same again. I don't understand anything about the war, other than that I know this is a horrible place to be and we're on our own. There's no one to help us," I whispered in fear.

"You're too young to be taking on the world, Rosina. The whole of Europe is in the same position as us but the war cannot last forever. We'll just have to be patient and be grateful for small mercies." I smiled at Papa, my rock.

I had had a few days off but, I was looking forward to going back to work.

"Do you know, since those soldiers came to our house, I am frightened stiff to go out on my own. It never bothered me before but that young soldier who we keep meeting really worries me," I told Colet. "I've told Hugo about my situation and how worried I am about walking home alone."

She nodded in sympathy. "I agree, Rosina, I've been seriously thinking of resigning, as I'm terrified of walking home alone."

That same morning Hugo called a meeting in the restaurant. Once everyone was there, he shut the door and locked it. We all glanced at one another wondering why he was been so secretive.

Hugo clapped his hands. "May I have your attention please?" Everyone suddenly stopped talking. "I've heard disturbing news today. Regarding young girls being raped and left on the roadside. Now I know that quite a few of you have to walk home on your own late in the evening and are worried about this, which is understandable. I have asked the girls who live in the staff quarters, if they would do the evening shifts during the winter months and have the mornings off on a rota basis and they've all agreed to do it. That means the staff who live at home can leave before it gets too dark and the streets become too dangerous for young girls to walk alone. You will be safer in daylight."

Colet clasped my hand and we smiled at each other with great relief.

Hugo continued, "During the spring and summer months, we'll look at it again."

We expressed our gratitude to Hugo. Knowing we would not have to walk home in the hours of darkness, meant a huge burden had been lifted from our shoulders, especially since the 8 pm to 6 am curfew introduced by the army often changed, so as to confuse us. If anyone was caught out during the curfew hours, they were immediately taken away, and various punishments were carried out by the police who now worked under the strict authority of the German army.

Chapter Twenty-Five
Springtime

It had been a cold hard winter but now that spring had arrived, life was that little bit brighter; even the birds sounded cheerful as they played and tweeted in cloudless skies.

One day, when Sara came home from school, I noticed she was limping and in pain.

"What's wrong, Sara? Why are you limping?" She sat on the floor and pulled her shoes off. I took one look at her feet and was absolutely shocked.

"Oh you poor thing—you have some corns on your toes because your shoes are too small for you. Your heels look so sore as well. You must be in agony, Sara! Why didn't you tell me?"

"Well, it's only today my feet started to hurt, I took my socks off because my feet felt warm, then when I put my shoes back on my toes were really hurting," Sara replied as she wiped her wet nose with the back of her hand.

"It looks like you've been like this for some time, you need new shoes," I said as I filled a pan with warm water for her to bathe her feet in.

"Well, what am I going to wear? I've got no other shoes and I know we have no money to buy shoes," she asked helplessly.

I looked up, amazed at how she knew about our financial situation. Papa and I had never discussed money in front of Sara. She must have seen the look on my face. She looked sheepish as she said, "I heard you and Papa talking yesterday and you said that we only had enough money to buy some food for today."

"Well, that is true, we don't have enough money to buy you shoes, but there is an alternative," I said.

"What does alternative mean?"

"Well, it means to look for another way of solving the problem of the shoes," I replied, marvelling at how inquisitive her young little mind had become. Hesitating, I glanced at her, unsure how she would react to what I was about to tell her.

"Sara, you could wear Monica's shoes; she didn't take them all to England with her. She has a lovely pair of plain black shoes which would be suitable for school, and they have a little heel which would make you taller." I waited for the backlash but to my surprise she smiled.

"Will they fit me, Rosina?"

"If anything, they'll be too big but you can wear two pairs of socks in winter time or I can put some paper in the toe part until you grow into them. Shall I go and fetch them?" I asked.

"Yes please." Her eyes sparkled with delight which lifted my spirits.

I wondered if I should mention that the coat and skirt she had been wearing were made from Mamma's clothes. I decided against it.

I found some old bandages Mamma had washed and put neatly in the back of the drawer. I held them to my face—after all this time her presence still lingered and was a strong reminder of the influence she still had in our home.

Within a couple of weeks, her feet were back to normal. One day I caught her looking at her shoes in the mirror with a pleasant smile on her face. I did feel rather guilty. Mamma would never have let Sara's feet get into such a state. It hadn't crossed my mind that as Sara was growing, her feet were growing as well. I made sure that she was presentable for school but every bit of clothing we had, I had to repair time and time again.

Thankfully, summer came early that year and Sara pleaded to go down to the beach.

"You do realise there will be soldiers everywhere. I'm not even sure if we are allowed on the beach. Some girls from work tried to sunbathe the other day and were told to leave. But I'll check this afternoon when I go into work. I'm sure Colet would love to come as I know she loves the sun."

I did miss going to the beach which was almost on our doorstep. Before the war, we wouldn't think twice about an early morning dip before school but that was before the Nazis came.

"I have a day off tomorrow, Sara, so we'll go. If the soldiers stop us, we'll come home."

She was so excited. "I can't wait to go into the water and to build sandcastles." Sara's blue eyes sparkled with delight. "Shall I ask Joanne and Ellen if they would like to come?"

"Yes of course," I replied.

The following day the children and I strolled down to the beach. It was a beautiful day with not a cloud in sight; the sun felt warm on my face. We met Colet after her shift had finished. The girls had run on ahead and were already in the water by the time I got there.

"If I hadn't seen it for myself, I wouldn't have believed that there are no soldiers about," I whispered to Colet.

"I know. Where are they all? Not that I'm complaining," Colet said.

"I feel as free as the birds in the sky! It's lovely to relax, and not have beady eyes watching you all the time," I told Colet.

We both began to laugh, a slice of silliness in a crazy world.

We sat near the promenade so it would be easier to get off the beach should the bombers come.

"Oh, I hope there's no bombing, Rosina—we're sitting ducks, as Hugo likes to remind us," Colet said.

Despite the shadow of the Nazis, we had a wonderful time. Colet and I joined the girls in the water; it was cold to begin with but we soon got used to it. It felt so good to swim. This was my first dip in the water since Dieppe and I felt a little nervous but I was determined to overcome it.

We devoured our picnic, small as it was, but it felt like a feast because Colet had brought some leftover cakes from the hotel. Then we both helped the girls to make a sandcastle. We were really enjoying ourselves.

It was late afternoon and we were packing up to go home The girls had just had their last dip in the water and their bathing costumes were wet.

My stomach turned as I glanced across the English Channel. I whispered to Colet, "What's that in the sky?"

"Oh my God! There are planes coming towards us!" Colet shouted.

Everyone started screaming and I yelled at Sara and my nieces. "Put your shoes on but you'll have to dress later!"

It was terrifying! Everybody was running for the nearest shelter. The doors to the shelters were very narrow and people were trying to push their way in shouting and cursing. Within minutes, the beach was empty.

"Look, there's a shelter across the road!" I shouted. We grabbed the three girls' hands and ran as fast as we could. They were screaming hysterically. As we got nearer, we could see the shelter was filling up. Someone shouted, "You can't come in here; we're squashed as it is!"

"What's wrong with you?" I screamed. "Can't you see I have three young children here!" I tried to push the girls in to the shelter but the door was slammed in my face.

The roar of the engines was bloodcurdling and deafeningly loud.

Suddenly, Colet shouted at me, "Look, somebody's calling us from down the road!" A man was waving both arms in the air. By now we were terrified; the planes were so low and we were almost on our knees; we had to drag the girls along the pavements as they were frantic with fear.

Finally, we reached the shelter and two men pulled us in and quickly slammed the door tight. It was pitch dark inside as we all fell to the ground exhausted. We had to feel our way around to get the girls close to us.

They were all hysterical and Colet and I couldn't calm them down. We could feel the vibration of the bombs as they hit the earth. How could a wonderful relaxing afternoon turn into one of sheer terror in one moment? The men tried to calm the frantic screams of the children as the bombs rained down on us but it was difficult. I could feel their bodies shaking as I held them close.

Another of the men was trying to convince us all that what was happening was for the good of the country. "The American Airforce and the British Airforce are trying to immobilise the docks along the French, Belgian and Dutch coasts so that they will be out of action for the German Army to use," he said. I don't think anyone agreed that it was for our good while the bombs fell from the skies.

"It will soon be over!" another man shouted. And thankfully, not long afterwards, the all clear siren wailed and one of the men opened the door and we all couldn't get out quick enough. I thanked the men for looking after us. Our eyes soon adjusted to the brightness but it took longer for the girls to calm down; they were traumatised.

"It's going to take a long time for Sara to get over this," I whispered to Colet as we made our way home.

"I'm not sure if I will get over it soon either," said Colet. "I was really frightened in that shelter. I was convinced one of the bombs was going to hit us. They felt so close and the noise was horrendous!" When we eventually arrived home, Sara burst into tears again as she ran to Papa's side. I explained to Papa what had happened. The pain of watching his youngest remaining child suffer was etched across his increasingly weary face.

Sara stayed off school for a week because she was so distressed and very nervous. Any loud noise made her dash either to hide behind the chair or under the table; it was awful to watch. On many occasions, I picked her up onto my lap and she cuddled into me as we both fell asleep, exhausted.

The bombings continued sporadically throughout the year but more often, the planes flew over us to drop their bombs on some other poor cities beyond us.

Chapter Twenty-Six
The Changes

The new year roared in again with no let-up in the artic weather. Icicles hung from window ledges once more, snow was piled high along the sides of the roads and pavements were treacherous to walk on.

As I was standing over the sink looking out at our sparkling ice-covered lawn, I said to myself, "Any kind of warmth would be welcome right now."

Suddenly, I had a brilliant idea. But it would have to wait until I was back at work the next day and I could speak to Hugo, my boss.

"Could I borrow an electric fire from one of the empty rooms?" I asked Hugo the following day when I arrived at work.

"Yes, of course, you can have one. I don't know why I didn't think of it before," Hugo answered. "How have you been managing to keep warm with the weather so cold and the shortage of fuel?"

Hugo's concern touched my heart. "It's been very difficult. When Papa is out and about, he'll pick up bits of wood but I'm so nervous. If the soldiers should catch him, he would be punished. We've been going to bed early instead to keep warm," I replied.

Hugo shook his head in sympathy. "The only problem I can foresee, Rosina, is if all the rooms are full, I will need the fire back. We can't have our poor soldiers going cold, can we?" Hugo remarked bitterly.

"No, we certainly can't have that," I replied sardonically.

Our evenings were now a little warmer with the electric fire.

"This is a brilliant idea, Rosina," Papa said as he held his hands over the top of the fire.

"I agree with you, Papa," Sara smiled.

"We will have to be careful how often we use it. Hugo told me about someone that was caught and his fire was pulled apart and thrown out of the house along with the owner," I said.

"What happened to him?" Sara asked fearfully.

"I don't know, Sara, and I didn't ask. The people that work in the Municipal Offices will notice if our electric bills are suddenly higher then they will come and search the house and won't leave until they find the reason." I tried to express how serious it would be if we were caught.

With the arctic weather outside, 1943 was bad enough. But there also came a new frosty feel in our house as well. I noticed Papa going out more than usual and he would often breeze in well after dark. When I asked him where he had been all day, he almost bit my head off.

"Have I got to ask your permission to go out!" he snapped.

"Okay, okay! I'm only asking," I replied. "It's just I'm so frightened that you will be picked up by the Nazis and taken away. What would happen to Sara and me then? I'm just worried about you, Papa."

His big blue eyes softened and he put his arm around my shoulder.

"You shouldn't worry about me, Rosina, I can look after myself," but I noticed he was blushing.

"What's wrong, Papa? Tell me," I asked.

After a long pause, his reply took me by complete surprise.

"I've met a friend, a lady friend," he said sheepishly.

"What do you mean, a lady friend?" I spluttered.

"Don't look so suspicious, Rosina. She's lovely and kind. I've known her for a long time," Papa explained.

"How long?" I exclaimed.

"Oh, I don't know, quite a while." He hunched his shoulders. "She's just a friend, Rosina. She has two children: Saul, who's the same age as Sara, and Mina, who is four years younger."

Before he could continue, I pounced on him. "Are you sure she's just a friend? You seem to know all about her, Mamma hasn't been dead three years and you're out all hours seeing other women! How could you do this to us, Papa?"

He must have seen the disgust in my eyes.

"Please, Rosina, try to understand—I miss your Mamma dreadfully. I feel very lonely at times."

"You have us, so how can you be lonely?" I shouted as I ran out of the room and slammed the door.

He shouted after me, "She's just a friend!"

"So you say!" I screamed back.

Since our row, Papa stayed in most evenings but his daytime outings remained the same.

"Where does he go for hours on end? Is he visiting the other woman all day?" I asked myself. I hated the tension between us and I knew he was lonely, but the thought of another woman in our home was unthinkable.

For an hour each night we settled down in front of our little electric fire. If I was lucky enough to find some chocolate sweets in one of the shops on my way home from work, I would keep them as a treat for us in the evening, when we listened eagerly to our wireless, afraid to turn it up higher than a whisper. We hoped to hear some encouraging news from our friends at the BBC in London. But often, the broadcaster's voice would die away and sometimes we couldn't tune into any station that suited us. We felt so alone.

When we were able to receive news from the BBC Home Service in London, we could hear the happiness in the broadcaster's voice when relaying news of the constant bombing by the Allied Forces over Berlin and Frankfurt, which was wonderful news to us too. Papa was so excited.

"This war won't last long now that the Allied Air forces are bombing Germany day and night," he told us, looking more cheerful than I'd seen him in a long time.

"Does this mean there will be more planes flying over Oostende?" I asked, dreading the answer. "I would expect so but, if the end is in sight who are we to grumble?"

The reality of occupation raised its ugly head when we heard of young boys, who were listening outside people's homes, hoping to catch them with their wireless sets on loudly enough to be heard outside. This was especially cruel to some of the elderly, who were hard of hearing, and had to turn their sets up louder. Of course they were breaching the law by just having a wireless set. Most people had more than one wireless and they were well hidden in their homes. The wireless was our saviour—our only link to the outside world. These young hooligans would contact the Gestapo and they didn't care who they were spying on. Even if they were ill or elderly, they would be beaten and flogged. These boys just wanted recognition from the Nazis to give them a feeling of power and control.

We began to question every word that passed our lips. We never confided in anyone that we weren't certain of. Betrayal of their own people meant nothing to some. It was heart breaking to think that our people would stoop so low.

"You must be very careful, Papa. Look how they treated you when they came to the house," I reminded him.

"I know; I must remember to keep the volume low," Papa replied.

The next day I was looking forward to a relaxing morning. I had become quite resourceful at unpicking old garments and basically turning rags to riches, which Mamma had done constantly. We were always well-dressed and clean and tidy. I don't know how she had coped when she had fifteen children, although many had not survived the great war due to lack of food and medication.

After walking Sara and her friend Katlyn to school, I hurried home. I wasn't sure how Sara would react to having skirts made out of Mamma's clothes. Even though she had been wearing such garments for a long time, I tended to make them when she was not around. I hadn't seen Papa all morning and I was just about to stop and make some lunch, when suddenly the kitchen door sprung open and in walked Papa with three strangers. Although I had never seen them before, I knew exactly who they were.

"How dare he do this without telling me," I muttered to myself.

Thoughts were running wild through my head. I was stunned into silence.

"Rosina, this is Heli and her two children, Saul and Mina." They all said nothing.

My reaction must have been obvious for Heli stepped forward, took hold of my hand with both of hers and shook it. I withdrew my hand just as quickly.

"Hello Rosina," Heli said. "I hope you don't mind us calling unannounced. Your Papa has told me so much about you. I thought it was time we met." She seemed friendly enough but I thought she had a sour smile. I still couldn't believe Papa could be so insensitive.

"Pleased to meet you," I replied with a forced smile.

Papa went out to the shed to look for some wood in the hope of keeping the fire burning.

There was a sudden transformation in Heli: her smile vanished and was quickly replaced by a harsh sternness. She looked at me and my clothes and I immediately knew we weren't going to get on.

She walked over to Mamma's chair, never taking her eyes off me. Then she sat down and crossed one leg over the other. I got up and walked over to the sink, pretending to be busy but I could feel her eyes on me. Her boldness was beyond belief. I tried so hard to keep calm and be as pleasant as I possibly could.

She got up and made her way over to the sink. She put her hand on my shoulder and tilted her head. "I was so sorry to hear about your Mamma and the rest of your family, but that's war for you," she said, keeping one hand on my shoulder. She lifted the other hand in the air. "We've all lost someone or other. I'm sure your Mamma wouldn't object to your Papa finding happiness again and not dwelling on the past."

I couldn't keep calm any longer; I turned to face this stranger with cold empty eyes. I picked her hand up and quickly threw it off my shoulder. Without raising my voice, I said, "How dare you come into my house and presume to know what my Mamma would want. You know nothing about us, so keep your opinions to yourself!"

Papa had just stepped into the kitchen.

"Rosina, don't speak to Heli like that!'

I turned to look at him and I saw someone I didn't recognise.

"Why didn't you let me know we were having guests, Papa. I could have made us all a cup of that disgusting coffee we now drink!"

"Okay, Rosina, there's no need to be so cynical. This is my house and I don't have to ask your permission when inviting friends over."

I caught Heli's smug smile behind Papa's back as he made it clear where I stood.

Just then, Sara walked in. I had forgotten she was due home from school at lunch time.

"Who are these people, Rosina?" she whispered, hiding behind me.

"I'll explain later. Go up to your bedroom for now," I told her.

Heli's daughter had been trying to talk to her Mamma and eventually, she skipped over and sat on her Mamma's lap. What she said next chilled me to the bone.

"Mamma, is this going to be our house?"

"Mina, go and play with Sara upstairs." She shooed her daughter away with her hand. I glared at Heli suspiciously, wondering if I had heard right.

Papa couldn't see past Heli's fake smile. I couldn't bear to look at him.

I was determined not to show Heli how upset I was. I opened the passage door and called, "Sara, I'm going over to Ada's; are you coming with me?"

She bounded down the stairs eagerly.

As I put my coat on, I looked at Papa, and whispered, "How could you?"

I caught hold of Sara's hand and closed the door behind us. A few seconds later, I heard it open and Papa called, "Come back, Rosina! Please—we'll talk about it."

I ignored him but before he shut the door, I heard Heli say, "Leave her, Jakop. She'll come around."

We both wrapped our coats tightly around us as we made our way to Ada's. The bitterly cold wind stung our faces, and the heavy snow, which had fallen the day before, had frozen in the severe frost, making it very slippery to walk on. Suddenly, Sara lost her footing and fell on to her back. She cried out in pain and I quickly picked her up.

"Who are those people?" Sara asked between sobs.

"Not now, Sara. Let's just get to Ada's so I can look at your back."

"Is Papa going to marry that woman and live in our house?" she persisted. I was trying to ignore her questions as I didn't want to give her false hope.

She looked up at me and said, "I do hope not. I don't want her to be my Mamma."

"Sara, she will never be our Mamma—always remember that. I think they're just friends of Papa's." I couldn't think straight; crazy thoughts were running through my head. I felt so angry with Papa for being so secretive; and I felt angry with Mamma for leaving us to fend on our own.

By the time we reached Ada's house, we were both in a terrible state.

"What's happened to Sara?" Ada asked with concern. I explained briefly the situation at home and how Sara had fallen. We checked her over; there was a red patch in the centre of her back so Ada filled a hot-water bottle and Sara held it on her back. Then she went through to see her nieces.

I welcomed the cosy, warm feeling as Ada wrapped my hands around a steaming cup of hot chocolate.

"Now tell me what's happened?" Ada whispered. I tried to explain calmly to Ada but I could no longer control my tears.

"A while ago, Papa met a woman friend. She has two children." Ada looked shocked. "They came to the house today without being invited," I gulped between sobs. "I never thought Papa would do that. He also told me that it was his house and he could bring whoever he wanted there."

"Well, I never expected he would ever do that. How long as this been going on?" Ada asked.

"I don't know! He's been staying out for hours and not coming home until after dark. But what worries me the most, is an innocent remark the little girl made; she asked her Mamma if they were going to live in our house. I'm sure they're planning to move in. Please, God, no! I can't cope with her there instead of Mamma. What am I going to do, Ada?"

I wept stormily then for Mamma, my sisters and my brother.

Ada took me in her arms and said, "Try not to read too much into what's happened today. The little girl may have been confused about what she heard."

Ada offered me a bowl of soup but I refused. My stomach was churning round in knots from fear and anxiety.

"I just don't know what to do, Ada."

"Well, for now do nothing. Don't go jumping to conclusions—wait and see what happens next."

Out of all Mamma's children, Ada was the one who resembled her the most. Her kindness knew no boundaries.

We stayed at Ada's until well into the evening, hoping that the woman and her kids would be gone before we got home. I knew I was taking a risk being out after dark, especially with Sara, but I couldn't face Papa that night. I was relieved to discover he had gone to bed by the time we arrived home.

When I finally got to bed, I lay there unable to sleep. Sara, on the other hand, had fallen asleep the minute her head hit the pillow. The fall had shaken her more than I realised. I was trying to piece together all that had been said. Mina must have got it wrong. I couldn't bear another family in our house. No one could replace Mamma or my sisters and brother. Something about Heli didn't ring true.

And I hoped Papa would realise sooner rather than later, that his friendship with this woman was a big mistake and be rid of her before she took over our house. I didn't know her but her appearance was enough to send a shiver of horror down my spine: she had harsh features; her hair was tightly pulled back with big clips, she was very thin with almost a skeletal look about her, she wore black pointed shoes which made her feet look too long.

I turned on my side hoping to fall asleep but I couldn't shake away the memory of how she made me feel like an outsider in my own home. Why bring her children and introduce them to me? There was one thing I was certain of; Ada missing that boat was a Godsend for me.

I was up at six the following morning and I took Sara to Ada's as I had to be in work for seven o'clock. Papa was still in bed so I avoided any further confrontation.

Walking down towards the hotel, I couldn't get Heli out of my mind. I pictured Papa and her together and it disgusted me.

I had forgotten that we were expecting a new batch of officers in by lunch time and so every room in the hotel had to be cleaned and all beds stripped and made up, cutlery had to be thoroughly polished and squeaky clean. All the fuss and commotion was for some General. Since the occupation, Belgium had been run by a Military Government and so everything had to be ship-shape for this General's visit. Hugo had kept us on our toes all morning so by lunchtime, Colet and I were shattered.

As the weeks quickly passed, I took on more hours in the hotel. With the extra money, I was able to save a small amount each week.

There had been no more sign of Heli and her kids since that awful day. Papa was very quiet and he didn't have much to say since the big introduction. I wanted to ask if he was still seeing her but I dared not for fear of another argument.

Walking home from work one day, I felt so worn out, being constantly at the beck and call of the Nazi soldiers, that I could hardly put one foot in front of the other. *I'm going to rest first before I start our evening meal*, I thought. I was also later than usual.

When I stepped into the kitchen, there was a wonderful aroma, one I had almost forgotten. Papa was frying herrings on the open fire.

"Where did you get all that fish, Papa? What a lovely smell and where did the coal come from? It's so warm in here, I had forgotten how cosy this room could be."

"I know, isn't it wonderful?" Papa replied. "Call Sara and we'll all sit down together and I'll tell you all about it."

As Sara and I sat at the table, Papa started to speak: "Yan called this morning—you remember him? He was my foreman when I was working. He brought two small bags of coal; he was always such a thoughtful man. I know we have the small electric fire but as you said, Rosina, we must be very careful if the electric bill spirals out of control."

"Where did the fish come from?" I asked searching his face.

"Don't look at me like that, Rosina. It was Heli who gave us the fish."

"Why am I not surprised?" I sneered.

Ignoring my sarcastic remark, he continued, "She brought it over this morning. Before you say anything, she had a box full of fish given to her by her friend's husband."

"She has got friends then?" I replied meanly and Sara burst out laughing.

"Sorry, Papa, I didn't mean that," I said quickly as I saw the pained look on Papa's face.

"Give me a break, girls. I'm trying my best to please you all. Anyway, there was too much fish for her so she thought of us, which was kind of her wasn't it?" There was no reply from Sara or me. He sighed heavily and then spoke again: "There is something else I need to tell you both. Please don't be angry with me."

"What is it, Papa?" I asked coldly; I just knew it involved Heli.

He glanced at us, then he pushed his meal aside.

"We're getting married," he announced.

"What!" I screamed.

He bowed his head and without looking at either of us, he whispered, "In two weeks at the registry office."

I was dumbstruck.

Sara stared across the table, her eyes brimming with tears. She looked so pathetic. Then with her index finger, she pointed furiously at me. "You said they would never get married," she said and I felt as if she had struck me. "I asked you if she was going to be our new Mamma and you told me she wouldn't. You lied to me, Rosina!"

"Listen to me, Sara," I pleaded. "She will never be your Mamma, even if they do get married. She will never take Mamma's place."

"I don't believe you, Rosina! When Mamma was missing, you said we would find her and we never did because she was dead! I will never believe anything you tell me again!" She jumped off the chair and started screaming and lashing out at Papa. "I won't live in this house if she is going to live here! She will never be my Mamma! I hate you, Papa, I hate you!"

She slammed the kitchen door and ran upstairs shouting. "I hate you both!"

I could hardly look at Papa. I knew the war had changed him but this I could not accept.

"Why do you have to marry her, Papa? You're only thinking of yourself. How could you do this to us? Don't you think we've gone through enough the last few years? How long have you known her?" I felt so confused as the questions that had been queuing up in my head tumbled out.

"I've known her for years," Papa said.

"Do you mean to tell me you were seeing her when Mamma was alive?" I shouted.

"No, no! Mamma knew Heli too—they both attended the same church."

"How am I going to win Sara's trust again? It's taken almost three years to put a smile back on that child's face. You've put this woman before your family, Papa."

I felt hurt and sorry at the same time. Losing his wife and most of his children had created a massive void in Papa's life which could never be filled.

"Was it Heli who persuaded you to get married?"

"No, not at all. We both want it. Don't worry about Sara—she'll come around—you wait and see. She'll forgive you before she'll forgive me. Sara looks up to you and relies on you for everything," Papa said, getting out of his chair to fill the kettle then resting it on the fire. "Shall I make us both a cup of coffee?" he asked.

"No, not for me," I snapped as I gave the dustbin the rest of the fish.

"I take it you've discussed the living arrangements?" I said coldly.

"Yes, we will live in this house," he answered.

"And where is everyone going to sleep?"

"Well…" he hesitated before continuing, "Heli thought her son could sleep up in the attic and Mina, Sara and you in the other bedroom."

Angrily, I blurted out my opinion of these arrangements: "You've obviously not thought about Sara or me! Have you stopped to think that I may want a bedroom of my own? I'm seventeen this year, Papa, and I would like a bit of privacy. You've just gone ahead and let Heli do all the arranging. How on earth are we going to manage on my measly pay?" I kept ranting on about how thoughtless he was being. "There will be three more mouths to feed," I reminded him.

"Heli has a small income each week and you have had a rise as well so we should manage," he said quietly. "I'm sorry, Rosina. I should have told you and Sara before we decided to get married."

"Yes, you should have." I opened the passage door but before I closed it behind me, I glanced back at him. "Papa, I hope you don't expect me to hand over all my hard-earned wages to your future wife because I won't. I've been doing fine without her." Then I closed the door behind me and I ran up the stairs two at a time. I could hear Sara sobbing and when I opened the door she was face down on her pillow.

"Go away, Rosina. I don't want to speak to you ever again," she cried.

"Not ever again," I said with a smile. "Oh, sweetheart, I knew as much as you did. I had no idea Papa was getting married."

I turned her over onto her back. "Try not to get so upset. You have me and you have Ada; you have school in the morning and you can go and stay with Ada until I come home from work."

She sat up and put her arms around my neck. "I wish Mamma was here. It's not fair that she had to die and leave us all on our own."

"You're not on your own, Sara—always remember that. And I feel exactly the same—I wish Mamma was here too."

The day of the marriage dawned. I couldn't call it a celebration as there was nothing to celebrate. Sara and I were in no mood to attend but we did for Papa's sake. I managed to alter one of Monica's dresses for Sara to wear.

After the service, Papa called me over, "Would you mind looking after the children, Rosina, for Heli and me to spend some time on our own. We'll be home tomorrow morning."

I could feel the heat rising in my cheeks. I felt so embarrassed that I couldn't even look at Papa.

"Yes, I'll look after them as long as you are back by eight-thirty in the morning because I've got to be in work by nine," I replied, knowing there was a hard edge to my voice but feeling no remorse. "Don't forget, Papa."

"I won't, and thank you," he replied.

As the weeks passed, Sara and I had to learn to get along with the new members of our household as best we could. To my surprise, Heli kept the place tidy and clean, which was a great help for me now that we had double the washing and ironing and double the mouths to feed. However, what I noticed, and it concerned me, was how small the portions of food were that Heli was dishing out each day to Sara and me. Saul and Mina were given much larger portions. Her children were never hungry in between meals but Sara was constantly looking for food.

I was at work most days so I didn't see the lunch time portions of food. Then one day I was off work with a heavy cold and I had stayed in bed all morning. I came down at lunch time.

"Oh, Rosina." Heli looked surprised. "You're down. I thought you were staying in bed all day so I didn't include you for lunch."

"Don't worry about me; I'll have some bread with jam," I said as I began to spread a tiny bit of jam on two slices of bread.

"Rosina, just one slice of bread and a thin spreading of jam! That's all you are allowed," Heli said sharply.

"Why only one slice of bread? That's not fair, you're all having fish as well as the bread!" I answered crossly.

"Well, that's the rule in this house—take it or leave it!" She threw me a filthy look.

Up until this point, Papa had never interfered with Heli's running of the house but that day, to my surprise, he did.

"Rosina, pour yourself a cup of coffee and take two slices of bread. There is a scraping of butter left so you have it. And then go back to bed—you're not looking well at all," Papa said.

Heli started to object but Papa put his hand up.

"That's enough, Heli! Can't you see how ill the girl looks? She needs nourishment."

"Thank you, Papa," I said gratefully as I closed the door and went back to bed.

I was in bed for three days and in all that time, Heli never once came upstairs to ask if I wanted a hot drink or something to eat. However, Sara brought me hot drinks and Papa made some sandwiches. I had plenty of time to mull over the fact that Heli was making sure her children got enough to eat, while Sara went hungry.

"I will deal with it when I am well enough," I told myself.

About a week after returning to work, I was in the kitchen having my lunch as normal when suddenly, I had the idea that I could bring some of my meal from work home for Sara. I had previously done that but was forced to stop because the soldiers had been searching everyone who left the hotel. However, these searches seemed to have stopped for now so I could try again. It would have to be something cold of course, and I could only do it if I was on a twelve hour shift which entitled me to a meal. As long as I was able to sneak some of my own meal out for Sara, I would.

I mentioned it to Sara that evening when we were on our own in the bedroom. She loved the idea, but was concerned that I was only having half my lunch.

"That's okay, Sara. I'm still having more than enough. I can only bring cold food home as long as you don't mind."

"Oh, Rosina, I don't mind as long as it's food," she said laughing.

I realised just how hungry she had been, when I watched how she devoured the cold snacks I brought her. I felt so sad watching her, knowing Mamma would never have allowed her children to be deprived of food. I was very careful not to show Heli what I was doing.

One evening when Mina and Sara had gone to bed, Papa and Heli were seated on the fireside chairs but with no fire to warm them. I thought this was my chance to bring up the monitoring of our food every day.

"Heli," I said hesitantly, "have you noticed that Sara is hungry all the time? I was wondering if she's eating all her food?" I continued trying to sound as innocent as I could.

"No, I haven't noticed," she replied, keeping her eyes down on an old newspaper she was reading.

"Heli, when I was off work, I did notice Saul having larger portions on his plate than Sara, yet they're both the same age," I challenged her. Anger was making me feel braver.

She put the old paper down on her lap then glanced up at me over the rim of her glasses.

"Are you accusing me of giving my children larger meals than Sara?" She turned to Papa. "Jakop, did you hear that? I don't give extra food to my children, do I?"

"No, dear," was all Papa would say, hiding behind his newspaper.

"Well, Heli," I said accusingly, "I see a huge change in Sara. She's become quiet and withdrawn; she's losing weight and has dark circles under her eyes and she's not sleeping because she's so hungry. I don't hear Saul and Mina complaining and this has only happened since you came here to live."

"That's enough, Rosina, drop the subject now," Papa demanded.

I did but the question hung in the air. What I didn't understand was how they could afford to go out as often as they did when money was so scarce. The spring nights made for later curfews and Papa and Heli were staying out longer in the evenings. I'm sure they were drunk sometimes and it worried me so much that I couldn't sleep until they were home. Papa had changed; I had lost him the day he met Heli. He now had his new readymade family, which didn't include Sara and me.

Monica was often in my thoughts and I wondered what she would make of Papa's new wife. At least she was well away from it. Britain may be at war but they didn't have the evil Nazis constantly watching them, controlling them and stealing their food. I hadn't had any contact with Monica since her letter at the beginning of the war. I supposed she hadn't received mine. All I knew was that Monica and my other relatives were staying in a small village in Wales.

The hot days of summer and the late curfews were easier to cope with during occupation. Some evenings Sara and I would stroll down to the promenade. If we were lucky we'd stop and buy an apple but that was rare. When there were no soldiers about we would chance it and walk along the water's edge; the sea felt fantastic around our feet.

We were constantly looking for food. There was never any waste; as long as it filled a gap in our stomachs, we would eat it. The hunger pains would live with me long after this cruel war was over.

Day after day, the Americans flew over Oostende heading for Germany and the British did their stint during the night. We listened to the wireless religiously; we'd rejoice when hearing what damage the bombing had done to railway tracks and military installations in Germany.

I never thought I would hear myself say how good it felt that the Germans were suffering now, like we had for the last three years.

The only trouble was we never had any peace. I was always worried a stray bomb would drop on us. It was worse at night with our bedrooms cloaked in darkness and the eerie drone of the engines flying over us.

Hope was our only light in a world of darkness.

One night when Papa and Heli were out and we were all sound asleep, Sara woke screaming.

"Rosina, I've got a bad pain in my tummy and I feel sick!"

"Do you feel hungry?" I asked.

"Yes, my tummy is hurting," she moaned.

I went downstairs to see what food I could bring her. I managed to find more than half a loaf in the pantry and then I noticed, behind some boxes, three jugs of milk and some butter. I wondered why Heli was hiding all this food. Surely she wasn't just giving it to her children? I cut a medium slice of bread for Sara then I poured her half a glass of milk as well.

"There—eat this, Sara," I said when I came back upstairs. "Eat it slowly and try not to wake Mina."

After she finished, I hid the plate and glass in my cupboard.

"If you should wake in pain again, drink some water—that may help. Now try and go back to sleep."

The thought of Heli hiding food from Sara and me troubled me greatly and I struggled to get back to sleep.

I must have fallen into a deep sleep because the next thing someone had their hands on my shoulders and was shaking me. I thought I was dreaming at first until I heard Heli's voice.

"Rosina, wake up, Rosina! I want you downstairs this minute. I need to speak to you."

"What's wrong? Is Papa ill?" I said and sat up and rubbed my eyes.

"No, your Papa isn't ill. Get up this minute!" Heli whispered in a rough voice.

"Whatever it is, can't it wait until morning?" I tried to lie back down but she caught hold of my arm and pulled me up to a sitting position.

"No, it can't wait—I want you downstairs now!" I found a cardigan and wrapped it around me then followed her down the stairs, wondering what was so important to get me out of bed so late in the night.

She stood in the kitchen arms folded.

"Answer me truthfully!" she shouted.

"I will if I can," I said, still in slumber land.

"When we went out tonight, did you help yourself to bread and milk?" She glared at me with her steely eyes.

I looked at her, astonished at what she had just said.

"You dragged me out of bed just to ask me if I've had bread and milk? Yes, I've had some. I felt hungry so I cut a thin slice of bread and drank a tiny drop of milk. There, I've told you. Now I'm going back to bed."

"Oh no, you don't!" she roared." You're not getting away that easy." As quick as a flash, she stood in the door way stopping me from going upstairs.

"Let me pass, Heli. Some of us have to be up early to go to work," I said loudly.

"Don't you raise your voice to me!" she shouted back.

174

"Why is it so important that you have to drag me out of bed at this ungodly hour? Couldn't this have waited until morning?" I was beginning to lose my patience but the look on her face told me this wasn't over.

"You have the cheek to stand there and tell me a bare-faced lie!" she screamed.

Her madness was beginning to frighten me. I looked at her and asked myself where had Papa met this horrible person? She pointed to her chest with her index finger.

"I know! You had more than a thin slice of bread and I also know you had half a glass of milk!" Heli announced.

"Who cares what I had!" I shouted back at her. Suddenly, I realised what she had done and I was horrified.

"You've marked the bread and the milk!" I was speechless. "How dare you do that when I'm the only one that goes out to work. You have no right to do that to me in my own house!" I raised my voice to her.

"I have every right—I look after this house how I see fit! And yes, I did mark the bread and the milk!"

The arrogance etched on this woman's face was absolutely brazen. Defiantly, she laughed. "Well Rosina, it's like this: when we go out I make sure the bread, the milk and any other food that may be in the pantry is marked so that I know exactly every tiny morsel of food that passes your lips!" she snarled.

I couldn't believe what I was hearing—how this woman had the gall to scheme and snake her way into our lives and lay down rules without any regard for Sara and me. Obviously, Papa was unaware of her cunningness.

"What did Papa ever see in you?" I spat at her.

"Watch your tongue, my girl!" she retorted.

"I'm not your girl and the sooner you realise you're not our mother, the better!"

She walked over to the pantry and pulled out a bucket and a bar of carbolic soap. I wondered why on earth she was bringing them out in the middle of the night.

"You are a very selfish, thoughtless girl!" she hissed.

I walked up to her, inches from her face. "If you had taken the time to get to know me, you would have seen that I am neither thoughtless or selfish. You walked into our house and owned it on your first visit," I reminded her.

"Who said that was my first visit?" Mockingly, she glared at me then continued. "I have been coming here for weeks, while you were at work! Ask your Papa if you don't believe me," she sneered.

That hurt. How could Papa have been so sly? I tried so hard to control my feelings and not show her how upset I was. I knew she was trying her best to make me feel that Papa didn't love me.

I made my way to the passage door. I turned to her and shook my head. "I knew the moment you walked into our lives that Sara and I meant nothing to you. I can see now why Sara is so hungry all the time!" I glared at her. "Well, this has to stop. I'm the breadwinner in this house. Not only do you have the audacity to mark the food but when you and Papa go out, you spend my hard-earned money on drink."

"Where do you think you're going?" She put the kitchen chairs on top of the table. "You will wash this floor now. Get down on your hands and knees and you make sure this floor is squeaky clean. I want each tile and the grooves spotless," she demanded.

"If you think I'm scrubbing floors in the middle of the night, you can think again." I opened the door to go upstairs.

"If you don't do as I say, you leave me no alternative but to get Sara down here, and I will ask her if she had bread and milk tonight."

I turned on her quickly. "You leave Sara out of this—it has nothing to do with her!"

"You wash this floor or I will wake Sara." She stood, resolute and seething with rage.

"Okay, okay!" I put my arms up in surrender, unable to bear the thought of Sara getting dragged into our fight.

Without another word, I poured the water from the kettle into the bucket and with the soap-suds and brush, I began to scrub the floor.

One by one I cleaned each tile, falling tears mingling with the soap suds. I thought of Mamma: she would have been horrified if she could see me scrubbing the kitchen floor in the middle of the night with this lunatic standing over me.

Heli stayed until the very last tile was done. I picked the bucket up and threw the dirty water down the sink.

As I made my way to the stairs, I stopped in front of her. "This is the last time I will ever do anything for you. I won't forget this and in future, if Sara and

I are hungry I won't hesitate to eat my bread and drink my milk regardless of what you or Papa says!"

Any thought of sleep was abandoned that night. I wakened Sara early and took her to Ada's before Heli was up. I did not want Sara knowing what had happened during the night.

When I came home from work, Heli was out and had taken her two children with her. I was desperate to speak to Papa about the night before, especially while Sara was still at Ada's.

"Papa, I need to talk to you now while Heli is out."

Papa looked up from the newspaper he was reading.

"What's wrong, Rosina? Don't tell me you and Heli have been arguing again?"

"Has she told you what happened last night?" I asked, aware that this discussion hadn't got off to a good start.

"No, what happened?" He looked bewildered.

"Are you aware that Heli marks the bread and the milk jug whenever she goes out, so that she will know if Sara or I have had something to eat or drink?" I said.

Papa was dumbstruck and I knew by his expression that this was the first he knew of his wife's conniving ways.

I told him and about Sara screaming with hunger pains, and how I went to find something for her to eat.

"Papa, I couldn't believe what I found: three bottles of milk and over half a loaf of bread hidden behind some boxes. I cut some bread and poured some milk into a cup then took it up to Sara. When you arrived home, Heli must have checked the pantry because she woke me and literally dragged me down the stairs, just because my sister was starving. My punishment was to scrub the kitchen floor, in the middle of the night and she called me a selfish, thoughtless girl."

I could no longer control myself and my tears fell unchecked.

"She called you selfish?" Papa put his arms around me. "You are not selfish or thoughtless." He looked pained as he continued, "Oh, Rosina, my darling girl, both you and Sara have been through so much. I will need to speak to Heli, this must stop. But," he hesitated, "I must be careful—I don't want to be seen as accusing her of favouritism."

177

"But, Papa," I protested, "she is favouring her children over Sara and me! It shouldn't be that way; we are part of this family whether she likes it or not. We should be treated equally but we feel unwanted in our own home," I said tearfully.

I woke the following morning to the sound of the fire being raked and for a minute I thought it was Mamma; she was always up first and we would come down to the fire lit, table laid and a lovely warm smile to welcome us all.

I missed her dreadfully and Heli's invasion of my mother's home made it even harder to come to terms with losing her.

I dragged myself out of bed, noticing that Sara and Mina must have gone downstairs already. I washed in cold water and quickly dressed.

I opened the kitchen door to find the table looking full of wonderful food. There was sliced bread, a small pot of jam and standing there beside the jam was a mouth-watering pot of butter all waiting to be eaten. Heli was putting sticks and coal on the fire. She looked up and smiled.

"Oh, Rosina, I didn't hear you come down. Can I pour you a cup of coffee?"

"No, thank you," I said, too astonished to challenge her on her sudden change in behaviour.

Sara, Mina and Saul were seated around the table. Heli was acting as if this was what breakfast looked like every morning.

"Look, Rosina, isn't it great," Sara smiled, pointing to the table.

"Yes, it's nice, for a change, Sara," I managed to mutter, determined not to confront Heli in front of the children. "I will be leaving soon and I'll take you over to Ada's on my way to work."

"Okay," she said in between mouthfuls of bread and butter. I couldn't help but enjoy seeing Sara laughing while eating her third slice of bread.

After dropping Sara at Ada's, I made my way to work mulling over the contrast between how nasty Heli had been the other night and how totally different she was this morning. She was acting as if nothing had happened. I wondered what Papa had said to her.

"Well, I won't be persuaded to forgive her that easily," I told myself. I didn't expect her motherly love to last and I was right. Within a week, Heli was back to her old selfish ways. Sara and I tried to stay out of her road as much as possible and I still kept bringing the small amounts of food from the hotel for Sara. When I thought back to the night Sara woke up screaming, I realised it was a time when I had been unable to bring any food home from the hotel for about three days because one of the ovens had broken down. It was further proof that Sara hadn't eaten much during those days.

Chapter Twenty-Seven
Hope Grows

I missed the old Oostende, the lazy days of summer, splashing along the water's edge and relaxing on our golden beaches. We were once the gateway to Europe. I hoped and prayed we would be again one day. I used to sit and watch the ferries from England cruise into port. I wondered why the ships made a complete turn outside the harbour and then steered in backwards. One day Papa told me it was because the harbour was too small for the ships to turn. I missed it all.

Lately there seemed to be even more than usual bomb-laden planes heading for Germany day and night. We tried to tune into any station we could but more often than not the wireless would crackle or die on us.

"The bombing can't go on forever; soon the Germans must crumble and when that day comes we will be waiting and cheering for the liberation," Papa announced.

July brought glorious weather. I enjoyed sitting in the back garden, sewing or knitting as I saw to Sara's needs.

Sometimes after everyone had gone to bed, I would open the kitchen door and stand there watching the planes fly low in formations of hundreds. They lit up the skies like thousands of stars watching over us: fathers, sons and brothers, all risking their lives to free us from the hardship and the cruel suffering that dominated Europe. While they flew over I felt a sense of safety, but once our allied friends had passed, the shadows of darkness spread once again and filled me with fear.

One particular night the planes flying over Oostende were endless. The following day we heard on the wireless there had been heavy bombing in Hamburg. I felt my heart lift with joy and then was startled; I wouldn't have dreamt of having such wicked thoughts before the war. But our lives had changed forever and there was no room for sentiment; the war had made me stronger and wiser in all aspects of life.

All too soon, our summer sun left us and drifted south, while the autumn winds began to undress the trees. The waves along the North Sea coast battered our golden beaches once again.

The thought of another winter under such harsh conditions worried me. In the autumn of 1943, the BBC home service was constantly broadcasting the slow demise of Berlin and Frankfurt. This gave us fresh hope, but nothing had changed here in Oostende. We were still looking for food and cutting down what was left of the trees, while trying not to get caught. The Nazis still caused fear in us on a daily basis.

Chapter Twenty-Eight
The Beginning of the End

Winter of 1944 was almost over. It had been a bitterly cold, endless season, with less food and often no fire for days and that meant no hot drinks. I even missed the foul coffee ersatz—at least you had warmth slithering down your throat. The small electric fire didn't throw out much heat with six bodies around it. I had no room to call my own and longed for privacy. Life was miserable.

Papa was constantly talking about the bombing of Germany. "Something is going to happen this year, Rosina. I can feel it in my bones," he said.

"Oh, Papa, how can you feel it in your bones?" I laughed.

"Haven't you been listening to the wireless?" he replied.

"When do I have the time to listen to the wireless? I'm at work most of the time," I reminded him.

However, Papa was right; things were changing and there was a spring in everyone's step. We weren't quite sure what was changing but there were rumours all over Oostende. There were also coded messages on the wireless which we didn't understand and leaflets were dropped from planes telling us to be ready.

"Ready for what, Papa?" I asked one day.

"Rosina, I'm convinced the end of the war is near," he said happily.

He poured us both a cup of coffee then sat in his chair. As he lit his pipe, he spoke of the years gone by and felt that the worse was over. I hoped he was right.

He seemed more content these days and it was lovely for me to have him all to myself for a change, and I think he felt the same.

"Have you noticed, Rosina, that there doesn't seem to be so many soldiers on the streets?" he pondered.

"Yes, I noticed on my way home from work yesterday, but there's still no let-up in the food rationing; in fact I think it's worse now. Every day I dream about when freedom will finally be ours."

Papa said, "Only the other day, I sat here for ages. It must have been at least two hours. Heli was out and I had the house to myself for once." He smiled sadly as he glanced over to me. "I cast my mind back to the day Poland was invaded. That was the beginning of the end for all of Europe. Do you remember the soul-destroying decisions we had to make about whether to leave Oostende?"

The tears were trickling down his cheeks. I sat on the floor by his chair, holding his hand. "I must admit, my dear, we made the wrong decision. I cannot blame Marie even though she desperately wanted to leave, but look how it worked out for her. God rest her soul. Little Ellie will grow up without her Mamma." He put both hands over his face and cried bitterly.

"Oh, Papa, you mustn't blame yourself for the past. I know it was torture for you; it was for me too; remember I was there as well," I said.

"Oh, my darling, I would never have been able to carry on if it hadn't been for you and Sara." His spirit was sinking very low.

"You've survived, Papa. Every day was a struggle for us, not knowing if we would make it, but we have," I tried to reassure him.

"I often think about that evening when the Gestapo came to our home. I was really frightened for all of us and I didn't want to show you how serious the situation was."

This was the first time Papa had mentioned that terrifying night.

"I thought they were going to kill us, Papa. The way you were treated was horrendous!" I confessed. "No one would have found us, maybe for days, if they had killed us. I'm almost eighteen now, Papa, but I was pushed into adulthood that dreadful night. But it also taught me to be courageous and stand up for what I believe in."

Chapter Twenty-Nine
The Allies Arrive, 6 June 1944

I couldn't believe what I was hearing on the wireless. "Oh Papa, where are you? Come quickly!" I shouted loudly.

"What is so urgent?" he said as he came through the door from the back garden.

"The first allied troops have landed on the beaches of Normandy," I gasped in excitement, but by the time Papa had come into the kitchen, the broadcaster's voice had faded away and then the wireless went dead.

"Oh, no, no, the Germans have cut us off!" I screamed at the wireless. "Oh, Papa, you know what this means? The allies have come to free us!"

Papa dropped the clothes he had been carrying onto the floor and leaped over to the wireless. He began to fiddle with the radio, clearly beside himself.

"Calm down! You're going to give yourself a heart attack," I said, trying to make him sit but, knowing he wouldn't.

"I want to know what's happening! Don't you, Rosina?"

"Yes, of course I do. I told you what the broadcaster said but we'll just have to be patient until we can hear more," I said with more calmness in my voice than I actually felt. "I'm off to work now. I'll pick Sara up from Ada's on my way home"

"I told you something big was going to happen this year," Papa remarked. "I could tell by the constant bombing of Germany."

Papa decided to come with me, hoping he would learn more about what had happened down in the town. He knew the Germans would do everything in their power to stop us hearing anymore broadcasts from the BBC in London if, indeed, the Allied troops were making progress through our cities and towns.

I hardly dared believe that this could mean freedom and I wondered how long we would have to wait for it to be ours.

I hurried to work as fast as I could. I was very late but for once I didn't care; I was flying high. As I walked through the doors into the foyer of the hotel, the atmosphere of joy and excitement hit me, but no one dare openly show it for fear of reprisal.

The soldiers had a menacing look about them with helmets low over their faces and rifles at the ready.

Hugo was practically bouncing off the ceiling with happiness, until a soldier appeared and then he instantly changed; we all did, but inside I wanted to shout to the heavens.

Hugo pulled me aside and whispered, "Be careful what you say and do, Rosina. The soldiers are ready to pounce at the most trivial of problems. They obviously know what's going on in France." Hugo smiled as he walked away.

"Thank you, Lord, for this day. I shall remember it for as long as I live," I prayed under my breath.

As the weeks rolled on, we heard more and more news of the troops advancing inland through France. But we also heard the sad news that thousands of troops had been slaughtered and many more wounded. The only way we got to hear any good news was by word of mouth on the streets. Now and again the BBC would throw out a word or two of the successes the Allies were achieving.

The troops were constantly on my mind; whilst we slept, they fought tooth and nail to give us the freedom we so longed for. We could almost grasp the hand of freedom, but the German army stood their ground and fought for their lives. They were unable to match the might of the fierce Allies however, as they advanced through towns and cities, flattening anything and everything that stood in their way.

I will never forget the day that we heard that Canadian troops had crossed the border into Belgium. It was September 1944, Papa and I were in the kitchen preparing lunch when the news came from our wireless.

We both stood and stared at each other, hardly daring to believe what we had just heard. Papa's eyes shone with tears of joy while I stood rooted to the spot, trembling.

"Could it really be true, Papa? Are we free at last?" I breathed.

Papa almost jumped over to where I was standing, grabbed me around the waist and then picked me up in the air!

"Yes, you heard right! They are on their way and soon the whole country will be liberated, my darling Rose!" Very rarely did Papa call me Rose these days, and his affection compounded my joy.

As we rejoiced, Heli walked through the door, bringing an icy breeze with her.

"What's all the shouting about?" Heli stared at the two of us.

"Haven't you heard the news? The Allies have crossed the border into Belgium!" Papa sang out.

"So what?" Heli shrugged her shoulders.

"What's wrong with you, woman? Don't you want the war to end?" Papa questioned.

"Of course I do, but I can't be happy until the Nazis have all gone," she answered, dampening our jubilation. I resented her intrusion into Papa's and my celebration.

We soon heard that Brussels was liberated and as the days passed, Antwerp and Ghent were also freed from the Nazis' grip: But not without a wall of German soldiers fighting until the bitter end.

9 September 1944

One morning I was outside the hotel brushing the steps. We'd had gusts of wind lately and the autumn leaves had gathered. All of a sudden I could hear loud noises coming from further up the road. I looked up and at first I thought my eyes were deceiving me. There were soldiers marching either side of their tanks. I thought it must be the Germans reminding us they weren't beaten yet but, as they came nearer, I could see they were not German tanks. They were Canadian soldiers, flying flags from their tanks and people were following them and rejoicing. I threw the brush on the ground and ran into the foyer where Hugo was talking to the receptionist.

I shouted as loud as I could, "The Canadians are here! Quick—the Canadians are here!"

Everyone ran outside, cheering and crying. We couldn't believe what we were seeing. I felt so overwhelmed that I just sat on the pavement and cried: I cried for Mamma, Marie, Louisa and poor Joseph. I felt so lonely amongst the crowds.

"Oh, how I wish you were here to see all this, Mamma," I wept.

Just then, someone caught hold of me under my arms and threw me up in the air.

It was Hugo.

"Rosina, what are you doing sitting on the pavement crying? You should be rejoicing with everyone else." I took my handkerchief from my pinafore dress and quickly wiped my eyes.

"Oh, Hugo, I didn't know what to do so I sat on the floor and cried," I laughed, feeling foolish.

Everyone was dancing and hugging each other and there were ribbons and balloons flying everywhere. I had no idea where they came from! Someone ran out from the hotel with plates of cakes to give to the soldiers. Then they were handed cigarettes and cognac.

Suddenly, I recognised someone laughing; it was Colet. We both hugged each other and shouted happily.

"Can you believe this? Where has all the food come from?" I asked Colet.

"You know how generous Hugo can be," she replied.

"I've got to pinch myself to know this is real," I shouted to Colet over the noise of the crowd and she grabbed my hand and we danced our way through the crowds.

It was pitch black outside by the time I was ready to go home. As Colet and I walked up the road, for the first time in four long years, I wasn't afraid. Instead of soldiers patrolling the streets, there were people still out celebrating.

"We're free at last!" I heard someone call and Colet and I laughed and cheered back. All sorts of thoughts were running through my head. No more Nazis stealing our food, no more humiliation while they searched us; starvation would soon be a thing of the past, life would be worth living again. The feeling of relief was overwhelming.

Again, my thoughts turned to Mamma and my brother and sisters. How I wished they could share in this magical moment.

It was past midnight when Colet and I parted ways at my house. The light was still on in the kitchen and Papa and Heli were both sitting by the fire asleep. They had obviously waited up for me.

As I shut the door, Papa stirred. "Rosina, you're home, did you see the soldiers?"

"Yes, Papa. I was brushing the steps when they went past, and I ran screaming into the foyer to call everyone. The hotel has been full all night and it's been absolute madness, but I've enjoyed every minute of it. I'm so happy, Papa! I can't believe the Nazis will soon be gone." Suddenly, exhaustion caught up with me. "I'm going to bed now—I could sleep for a week! Oh, by the way, I don't have to be in work until 10 o'clock, Hugo told me to have a lie-in so don't wake me up early. Goodnight, Papa." I hugged him and kissed his almost bald head.

Before I reached the bottom step, Papa called out, "We made it, my darling Rose!"

"Yes, Papa, we did. And we won."

Chapter Thirty
The Victory

Christmas 1944 was the happiest since before Mamma had died. There was still a shortage of food and fuel to light the fires. But we were free to do as we like. By February 1945, the whole of Belgium was liberated.

Then we heard that the Allies had crossed into Germany and we knew that it would only be a matter of time before the victory was complete. We didn't know until months later that there were many of our own people who lived on our street, people who were our neighbours, were involved with the underground movement. I felt proud to even know these people who had risked their lives to help others. We later learned that there were many Jews and orphaned children who had been moved around so as to confuse the Germans. I hoped with all my heart that they'd made it to a safe place.

We also learned that there were many people who had collaborated with the Germans. On my way to work one day, I witnessed a woman having her hair shaved off because she had betrayed her country. I shivered with horror as I listened to her screams and saw the wild terror in her eyes.

For some reason, the rationing was worse and we couldn't understand why. With the war over, we all assumed there would be plenty of food in the shops, but in fact there was less food available. It was really only the herring which the fishermen caught and sold that kept us alive.

"We must be patient," Papa said. "The country needs to grow food again. It will be a long time before life gets back to normal, if it ever does."

"Oh don't say that, Papa," I sighed.

The fact that I could walk down the street on my own and not be afraid any more, not just of that one soldier who had terrified me so much, but of any soldiers or enemies, was heaven to me.

Every October for many years, a massive fair had come to Oostende. It was a ritual that everyone attended young and the old. After the invasion everything stopped and so did the fair but, now it was back; to everyone's delight.

Sara wanted to go to the fair on her own but Papa and I were still worried about Sara walking the streets alone. She impatiently waited for me to get ready to accompany her.

"Hurry, Rosina!" she said, hovering at the bedroom door as I tied my hair back.

As soon as I was ready, Sara grabbed my hand and dragged me out the door and down the street. As we got nearer, we could hear the music and it gave us such a thrill that we ran the rest of the way.

Everybody looked so happy and relaxed. It was so wonderful to be part of this moment in time. I would relish it forever.

Sara saw some of her friends and ran to meet them. I shouted after her, "I want you back at the entrance at ten o'clock! Do you hear me, Sara?" She merely waved her hand at me.

I walked around the fair several times hoping to spot Colet, but she was nowhere to be seen.

I went to stand next to the dodgem cars; suddenly, someone tapped me on the shoulder. I turned quickly and almost lost my footing. Assuming that it had been Colet, I was just about to tell her off, but instead I fell into the arms of a handsome stranger. I was so embarrassed that I just stood there, stunned and with heat rising rapidly in my face.

The stranger introduced himself. "Hi, my name is John. I'm a soldier with the British army. And who are you, my little beauty?" He dazzled me with his intense brown eyes. I couldn't speak but I couldn't take my eyes off him either. His alluring smile awakened emotions in me that I had never experienced before. How could I allow a total stranger to get inside my head? I knew in that moment that love at first sight was possible.

"Would you like to come on the dodgems with me?" he asked in a voice that sounded very different from that of the BBC announcers, seemingly unaware of the impact he was having on me.

I was still rooted to the ground and I just nodded my head up and down. He laughed as he took my hand and helped me into the dodgem car. He made me feel so special; I felt as if he only had eyes for me and I didn't want that feeling to end. I kept giving him sideways glances every now and again as we drove around in the car. I expected him to walk away once the ride was over but he didn't. There was a language barrier: My broken English was evidently not as good as my ability to understand it being spoken, and his strange lilt when speaking but, it didn't stop us having fun. I could not believe he had picked me out of all the pretty girls in the fair.

He was like a film star, with chocolate brown eyes and jet black, wavy hair to complement his Errol Flynn moustache. He seemed to enjoy trying to understand the Flemish language and struck me as so very gentlemanly. I couldn't believe how well we got on, considering we did not know each other.

Then all too soon it was ten o'clock. I pointed to my wrist then I put up ten fingers as I walked to the entrance of the fair. He looked down at me with a sparkle in his deep, dark eyes.

"I will walk you and your sister home," he announced.

As he caught hold of my hand, a sudden surge of emotions rose within my body. This was something new to me. I had only fleeting friendships with boys previously but, I knew this man was going to be more than just a friend to me. As we approached the entrance of the fair, we saw Sara who was already there waiting for me. She gazed intently at John.

"Who's that stranger holding your hand, Rosina? You shouldn't let him do that," she whispered under her breath.

"Be quiet, Sara, you're being rude," I said as I introduced John to her.

John held out his hand but Sara was a little dubious, hiding behind my back until his smile softened Sara's guard. She held out her little hand and said with a smile, "How do you do?"

I looked at her, startled.

"Where did that come from?" I asked her.

"School," she replied, and we all laughed.

Chapter Thirty-One
The Big Romance

The weeks that followed were the most breath-taking weeks of my entire life. My feet never touched the ground. The only time John and I didn't see each other was when he was on duty, or I was in work.

We couldn't get enough of each other and we loved learning more about each other. I discovered that he was Welsh and that he had been brought up in a tiny village there.

To my surprise, Sara seemed sad about my relationship with John.

"Rosina, are you going to marry John and move to Wales?"

"Oh, my darling Sara, I don't know. It's too early to even think about marriage. I don't know him that well, but...I will let you into a little secret...I haven't told anyone else: I love him and I've loved him from the moment I met him. But I haven't dared tell him." I caught hold of both Sara's hands and hugged her. "You will be the first to know, Sara, if our relationship becomes more serious."

I also reminded her that she would soon be a teenager. "And I'm the last person you will want to hang around with. You're growing up now, Sara. You'll soon have a boyfriend of your own."

"No I won't, I don't like the boys in school," she replied.

I assured there would be plenty of boys outside of school as well. Reminding her of her approaching teenage years seemed to cheer her up.

I suddenly thought about what Sara had just said.

What would I do if John did ask me to marry him? I asked myself. I knew nothing about this man, only that I had fallen deeply in love with him. I had been so wrapped up in my own feelings about John that I had automatically assumed he loved me just as much.

"Anyway Sara, he's a soldier and he'll most probably go back to Britain and forget all about me," I said. She pulled away from me, seemingly happier than she had been at the start of our little chat, but I did feel awful, as I remembered telling her that I would never leave her. At least, I comforted myself, Heli was beginning to slacken her strictness about how much food we were allowed.

One evening I brought John home to meet Papa and Heli. I felt so nervous about how Papa would react. The evening went better than I had expected. Heli even offered him a cup of tea.

"You're honoured, John," I said.

Heli laughed. "I was given a bag of British tea only this morning and we haven't tasted it yet."

"Thank you, Heli," John said, giving Heli one of his heart-stopping smiles. "I hope you don't think it rude of me to call you Heli on my first visit to your home."

"Not at all, John," Heli replied, smiling back in a way that I barely recognised. I couldn't believe how friendly she was to John. Was she conniving how to get rid of me, so there would be one less mouth to feed if I was to marry John and move to Wales?

Papa was very quiet but when John offered us some chocolate to have with our tea, he seemed to come around.

"When do you think you'll be heading home, John?" Papa asked.

"I'm not sure yet. I have to accompany some German prisoners back to Germany early in the New Year but that's all the information I've been given so far," John explained. I was on edge, hoping Papa wouldn't ask him about his plans regarding me.

After John had left, Papa spoke to me, "He's a British soldier, Rosina—he will love you and leave you and then what are you going to do? He'll go back to Britain and you will be left with a broken heart."

"Oh, Papa, please don't spoil it for me! I feel so relaxed with him, like I've known him for years. I'm nineteen now and I know what I'm doing."

"Tread carefully, Rosina," was all Papa would say.

I was amazed at how kind John was to us all. On each visit he would shower us with gifts: cigars for Papa, stockings for Heli and me, the most chocolate Sara had ever seen in her young life. When we were alone he would bring out perfume and sweet smelling soaps which were luxuries I had forgotten all about. On one occasion, John gave me a beautiful coloured scarf. The most appreciated gift of all was coffee; I had longed for real coffee for the five long years we had to endure the muck that substituted it. At first I never asked where all the gifts came from.

Until one day, just as John was leaving, I did ask him. Without saying a word, he grabbed me and pulled me close to him; his intense passion sent shivers rippling down my spine. He kissed me so long and hard that it took my breath away.

Afterwards, he calmly pulled out a packet of cigarettes and lit one, and I thought he was going to ignore my question.

He leaned against the wall and exhaled the grey smoke up to a star filled sky. "Being a soldier, we get perks," he eventually said.

"What are perks, John?" I asked and he started laughing which made me feel embarrassed.

"Perks are what the soldiers are offered. They're free but sometimes I have to pay if I buy something from the black market," he explained.

"But the black market is very expensive, isn't it?" I asked.

"Yes, it is, but being a soldier, we know where to go. And anyway, you're worth it."

His charm silenced any further questions and I leaned into the crook of his strong arm.

Even Papa was beginning to come around to John because he could see how kind he was to me. I didn't care what Heli thought but it was a relief that she was being friendly to John and, surprisingly, me.

I loved every moment I had with John and that was all that mattered. I never wanted it to end. I knew Christmas was fast approaching and I was worried he would go away on leave and I'd never see him again. I would be left heartbroken.

One evening when Heli and Papa had gone out and the children were in bed, it was as if he read my mind.

"I'm staying in Oostende for Christmas," he began. "Would it be presumptuous of me to ask if I could visit you over the holiday season?"

I was just about to answer him, a smile and a welcome on my lips, when he put his hand up, before continuing. "As I mentioned before, my platoon will be escorting a lorry full of German prisoners back to Germany. I'm not sure if we are leaving before New Year or just after but I will let you know." He must have noticed my tearful eyes for he said, "Don't be sad. I will come back, you have my word on that."

"What if you get shot, John?" I said worry etched on my brow but he just smiled.

"I won't get shot. Hitler is dead and there is no army in Germany at the moment."

Over the festive season, I clung to him like glue. With the rations we already had and the food John brought, it was the best Christmas since before the war.

On the night before John had to leave for Germany, we went for a long walk along the promenade. It was freezing but I didn't mind, as long as I was with him. Suddenly, he stopped and turned towards me, making me wonder what was wrong. Was he going to tell me it was over? That on his return from Germany he would be leaving for Wales. I was shaking, not sure if it was the bitterly cold wind that swept recklessly over us from the sea, or my beating heart. I bit down on my lip desperately trying to hide all the frantic emotions rushing around in my head. He looked at me, then put the palm of his hand on mine.

"What is it, John? What are you trying to say?" I asked.

"What I'm about to ask you, I want you to think long and hard, while I'm away." He studied my face and for a moment I didn't know whether to run or stay rooted to the spot.

"Rosina. Would you do me the honour of becoming my wife when I return from Germany? You don't have to give me an answer right now." John gently stroked my hair which caused shivers throughout my body. "We've only known each other a short time but I feel I've known you forever. My love for you is deeper than I've ever known."

I was speechless. I couldn't believe what was happening to me. I kissed his face over and over while we both laughed and cried.

"I don't need to think long and hard," I said. "Yes, yes, yes! Of course, I will marry you. I love you too, John," I cried.

John told me that he needed to seek my father's permission but he wondered if it would be better if I prepared Papa by speaking to him first. "After all, you are only nineteen years old and I'm twenty-eight and a soldier in the British Army. Your Papa could think I'm too old for you, which I suppose I am," John said.

The age gap didn't matter to me but I agreed to speak to Papa that evening. "But my answer won't change, regardless of what Papa thinks," I told John.

"Where will we live, John? We need a place of our own," I asked. I knew in my heart that as well as my deep desire to be with John, I was also rejoicing that I would get away from living with Heli which I had always hated.

John told me about an apartment he had seen in the town above a furniture shop and we agreed to enquire about it the next day when we met.

That evening I spoke to Sara first, even though it was late. She had stayed awake, waiting for me to come to bed.

"Sara," I hesitated. "John has asked me to marry him and I've said yes." I took her in my arms. "I hope you're not too sad but you're thirteen now—a young girl in your own right and life is for living. The war is over and we have our freedom back at last, so enjoy it with your friends." I wiped the tears that were shining in her eyes.

"I'll make you a new dress for the wedding. We'll take a look in the shops and see what's in fashion. I should look for something for myself too," I said to her.

She looked at me with one of her cheeky smiles.

"It's not going to be one of Mamma's coats then." She glanced at me then burst out laughing. My eyes almost popped out of my head. I was astonished at how she had kept quiet about the fact that she knew I had been using old clothes to make her outfits.

"You knew about that? I thought I had been very discreet."

"Of course, I knew—I'm not stupid, Rosina," she laughed.

I gained fresh admiration for this little sister of mine who had been more resilient and uncomplaining than I had given her credit for.

"You're okay about me getting married?" I asked anxiously.

"Of course I am, Rosina. I couldn't be happier for you," she said as I hugged and kissed her.

Papa was still downstairs. Thankfully, Heli had gone to bed, so I knew this was my chance to speak to him.

"I have something to ask you, Papa," I began. My words tumbled out:

"John has asked me to marry him and I've said yes but I want your blessing, Papa."

He glanced up at me with a mist forming in his eyes. He looked a lost soul. It reminded me of the day we were told the devastating news about our family "Papa," I pleaded, "don't be sad. You're not going to lose me, even if I do eventually move to Wales. I will come to see you as often as I can. But I love

196

John and he loves me. We both know that we have a lot to learn about each other but the war is over now and we both feel life is too short to hang around waiting for the right moment." I looked at Papa expectantly.

"Say something, Papa."

His voice was quiet but I still could detect a hard edge to it. "Well, you seem to have made up your mind so it doesn't really matter what I say. But what makes you think he will come back for you after he has been in Germany? Soldiers are notorious for not keeping their word to a pretty girl who turns their head." He paused and then continued, "I just wonder, Rosina, would you have been so eager to leave the country if Mamma was still alive?"

"I cannot answer that, Papa. The world is a different place now. I love John and he loves me and that's all that matters," I spoke defiantly. "I'm meeting him in the morning before he goes to Germany so we can look at an apartment to rent." Papa looked away and busied himself with tidying away tea cups.

"Oh, Papa—can't you be happy that I have found true love?" I felt like I was begging him, desperate for his blessing.

"If he returns after his time in Germany, I will take his claims of true love more seriously. I will listen to what he has to say if he comes back." He had his back to me as he stood at the kitchen sink, but his voice sounded softer.

"Thank you, Papa. He will come back; I know he will."

The following morning, I met John outside the flat.

As soon as we entered the one-bedroomed apartment, we felt at home. It came furnished which made us act immediately and put a deposit down then and there. I felt I was dreaming because everything was going our way.

Later that day, we said our farewells as he left for Germany. Knowing we had a place we could call our own made the goodbye less painful.

I was disappointed that John and I couldn't spend New Year together. But then I thought of the many years of celebrations we would have together in the future.

A few days after the new year had begun, there was a knock on the front door. I knew straightaway that it would be John.

I opened the door and jumped straight into his arms. I couldn't stop kissing him.

Papa shouted from the kitchen, "Rosina, are you going to keep the boy on the doorstep all day?"

Papa offered John a cognac when he came into the living room and I was relieved to hear them greet each other amiably.

"How was the road to Germany, John?" Papa asked.

"Not a very pleasant sight to see. Germany will need rebuilding, as every country involved in the war will."

But Papa seemed to sense that John didn't want to elaborate any further, so he changed the subject.

"Tell me, John, what are your plans for the future?" Papa didn't believe in beating about the bush. "Rosina tells me you have an apartment downtown. Does that mean you will be staying in Oostende, maybe settle down here?" Papa said hopefully.

John smiled but he hesitated, "I don't think so. I will be de-mobbed sometime in May, and then we will go to Wales. There isn't much in the way of work here for me. But in Wales, there are jobs available."

"What part of Wales are you from, John?" Papa asked.

"I was born in a little village called Brynaman," John answered.

"Isn't that where Jack and Monica are staying? Really? What are the chances of that?" Papa asked. I could see his face soften and I knew he would find it easier to let me go if he knew I would be near to family.

"We moved away from Brynaman after my father died, but the village my mother lives in now is not far away," John continued.

"I'm sorry to hear you lost your father," Papa said softly.

I could tell John was eager to open up and tell Papa all about himself.

"It was a long time ago—I was just ten years old. He died in the coal mines in an accident with a runaway truck," John recounted.

Papa listened with genuine compassion as John told him about his father and how he and his mother had coped. He went on to tell us about how his mother had remarried a few years later.

When John had finished speaking, Papa looked at us both seriously.

"So you want to marry my daughter?" he said, directing his gaze at John.

"Yes I do, if I have your permission," John answered quickly.

"I hope your word is genuine," Papa began. "What I mean by that, John, is that I hope you will always love and cherish Rosina. You must remember that she will be a young girl in a strange country."

"I know it will be strange for her in the beginning but, I will take good care of her. You have my word on that," John replied, taking my hand in his.

"Then you have my blessing to marry, Rosina," Papa said.

I took one leap over to Papa and smothered him with kisses and hugs. "Thank you, thank you, Papa!" I cried.

Chapter Thirty-Two
The Wedding

We were married on 19 January 1946.

It was a wonderful day; the sun shone brightly, even though we were in the midst of winter. I found a lovely white dress for Sara, who kept it on for days, until it became too soiled to wear anymore. To my surprise, Heli bought me a beautiful cream satin blouse to match my cream skirt. Papa cried through the whole service, he told me later that he was thinking of Mamma and all the family we'd lost. I tried my best to keep my tears at bay.

I was sad that Colet couldn't come as she had moved to Canada with a Canadian solider she had fallen in love with during the war. But faithful Renata was there.

"I'm so happy that you have found true love, Rosina. After all you have been through," she said with tears in her eyes. "I've bought you a little gift to hang on the wall—it's a picture of Oostende to remind you of us all. Don't you forget to come and see me when you come to visit."

"I will never forget you," I said embracing her tightly. "You have been my second Mamma. Knowing that you were only a few doors away, made life much easier for me. You have been my strength throughout all the heartache. I truly love you, Renata."

As I pulled away from her, John approached and put his arms around me. "Are you happy, Mrs Jones?" he murmured into my ear as he kissed me.

"Ecstatic, Mr Jones," I replied, kissing him back.

We moved into our new apartment that same day and began our married life together.

I felt that life was bliss. Some days I had to pinch myself to feel that it was real. Our evenings together were perfect, cuddled up in our cosy apartment but, if I was truthful, I couldn't wait to go to Wales. But I had to be patient for John to complete his duty in the Army.

Within six weeks, I was pregnant and absolutely thrilled. I had visited the doctor who examined me and told me the baby would be due in October. I was so thrilled that I couldn't stop crying.

"Oh Mamma, I wish you were here to see how happy I am and with a baby due soon," I whispered to myself.

"I'm happy and I'm sad all at the same time," I laughed as I told John that he was going to be a Papa.

He picked me up and swung me around in joy. We were both laughing as we flopped onto the settee.

John suddenly sobered up. "Rosina, there is something I must tell you." All the laughter was gone from his eyes. "When we get to Wales and the baby is born, I will be Daddy or Father, but not Papa. You must remember that."

I laughed out loud but John couldn't see the funny side of it. "I'm serious, Rosina. I won't be called Papa."

"Okay John, don't be so stern. I will do as you've asked," I replied, unnerved by this strange request and sudden change in mood.

We were still on food rationing, which was difficult when trying to make a decent meal for John when he came home from work each day. I wrote to Monica telling her of my marriage to John and that I was now pregnant. She was surprised, but thrilled for me. She also told me that Jack would be coming back to Oostende from Wales but she wasn't sure when. She was amazed that I had married a man who was born in Brynaman where they had spent the war years. It seemed an impossible coincidence.

One day when John came home from work, he seemed happier than usual. I'd certainly not heard him whistling before.

"I've had word about my de-mob papers," John said. "They haven't come through yet, but they reckon it will be around about May when I am able to leave the army."

"What does that mean for us, John?" I asked nervously.

"We will have to go to Britain as there will be no job here for me," he replied.

"I should tell Papa soon. It's March already and I can also give him the good news about the baby. It will give him time to get used to the idea of us leaving," I said. "I know it will be hard for Papa but I'm really looking forward to moving to Wales."

"Rosina, it's nothing like Oostende," John said, and his good mood seemed to have disappeared.

"It can't be that bad surely?" I said.

John frowned. "It's a little staid," was all he would say but I could tell there was something else on his mind. I was beginning to read his moods. I always knew when he needed to get something off his chest.

"Are you feeling ill, John? You seem far away," I said. He looked at me then caught hold of both my hands.

"There is something I need to tell you. When will you be writing to Monica again?" he asked. I thought that was an odd question to ask me.

"Soon, I suppose—it's my turn to write. Why do you want to know?"

"Don't be annoyed now when I tell you that my mother and stepfather don't know that I am married," he said. I gasped in horror.

"You mean, they don't know about me! Oh, John, how could you be so deceitful?" I ran to the bedroom crying.

He ran after me, and tried to take me in his arms but I wouldn't let him.

"Please let me explain, Rosina," he pleaded.

"Why would you not tell your own mother that you were getting married?" I demanded, as I curled up on the bed and turned my back on him.

"Please listen to me, Rosina. My mother is very old-fashioned and I would rather tell her face to face that I am married."

I stayed in the bedroom for the rest of the evening. I couldn't look at John, let alone talk to him.

The following day I was off work and John had the morning off too. I decided I had to confront him about his refusal to tell his mother about me. I told myself that it was normal for couples to quarrel, but feared that this might be just the first of many.

"Are you sorry you married me, John?" I said as he walked into the kitchen and I handed him a cup of freshly made coffee. "Please be honest with me. I would rather know the truth before I go to Wales." The tears were bubbling in my eyes.

"Of course not. I am so glad that you married me," he said, as he met my gaze. "I love you. But you're a very different kind of girl to what they are used to in Wales. For a start you're foreign and also you're a Catholic but above all, you're young and beautiful, just not what they are used to at all." He came over to hold me but, I pulled away, still hurt and angry.

"What has Monica got to do with this? And why did you want to know when I'm writing to her again?" I asked.

John sheepishly explained that he wanted me to stay with Monica, who was now living in London, while he went to Wales to break the news of our marriage to his mother.

"Where are we going to live when we get to Wales?" I asked. Now dreading that I knew what his answer would be.

His hands were sweating. "Well, with Mam I expect, for now."

"How could you keep this from me all this time, John?" I asked sulkily, refusing to let the bad feeling between us be healed. There was no convincing answer from him.

Chapter Thirty-Three
To Wales

Heli and Papa were both dozing by the fire when I walked into their kitchen.

"What a nice surprise," Papa said. "I'll put some coffee on, shall I? At last we have had some decent coffee in the shops."

Heli got up, filled the kettle and placed it on the fire.

I didn't even wait until I was seated before I blurted out my news.

"I'm pregnant!" I said excitedly. "The baby is due in October."

I knew Papa would be pleased, but Heli's reaction really surprised me. She stood behind Papa as he hugged me and I could see genuine joy in her eyes as she warmly congratulated me.

"There is something else I need to tell you," I said hesitantly as Papa poured the boiling water into the coffee pot. "It looks like we will be leaving for Wales in May."

"I expected this, Rosina," Papa sighed. "There's no reason for the soldiers to be here anymore, is there?" He poured three cups of coffee then sat back on his chair. I was relieved when he smiled over at me.

"How do you feel about moving to another country, Rosina?" Heli asked.

"I have mixed feelings," I said, willing to open up to this woman who I was usually on my guard against.

"I'm looking forward to going to Britain but I don't know about living in Wales. Apparently, they are a little behind the times but I hope I will settle there."

Heli smiled as she handed me a cup of coffee, and I recognised the Heli of old as I saw that familiar scheming look in her eyes. She would be quite glad to have me on the other side of the Channel. Her earlier warmth hadn't lasted long.

The weeks rolled by so fast and before I knew it, I was handing my notice in at the hotel. Hugo was sad to see me leave but he was overjoyed to see that I had found love and happiness.

"Well Rosina, I hope you and your baby will come to visit us when you're over to see your family," Hugo said, giving me a beautiful bunch of flowers and a little extra money in my last wage. I felt so overwhelmed I couldn't hold back the tears.

"I won't forget you, Hugo!" I cried as I embraced him goodbye. "For the last five years, working in this hotel has been a lifeline for me. A second home if you like, as well as a distraction during the horror of the war," I said smiling. "It's helped me keep my sanity in the evil madness that engulfed our country. You and all the friends I've made here are just like a second family to me. I will miss you all."

What I didn't realise was that quite a few of the staff were standing behind me and suddenly burst into applause. I was so embarrassed, I felt the heat rise in my neck and cheeks. Everyone came over to hug me and some even gave me little gifts, which I knew they could ill afford.

After I said my goodbyes, I walked out of the hotel and left my old life behind. It seemed very final. I called in to say my goodbyes to Renata, we both cried as we hugged each other. "I will miss you dearly, Renata."

"Don't you forget to bring your baby around to see me when you come back for a holiday."

"I will," I said as I left.

I did wonder about my future for a fleeting moment. If I had been able to choose how my life had worked out, I would have chosen to stay in Oostende, but Mamma and the rest of my siblings would have survived the war too—and I had to learn to live my life without them. I knew I could adjust to life in a new country.

John was already back and cooking our evening meal when I arrived home.

"What a wonderful smell," I said as I went up behind him and put my arms around his waist, marvelling at how happy I felt at that moment.

As we sat at the table enjoying our dinner, I commented on what a good cook he was.

"Well, when you're in the army sometimes you had no choice: cook for yourself or starve."

After I took my last mouthful, I sat back contentedly and told John, "That was the best meal I've had in a long time."

John didn't acknowledge me but went very quiet and seemed very tense. I asked him what was wrong, not prepared for what came next.

"You didn't waste any time finishing your meal, did you?" he shouted. "You eat a lot for a woman."

"What do you mean by that?" I spluttered. "You put the food on my plate!"

"Yes, but I didn't think you'd eat it all." By now, he was very angry.

"That's ridiculous, John! If you'd wanted to save some of the food, you shouldn't have given me so much. I'm well used to going without—I had to put up with meagre rations for five years."

"Are you trying to be funny?" John snapped.

"No I'm not," I said, struggling to keep my composure. "I just don't understand why you are making such a fuss."

"I'm going to lie down," he said, and he slammed the door behind him.

We didn't speak to each other again until the next morning. I spent the rest of the evening feeling bewildered by his reaction. I wept quietly as I thought of the shadow it had cast over our happy news about the baby.

The next morning, I decided to start sorting through our possessions, deciding what to take to Britain and what to leave behind. It was already the end of April so we would be leaving in a just a few weeks.

I called John's name as I went into the kitchen, hoping that with the dawn of a new day we could amends. There was no sign of him and I felt panic rise up within me. But a few minutes later, he appeared at the door with fresh milk and bread.

"Oh, there you are," I said, trying to smile brightly but he didn't return my smile.

"You make the coffee. I'll make us some toast," was all he said.

After breakfast John lit a cigarette, got up from the table and sat by the fire. I too lit a cigarette; I had started smoking on my wedding day. I made myself comfortable on the settee, trying to think about what I could say to clear the air.

Before I had a chance to speak, John spoke: "Have you had a reply from Monica yet?"

I told him that I'd heard from her the day before, and that she wanted to know what date we were arriving in London.

"I'll know once I hear about my de-mob," he said. His tone softened. "You'll have time to spend with your sister after all these years apart, while I go to Wales and try to find somewhere for us to live."

I could tell he was trying to make amends, but I was only reminded of the fact that he still hadn't told his mother about me.

"I'm not looking forward to meeting your mother, John. We have nowhere to live and I'm expecting a baby in October, what were you thinking? I'm so worried," I told him, pouring my third cup of coffee. I immediately regretted my honesty, wishing I had just kept my concerns to myself.

"That's why I thought it would be easier for me to go to Wales and make arrangements, rather than both of us just turn up on Mam's door!" he growled.

"What if you decide not to come back to London to fetch me?" I said, knowing I was being irrational.

John grabbed me and held me close. "Of course, I'll come back!" he said fiercely. "I love you, don't I?" I didn't know what to think or feel: one part of me welcomed his touch and the declaration of his love but the other part of me feared this man and the unpredictability of his moods.

The day of our departure arrived quickly and all the family came down to the docks to see us off. We had a small gathering the previous night, which Renata attended; I was so glad she had. So I could say my goodbyes to her. I didn't expect to see them all again that morning. But I welcomed their presence as I was very anxious about my journey across the English Channel. The last time I had sailed on a boat was a terrible turning point in my life. By the time we got to the ferry, I was shaking and my teeth were chattering so much I could hardly speak.

John hadn't noticed how frightened I was until Papa nudged him. "Go to her, John; look, she's terrified. Consider what happened to her at Dieppe."

John caught hold of my arm and helped me up the gangplank. "Don't be afraid, Rosina. This time it will be different: there are no bombs or Germans to frighten you, the sea is very calm and if you haven't noticed, this is a bigger ship than the last one you were on."

"Just hold me tight, John. I don't like the thought of the water beneath me. I don't know what I would do if there was a storm," I cried.

"You won't fall—not while I'm holding you," John laughed as he lifted me on to the ship. "When the ship leaves the dock, we'll go and stand on the upper deck; it's not so stuffy up there."

Suddenly, I noticed Sara who had been very quiet and when I went over to her, she burst out crying.

"I'm never going to see you again, Rosina. How will I cope on my own? I don't like Heli," she wailed as she flung her head onto my chest. I put my arms around her and held her tight and beckoned for Ada to come over.

"You know, Sara," Ada said, putting her arm around my younger sister's shoulder, "my door is open to you at any hour of the day. And now that your big brother Jack is back, you can get to know each other again."

It was time to say our last goodbyes. I hugged each member of my family in turn. When it came to Papa, I was so overwhelmed and my tears fell unchecked. We had endured so much together since the war had begun.

"Oh, Papa, I'm going to miss you so much. Please look after yourself," I whispered into his ear. He held me tightly, reminding me of how safe and secure he used to make me feel as a child. I kissed him one last time. As I walked away, it broke my heart to see what the war years had done to him. He had aged dramatically and his sad, little face was forever imprinted on my mind.

As we sailed out of the harbour and dipped our way into the open sea, all those that I loved and cherished grew smaller and smaller as they stood, waving by the water's edge.

I turned to look for John, with tears flooding my eyes and doubt in my heart. I wondered if I was doing the right thing as I stepped into unknown territory. My only consolation was that I was leaving behind the misery of living with Heli.

John caught hold of my hand and said, "Come on, we'll go and have something to eat—they have a lovely cafeteria."

"Okay, but first I want to find out where they keep the life jackets—I'll feel safer sitting near them." I tried to be brave in front of John but I hadn't fully realised that the trauma of what had happened to me in Dieppe was affecting my mental wellbeing. I stood looking down at the dark, deep waters beneath me, terrible flashbacks of the bombs falling and the horror of being in the water invaded my memory.

I trembled as that dreadful memory of kicking away that little person, who could have been my beloved sister, came rushing back into my mind. I realised that the agony of losing my beloved Mamma and so many of my family in such a cruel and frightening way had changed me forever.

Chapter Thirty-Four
The Arrival

We arrived in Dover about mid-day. Everyone was rushing and pushing in their eagerness to get onto dry land.

We were lucky and got the last luggage trolley. I was so afraid I would lose John in the crowd that I tried to hang on to the trolley as we made our way to the passport area. Because I wasn't a British citizen, we were taken to another room where we had to show everything: our marriage certificate, passports and any other legal papers we had. We both had to fill in forms which were difficult for me to understand because they were written in English and what I had learned at school didn't help me much, but a lady came over and helped me. John tried to explain that I was pregnant and that we were going to miss our train, but they ignored him.

"I feel light-headed and my legs are weak, John. I can't stand much longer," I said and someone quickly got me a chair and a drink of water. John was losing his patience but finally, they let us go.

"We'll soon be on the train for Victoria station," John said. Thankfully, we just managed to catch it but it was very full; we found seats but not together. I kept my eye on John the whole time and I knew he was watching out for me as well.

When we got to Victoria Station, I couldn't believe that so many people could be in one place at the same time.

"Stay near to me, Rosina, or you'll get lost," John commanded.

"I'm trying, John, but you're walking so fast I can't keep up," I complained.

We trudged our way through the busy streets until we arrived at the underground station and we got on the train to Kensington. We would then have a short taxi journey to Monica's house.

It had been five long years since I had seen her, I was giddy with excitement but also anxious. We had been separated for so long and in such a cruel way.

When we arrived at the correct address, I took a deep breath, trying to calm myself, before knocking on Monica's front door.

As the door opened and I saw Monica standing in front of me, I just fell into her arms and we held each other tightly, crying and laughing at the same time.

"Oh Monica, you've changed! You're so grown up," I cried, dropping my luggage.

"And I could say exactly the same about you!" she laughed. "Look at you, an old married woman and soon-to-be mother."

When we eventually stepped into Monica's apartment, John had already brought the cases in and was sitting down. I introduced John to Monica.

"I'm delighted to meet you," he said, giving her one of his winning smiles. "If I didn't know better, I would have taken you for twins, you're so very much alike."

After supper and a great deal of chatting, John excused himself. He was leaving very early the next morning and wanted to get enough rest before another long journey.

The following morning John had left for Wales before I woke up. Monica had gone to work but would be home at lunch time. I thought I would be glad to be on my own but, I started to feel uneasy with John gone, and tormented myself with doubts, about whether he would come back to fetch me, or if I would be left to fend for myself as a single mother.

I went over to the kitchen sink to wash up the breakfast things in an attempt to distract myself, but what I saw as I looked out the window did nothing to lift my spirits. I realised that not one single building in the street below had escaped the German bombs. *Monica must have been terrified*, I thought to myself. I tried in vain to cheer myself up before my sister came home.

When Monica arrived home, we began to fill each other in on the five years we had lost to each other.

"We have lost so many loved ones, Monica," I said. "I didn't think I could endure anymore heartache and then Joseph was taken from us too. Papa's heart was broken and I don't believe he's ever fully recovered." Monica reached over and squeezed my hand, tears brimming in her eyes. I could see the last five years had taken their toll on her too.

"How are you managing in London?" I asked, changing the subject. "It's such a huge place."

"It is and at first, I found it frightening and very difficult to get around. We stayed in Wales for a while which was the right thing to do. It would have been too much of a change to come straight to London. Little Ellie and Jack were missing their Mammas and were terribly homesick. They weren't eating or sleeping, and they couldn't understand why they had to stay in Wales. It was an awful time, Rosina," Monica said, dabbing her eyes gently.

She continued: "Then as we all got used to the countryside and the animals that grazed in the never ending fields, Jack and Ellie began to settle but it was so different from what they had been used to. The people were friendly and helped us in whatever way they could. Both children started school together even though Jack was older than Ellie. They were moral support for one another."

Monica went on to explain that in order to find work, she had to move to London. Once Jack and Ellie began to learn English and make friends, she felt able to leave them and came to London finding work as a telephonist. She started off living with a couple in a large Kensington apartment but, the previous year she had moved into a place of her own.

"But that's enough about me," Monica smiled. "How are you? You're facing huge changes: moving to a new country and impending motherhood. Are you happy, Rosina?"

"Yes, I am happy," I told her, although I wasn't being entirely honest.

"Is there anything worrying you? You seem restless." Monica could always read me like a book.

"I just feel lost without John," I admitted. "Since we met, we've hardly been apart. I'm not looking forward to meeting John's parents. It will be difficult in the beginning, but I have my baby to look forward to in the autumn."

I tried to keep my voice as light as I could. In the past, Monica and I had always confided in each other but, I didn't know if I should tell her why John had gone to Wales before me. I had kept it to myself for all these months, I was desperate to unburden myself.

When I began to tell Monica my story, I was close to tears. She was angry with John and couldn't believe how deceitful he had been.

"Surely the two of you discussed this before you got married?" she exclaimed.

"No, we didn't. I took it for granted that he had written to his family," I replied.

"How long did you know him? Before you were married?" Monica asked.

"Three months," I said but I couldn't look at Monica.

"What! Three months? Rosina, what were you thinking? You hardly know him." Monica was obviously shocked.

"It was love at first sight for me. I guess I was blinded by his looks and personality and I assumed he had made all the arrangements in Wales," I said sadly.

"Obviously not!" Monica exclaimed.

"If I am being truthful, I don't think I would have been so hasty in marrying John if Mamma had still been alive but, it was a way out of the life I was in," I said and I realised this was the first time I had admitted this even to myself. "It had been so difficult living under German occupation, always looking over your shoulder. I can see London has been flattened but you haven't had the Nazis watching your every move, stealing the little bit of food you'd just bought from the shop. Life was hell, Monica. Then Papa got married again, which was a shock to us all," I explained.

"What is she like, Rosina?" Monica asked.

I didn't hold back in telling Monica exactly what I thought of Heli and how she let Sara go hungry while her own children were well fed.

When John hadn't arrived back in London after four days, I began to panic. I packed my case ready to return to Belgium, dreading having to face Papa and Heli, and the idea of bringing up a baby on my own didn't bear thinking about.

But on the fifth day, late in the morning, there was a knock on the door. Monica and I looked at each other and my heart was racing as she opened the door and John stepped in. I ran into his arms.

"Where have you been? I almost gave up on you." I was hysterical, hitting him and crying at the same time.

"I'm sorry, it took me longer than I thought it would. I've been looking for somewhere for us to live," he explained. He hesitated and looked away before continuing, "But there is nothing at the moment so we are going to have to live with my mother until we can find a place of our own."

Monica looked at me and shook her head behind John's back. I said nothing but anger simmered within me.

I was up early the following morning when Monica was getting ready for work.

We hugged and kissed each other many times, struggling to say goodbye after only just being reunited.

"I will write to you regularly!" I promised her. "Thank you for the last few days—they were wonderful. I will miss you greatly." She gave me one final embrace before leaving her apartment.

On the train journey to Wales, I began to feel very nervous; my mouth was so dry I found it hard to speak. John fetched me a glass of water.

"What are your folks like, John? I know I've asked you this time and time again but I never get a straight answer from you. They must be very kind to let us live with them," I said, willing it to be true.

John didn't comment, which I found odd; he just smiled.

As we pulled into Swansea station I was shocked by the state of the city; there were derelict buildings and shattered glass everywhere.

John explained that Swansea had a sea-port, just like in Oostende, and the German Luftwaffe had tried to bomb docks throughout the country.

"I would love to go down to the seafront one day. Maybe you could take me?" I said but John seemed far away and there was no answer.

"I hope your mother will like me, John?" My stomach was in knots.

"Of course she will," he said. "Don't worry, we'll have our own place soon."

Chapter Thirty-Five
Meeting the Family

"So you're Rosina then?" John's stepfather shook hands with me.

"Yes, I'm pleased to meet you," I said, as brightly as I could. "John has told me so much about you both."

John's mother totally ignored my handshake.

"Take her luggage upstairs, Johnny," she snapped.

"My name is Rosina," I reminded her.

It was as if I hadn't spoken.

"Johnny, do as I say, and then show her where everything is then make her a cup of tea. I'm busy; they'll all be home soon for their dinner."

"Do you have coffee, John? I would much prefer it," I asked.

Before John could answer, his mother shouted from the scullery, "We don't use that muck in this house! It's tea or water."

I followed John up a narrow flight of stairs. The walls were decorated in a very dark brown leaf design, which I felt was closing in on me as we reached the top of the stairs. To the left there was a long, dark, narrow corridor with the same design on the walls and a dimly lit shade which hung from the ceiling. John turned in the opposite direction and climbed up two more steps into a very small bedroom which was to be ours.

"Oh, it's dark in here," I said as I opened the curtains as wide as I could. I tried to open the window but it was very stiff. I turned to ask John for help but he had bolted out of the room and down the stairs, leaving me to lift the cases onto the bed.

There was a rough, woollen blanket, which had seen better days, folded on the bed; one pillow and pillowcase each; and one grubby sheet that lay on the bed for me to make up. I sat down and looked around. It was hard not to form the conclusion that I would not enjoy living here, especially after the cold reception from John's mother.

I could hear voices drifting upstairs and listened as John asked his mother what was for tea.

"It's laver bread for tea, Johnny," his mother told him. "It's your favourite. I was hoping the butcher would have some left, and when I mentioned that you were just back from the war, he gave me a little bit extra. But there's only one slice of bacon and one slice of bread left."

"Oh Mam, is that all? My stomach thinks my throat's been cut," Johnny laughed,

"I can't help that, there's an extra mouth to feed now. The war may be over but we are still on food rationing," she retorted.

"I know. It's the same all over Europe, Mam. Rosina has had a particularly bad time of it in Belgium with the Germans breathing down their necks."

"Yes well, it's been terrible here too," his mother replied.

I must have fallen asleep and when I woke, I wondered where I was for a minute. My cup of tea was stone cold on the floor. Alongside it was a dry piece of bread with the ends curled up and no butter. I called John.

"Will you come upstairs?"

"You're awake?" He bent over to kiss me, but I turned my head away.

"Why didn't you wake me when you brought the tea up?" I said irritably.

"I didn't want to wake you, you looked so peaceful."

"I haven't eaten since we left Monica's this morning. You seem to forget that I'm pregnant," I said more loudly than I intended.

"Keep your voice down," John snapped. "Nobody knows you're pregnant, and I would appreciate you not mentioning it just yet!"

I put my hand over my mouth to stop myself from screaming at him.

"How could you do this to me, John? First our marriage and now my baby! Are you ashamed of me? Because it certainly seems that way: I've had enough of your deceitfulness. I might as well go back home." Tears were running down my face. "We've only been here a few hours and I'm miserable already!" I couldn't look at him.

"This is your home now, Rosina. Not Belgium," he reminded me.

"Well, it doesn't feel like home! Your mother has shunned me. My family didn't treat you the way your mother is treating me. I'm leaving first thing in the morning," I announced in a stern voice.

John just laughed and said, "Firstly, it's my baby too so you will stay in this country." John's eyes softened. "And secondly, I love you and I don't want you to leave." He took me in his arms.

"Oh, John, why didn't we stay in Belgium? At least we had a home there," I said, resting my head on his shoulder.

"We may have had a home, Rosina, but there was no job suitable for me. You couldn't have kept on working once the baby had arrived. At least here, there is more chance of me getting a job and hopefully just down the road from here," he said.

"What do you mean just down the road?" I asked.

"Well, there is a big factory called the Sheet-mills. I'm going to call there tomorrow morning to see if they have any jobs available."

John kissed me on the neck. "I'll pop down and make you another cup of tea and find out if there is something a bit more substantial than one slice of dry bread. I don't think you would like laver bread," John remarked.

I couldn't be bothered to ask what it was. After John left, I began to unpack the cases and when he came back up to the bedroom, he had a warm cup of tea and two cheese sandwiches spread thinly with butter. Behind John was one of his sisters, who immediately came over and hugged me.

"How are you, Rosina? I'm so happy to meet you. I'm Heather," she said smiling warmly. I thought how genuine she appeared and she was very pretty, with long blonde locks. "You must be feeling very tired after your long journey?"

"Yes, I am," I answered but John looked at me with pleading eyes.

"You could come down and meet the rest of the family?" he begged.

"I think I will stay up here and have an early night, John. I feel utterly exhausted." I looked at Heather. "Would you be so kind as to pass on my apologies?"

"Of course I will. It's very understandable; it's your first day here and having to meet all the family is a little intimidating. I'll see you tomorrow, Rosina," she said, smiling.

When Heather left the room, I looked at John. "How many sisters are down there?" I asked anxiously.

"I have five sisters and two brothers, but one of my brothers is still abroad and Ethel is away for a few weeks."

"Oh, John, no wonder your mother has given me a frosty welcome. Where is everyone going to sleep?" I queried, shocked at John's calmness.

"I don't know. Maybe Mam has made up beds downstairs in the front room." He stood restlessly like a naughty little boy waiting to be excused.

"Why have you never talked about your family? I had no idea you had so many siblings. I feel like I know nothing about you. I've told you all there is to know about my family." I scanned his face.

"Well, I thought I had told you," he said, clearly trying to avoid meeting my eye.

"No, John, you've never mentioned your family, and more fool me for not asking," I said but he just laughed.

"Anyway, you know all you need to know about me," he joked.

"That's not an answer," I retorted. "I have a terrible headache and I'm too exhausted to do anything else today. You go down and enjoy your family—you have years of catching up to do. How long is it since you saw them last?"

"It must be over eighteen months since I was last home. With all the preparation for D-Day, no one was allowed any leave," he explained.

"Enjoy getting to know them again," I said and kissed him goodnight.

I woke the following morning and had to dash to the bathroom. I got there just in time. I wondered what John's mother would say if she caught me vomiting every morning. *But surely, she will be happy*, I thought; *this is her first grandchild after all.*

John was awake when I came back to bed. I crawled in between the sheets and turned to face him.

"How am I to hide my bulging belly from everyone, John? It's not fair that I am put in this position; this should be a happy time for us and for your family."

"I know, just give them time to get used to the fact that I am married and more to the point, got married in Belgium."

"And to a Catholic," I butted in.

"Well, yes, it did come as quite a shock to Mam but I will tell them all soon."

Today was Saturday and John reminded me that the whole family would be home.

"Some of my sisters can be funny. Don't take any notice of them."

"What do you mean funny? Will they laugh at me?"

"No, no but they can be stuck up." John didn't elaborate so it seemed I would have to find out on my own.

As the weeks passed, I got to know John's sisters, and quickly found out what John meant about some of them being stuck up, apart from Heather, who had welcomed me that first night.

John had been offered a job in the factory down the road which I was very pleased about. We had managed to put away some savings from my wages when we lived in Belgium and with John's de-mob money from the Army, we had thought we were comfortably off, but that little pot of money was now dwindling fast.

After paying rent, there wasn't much left. I wanted to save some money for when my baby was born.

"John, tea is ready," his mam called up the stairs. "I've made yours and Rona's first before the rest of the family come home."

"Why does she insist on calling me Rona all the time? We've been here a month so she should know it by now," I said shortly.

The evening meal arrangement suited me. There were too many of them and only one of me. Each evening after our meal, I washed our dishes, made myself a cup of tea and went back upstairs before the rest of the family came home. I didn't want to feel in the way but how I longed for my own home and a cup of real coffee.

Life in Wales was very different, especially in this small village. There were no shops near enough for me to walk to and I was afraid to venture out too far in a strange place for fear of getting lost.

One morning as I was walking down the stairs for breakfast, I stopped halfway. I could hear voices and snippets of a conversation. Betty, one of John's sisters who liked to hear the sound of her own voice, was speaking to her mother.

"I'm sure Rosina is pregnant," I could hear her saying. "She's putting on weight, have you noticed, Mam?"

"No, I can't say I have but I don't see much of her as she stays in her room—which suits me," she admitted. "But I will ask Johnny when he comes home from work."

"The thought of a screaming baby in this house is unthinkable," Betty sneered.

I froze, then turned around and walked quietly back up the stairs despite being desperate for a cup of tea. I stayed there until John came home from work and I drank the water from the tap to stop my mouth being too dry. I had known in my heart that they knew I was pregnant.

John didn't come straight upstairs and I could hear raised voices downstairs between him and his mother.

"Tell me, Johnny, is Rona, I mean Rosina, pregnant? I want the truth. If she is, you will have to leave and soon," she said.

I heard John pleading with his mother. "Where are we going to live, Mam? You can't just throw us out. The baby is due in October."

"That's not my problem. You should have thought about that before you got the girl pregnant. You've made your bed, Johnny. Now lie in it," his Mam said coldly. "How dare you do this to me? It's bad enough that you have married a foreigner and couldn't be bothered to let us know for months." She paused and I thought her tirade was over, but then she started again. "Was she pregnant when you asked if you both could live here? You'd better tell me the truth, Johnny."

I heard John say, "We weren't sure then."

"I don't believe you," she snarled. "You knew damn well she was pregnant, and you also knew what my answer would have been."

I came downstairs, determined to back John up and explain that we were looking for a place so we could move out as soon as possible, but I didn't get the chance. She turned her eyes to me with sheer disgust and said with hatred in her voice, "Don't you stand there, little Miss Innocent—you are just as much to blame!"

Ignoring her vile tongue, I took a deep breath, walked over to her and tried to appeal to her good nature.

"Please, Megan, let us stay until John finds somewhere for us to live. He's out looking day after day. I can help with the ironing and the cleaning, or I can keep out of the way if you'd prefer that."

She couldn't look at me but she shook her head. "My answer is still no. I need the bedroom back."

"For whom, Mam?" John asked.

"Ethel is due home any day now. I can't have a crying baby here; we're overcrowded as it is."

Megan stood over the sink and began to peel potatoes. She kept shaking her head.

"I didn't expect this of you, Johnny, to come home from the war with a readymade family!"

She made me feel like an intruder and that I was to blame. I turned around to walk back upstairs but before I did, I glared at her, and in my best English I told her, "When I first met John, he was such a kind loving person, and I thought his family must be just like him. How wrong I was. This is John's baby, your first grandchild—how can you be so heartless? I love John with all my heart and I came over here to be with him in a strange country, hoping to start a new life with him and my baby." I couldn't carry on. I ran from the room sobbing.

It was a while before John came upstairs. When he did, he just sat on the bed and said nothing.

"I really thought she would have been happy for us with this being her first grandchild," I said to John but he completely ignored me.

Riled by his lack of response, I shouted at him, "I hope you are not blaming me for the mess we are in!" But he only shook his head.

"I'm so worried, John," I said, desperate for him to respond and reassure me in some way. "I have no clothes for the baby and now we have nowhere to live. I thought my life in Belgium was horrendous, living alongside the Nazis and with a ghastly stepmother but this is worse and now I have a baby to consider. Oh, John, you'll have to find somewhere for us to live and soon."

"I'll ask again at work tomorrow," he snapped.

I knew he was in a terrible temper, but I couldn't stop myself from provoking him further. "Don't take it out on me, John. You should have made some arrangements before we came to Wales and you should have told your parents. You have had long enough to sort something out."

He stood up; his eyes were raging in temper, his hand was curled into a fist.

I backed away and fell on to the bed. I was terrified as he leaned over with his fist only inches away from my face.

"If you don't shut up, I'll ram this fist down your throat!" he yelled.

I was hysterical and pulled the blankets over my head in an attempt to protect myself from my husband who seemed like a stranger to me.

I heard him slam the bedroom door and run downstairs.

"Oh, Mamma, what have I done? Who is this man I've married? I don't know anything about him," I cried quietly to myself. I eventually fell into a restless and troubled sleep.

When I woke, I felt so ill. The morning sickness was getting worse. I hadn't eaten anything the day before and no one had bothered to come and ask if I was hungry. I just made it to the bathroom in time but only water came up. I crawled back into bed, not knowing where John was and not particularly caring at that point in time.

I must have slept for hours because John woke me about mid-day with a cup of tea and two slices of toast but I couldn't look at him.

"I'm sorry about yesterday. I shouldn't have lost my temper with you," he said. "I never expected this from Mam."

I ignored him.

Two weeks after John's mam had asked us to get out, we still hadn't found somewhere to live. John had asked everyone he knew and when he wasn't in work he walked the streets looking to see if there were any empty buildings but the only ones that were empty were unsafe to live in.

The atmosphere in the house was unbearable. James, my stepfather-in-law, was the only one who understood our plight.

"I hope you will find somewhere to live soon," he said and taking hold of both my hands, he squeezed them with sympathy.

One afternoon when John was at work, I went for a walk. I couldn't bear to stay in the bedroom all day. I had helped with the chores in the morning but I had only spoken when I was spoken to.

I didn't know where I was going but I knew I had to stay near the house because I was afraid of getting lost. There were no shops and no cafés for me to sit in with a cup of coffee, and maybe get to know some of the people of the area. On my way back there was a lady brushing the path of her garden which was two doors up from Megan. She stopped as I was passing.

"Oh, hello. Are you Rosina, the Belgian lady?" She smiled. "My name is Mary. I hope you don't think I'm being nosy, but are you and your husband looking for a place to live?"

I wondered how she knew and I could see that she was obviously heavily pregnant too.

"Yes," I replied, delighted to speak to someone friendly.

"Well, I have a room you could rent. You'll be looking to find somewhere soon, as it can't be long until your baby is due."

"Thank you so much," I said. I knew it still wouldn't be a place of our own, but anything would be better than our current situation.

I told John about the lady's offer later that night, "Was it a woman that lives two doors down from us?" he asked and I told him that it was.

"If it is her, she has five children and another one on the way. She also has an alcoholic husband. No doubt she is desperate for the money. Are you sure you want to go there because I certainly don't!" John said, clearly annoyed.

"Well, where else are we going to live, John?" I snapped back.

"Oh we'll find somewhere soon," he replied.

"You're very relaxed considering the seriousness of our situation," I said bitterly.

"I'm tired, Rosina, we'll discuss it in the morning."

I gave up trying to make him see reason but I lay awake all night with worrying thoughts running through my head.

Chapter Thirty-Six
Two Doors Down

The following day the decision was made for me. We had no choice but to leave because John's eldest sister Ethel arrived back home.

She took an instant dislike to me. As John introduced me to her, I was just about to hold my hand out but stopped myself. She looked me up and down with such contempt, I had cold shivers down my spine.

"I know who she is," Ethel sneered. "She's the foreigner that thought she could just breeze in to our house, with a baby on the way and expect me to give up my bed. Who does she think she is?" Her expression as she looked at me was one of pure hatred. She turned on her heel and left the room.

"Rosina's my wife, Ethel. Don't be so rude to her," John shouted after her. It heartened me to hear him defending me.

But a few minutes later, Ethel returned and my heart sank. Her eyes were scrutinising my whole being, making me feel very uncomfortable.

"Don't you wear stockings?" She looked down at my legs. The other sisters laughed. "Every respectable woman wears stockings. It just shows where you came from." Her voice dripped with contempt. "Oh, and by the way," she continued, standing there with one hand on her hip, the other holding her cup of tea. "Did you have to get married because you were having a baby?"

"That's none of your business, Ethel." John glared at his sister.

She give him the once-over, then snidely remarked, "Not giving me a straight answer, Johnny, tells me you did." She couldn't have sounded more evil if she had been a Nazi officer standing in front of me.

"You don't belong here!" She clearly hadn't finished yet and my fear of her was starting to give way to anger. "We have had a terrible time during the war and we don't want to be reminded of it any longer. So foreigners and, especially Catholic foreigners who can't even speak our language, are not welcome here! I don't think you would have married her if she wasn't pregnant, would you, Johnny?" she sneered, waiting for an answer.

"How dare you judge me! You don't even know me!" I stood up and glared back at her. "John and I love each other and I didn't have to get pregnant to know that!"

The other sisters looked on, enjoying the show. Only Heather closed her eyes, embarrassed at what her eldest sister had said. I felt so humiliated but I wasn't going to back down to her and her accusations. "Don't worry, I won't stay here another day!" I shouted at her. John didn't say anything. I turned around and walked back upstairs in as dignified a manner as I could. I knew in that instant I had to leave. I had started to pack by the time John came into the room.

"What are you doing, Rosina?"

"What does it look like I'm doing?" I snapped.

He slammed the case shut. "And where do you think you're going to go?" he said.

"If I had enough money, I would be on the next train back to Belgium. I have never been so insulted in all my life. I have a loving family back home. I don't deserve this from your family or from you—I didn't hear you sticking up for me! How do you think I feel living here, John? Whenever I walk into a room everyone starts speaking in Welsh. My English is not good enough, especially when I have to defend myself to your sisters. I cannot live here anymore, so I am going to see that lady up the road in the morning. I'd rather live in a house filled with children and an alcoholic husband than stay here. You can do what you like."

My tirade was met with stony silence and then a slammed door. Me, and my morning sickness, were up early the following day. John had already gone to work. As soon as I'd had a cup of tea, I went around to see Mary about the room she had offered us.

I knocked on the door and I could hear children shouting and a baby crying. I grew up with younger siblings, so thought I could put up with the noise.

As Mary opened the door, I suddenly felt very nervous.

"Hello Mary, do you still have the room you offered me the other day?" I asked.

"Yes, of course I do. Come on in," she replied. I expected the place to be very untidy, but although there were some toys scattered on the floor, the house was homely and it brought back memories of Mamma and my brother and sisters.

Mary asked when I would like to move in and I told her that as soon as she could take me would suit me.

"That bad, is it? I can have the room ready by this evening," she said kindly.

I nodded gratefully and headed back to John's family home. Heather was the only one in the kitchen, which I was relieved about, she was the only member of the family who had shown me any kindness. I told her my plans and she listened sympathetically. "I'm so sorry for how my mam and sisters have treated you," she said. "It's inexcusable."

I wondered how this girl could be part of the same family as Ethel and Megan.

"Why don't I take you to the doctor's surgery later on and you can register yourself and the baby?" she offered.

I began to cry at finally receiving some kindness. "Thank you, Heather," I managed. "Let's do that after I've rested."

I lay down on the bed, going over and over in my mind the time when I first met John. He had been so loving and kind and he couldn't do enough for me. How deceitful and cunning his behaviour now seemed. I felt angry with myself that I had fallen for his charms. The dawning realisation that I had married a stranger made me feel weak and foolish.

I must have fallen asleep because the next moment John was shaking my shoulder. Startled, I awoke.

"Are you okay, Rosina?" John asked as he sat on the bed.

"No, I'm not okay, John." My earlier ruminations had made me determined to stand up for myself and take my future into my own hands. "I've made arrangements to move to Mary's house tonight. I know this isn't ideal, John, but I cannot stay here with your family a minute longer."

"Have you packed any of my clothes yet?" John said.

"No, I haven't. I wasn't sure if you were coming," I said warily.

"Of course, I'm coming. We're married, aren't we, and we stay together no matter what."

I held my arms open and cried into John's chest. I couldn't resist this man, despite his mercurial nature, and tried to shake the looming doubts and just be thankful that I wouldn't be leaving without him.

That night as I lay in John's arms in a stranger's bed, I couldn't stop crying. Mary was very kind and tried to help but she was still a stranger to me. I couldn't think of the future—it was too frightening.

We now had nothing: no home and nothing for the baby—I hadn't even bought a bib. Only Heather had shown any interest in me; everyone else just wanted to belittle me or avoid me. So much had been said in John's house that I vowed I would not forget or forgive them. And my fears about John reared his ugly head during the night watches. I never knew if his passion for me would be manifested in fierce kisses or a display of rage.

I must have fallen asleep because suddenly a child's distant cry woke me. It took me a while to remember where I was but when I did, I could only think what a mess my life had become and cried myself back to sleep.

Living in Mary's house was very distressing. Some of her children were school age but it was their annual holiday season so the house was always full. Someone was always hungry but Mary's cupboards were always empty. With no money and no help from her husband, I don't know how she managed. I helped as much as I could by feeding and dressing the younger children and I kept the ironing basket empty. As much as I liked Mary and found living with her preferable to living with John's family, I had to be realistic and I knew I couldn't stay there indefinitely.

Mary's baby was due in August, but had been told by the midwife that, since it was her sixth, it could very well come early.

Mary sighed as she sat down and put her legs up on a chair. "I will be glad when my baby is born. This pregnancy has been long and difficult. I have vowed this is my last—I don't want that drunken sod of a husband anywhere near me again," she announced in anger.

I felt so sorry for her because she had no one to help her either.

"I can't wait for my baby to be born too," I said, glancing down at my ever growing tummy.

Mary's husband was constantly drunk; some days he couldn't even form a four-word sentence. It angered me to seeing him buying bottles of whiskey and gin when the children often went without enough food. I made sure that Mary, not her husband, received our rent money.

We had lived in Mary's home for almost three weeks, when John came home from work with a smile on his face which was rare these days. He motioned me to follow him upstairs. I did and nearly tripped over one of the children's dolls on the floor. John just caught me in time or I would have fallen onto my stomach.

"I can't wait to get out of here," I whispered to John.

Once we got to our bedroom, John spoke in hushed tones: "I have found us somewhere else to live."

"Oh John, that's great," I said, overjoyed. "Is it a flat or a house?"

"No, no, it's someone that works with me, who has a three-bedroom house, and is offering to give us two furnished rooms upstairs. But we have to share the kitchen and bathroom," John explained.

"I don't mind that," I said feeling lighter than I had in months. "As much as I like Mary, two rooms will be so much better than one."

John told me that his colleague, Idris, had said we could move in the following week. His wife was also expecting a baby about a month before me, so John said he hoped we would be company for each other.

I told Mary that same evening. She was upset to see us leave but she understood our predicament.

"You must come and visit me when your baby is born," she said, drying the tears from her eyes. "I'm going to miss you, Rosina." I realised I had made a friend and been a friend to this woman who managed to remain cheerful despite her difficult circumstances.

"I will miss you too, Mary," I told her as I hugged her. "You have been a Godsend to us and I will always remember your kindness."

Chapter Thirty-Seven
The Next Move

The next day we moved into our new lodgings. I was excited about having more space and no noisy children running around. But my heart sank as I looked around our new home. The two rooms were small and the walls were covered in a dark green, striped paper which had seen better days. In the living room lay a small threadbare rug, which I would be getting rid of because it was filthy.

"I will not lay my baby on that," I told John.

There were two small armchairs, a tiny table with two stools and in one of the corners stood a small fire with only one bar. On closer inspection, I saw that the lead was worn, leaving the wires exposed. John agreed to look for a replacement.

"We can't use that, John, it's too dangerous," I exclaimed. All my previous excitement was fading quickly. My exasperation increased as I realised that despite being told the rooms came furnished, there was barely enough storage for one of us, never mind a baby too.

We went downstairs to speak to our new landlords. Gwen, the wife, seemed friendly enough but I took an instant dislike to her husband, Idris. When he shook my hand, he held on to it for far too long. I literally had to pull my hand away from him. He had this mad look in his eyes which made me feel very uneasy.

Thankfully, he was out working for most of the day, and I soon came to appreciate my new home, especially when I remembered living with John's family.

One day when I was out for a walk, I found a small wool shop where I bought lots of white wool and knitting needles. Knitting was my saviour as the days were long when John was at work.

I wrote frequently to Papa and Sara telling them a little about the area but I didn't mention that we had already moved twice. And we still had our mail sent to John's parents as I was too ashamed to tell my family about the hostility I had received from John's mother and sisters. I knew Papa would worry too much. I longed to see him. Monica was still in London and I wrote to her often as well but I didn't tell her about how unwelcome I had been made to feel.

When the weather was dry, I spent my days walking to familiarise myself with the area. I had registered with a doctor and made an appointment with the midwife, who told me my baby was due on October the fifteenth.

We were still on food rationing but I tried to make sure John had a substantial meal waiting for him when he got home from work; however, he still moaned that it wasn't enough.

One afternoon I had just settled down in the armchair with a cup of Camp coffee and my knitting, when there was a loud knock on the door.

"Who is it?" I asked nervously. There was no answer. I saw the door handle turn so I shouted again, "Who is it?"

"It's Idris," came the reply, and I felt a wave of fear pass over me.

I unlocked the door slowly and he pushed his way into the living room.

"I just called to see how you were settling in. With John at work a lot, I thought you might be lonely," he leered. My stomach lurched. His eyes never left me as he went to sit in one of the chairs.

"Idris," I said, trying to sound more bold than I felt, "would you mind leaving? I'm feeling very tired as my baby is due soon and I have been going to bed early."

The creepy smile vanished as he stood up. "You do realise this is my house and I can come and go as I please," he said, with a hard edge to his voice. "But I know when I'm not welcome," and he slammed the door shut behind him.

After he had gone, I began to shake. I jumped up and locked the door, then sat down and took deep breaths.

"Calm down, Rosina. This isn't good for the baby," I said to myself.

I lay down on the settee and fell asleep until I was wakened by another knock on the door.

"Who is it?" I said weakly.

"It's me, John. Who do you think it is?"

John wanted to know why I had locked the door and I told him about Idris' visit to "see if I was feeling lonely".

I studied John's face for a response. I could tell he didn't believe me.

"I can't imagine him talking like that," he eventually said. "If I go down and tell him not to come up when I'm not here, he will most probably throw us out."

I stood there shaking, too angry to speak.

"Look, if he calls again when I'm at work, don't answer the door," John said, calmly lighting up a cigarette.

"That's easier said than done,' I argued. "What happens when the baby is born? I will be up and down the stairs all the time."

"Just ignore him," John snapped.

It didn't take much for John to lose his temper so I decided to drop the subject for the time being.

Towards the end of September, Gwen gave birth to a baby girl, who they called Millie. She was beautiful, with jet-black hair, and I hardly ever heard her cry.

"I hope my baby will be as quiet as your Millie is," I said as I handed Gwen a white cardigan that I had knitted for the baby.

I always made sure Idris was out and John was upstairs when I called to see the baby.

I still had a fortnight to go before my baby was due and it seemed never ending, as I finished knitting a lemon cardigan. I looked over at John who was asleep in the chair. It was hard to feel angry with him when he looked so peaceful. I wondered if the long hours he worked could be the reason for his irritable moods.

John and I went for a walk one afternoon, as the nurse had said walking could help induce labour, and on the way home I began to have pain in my back. By the time we got home, the pain was stronger and just as we got to the front door, my waters broke.

"Quick, John," I breathed. "Call an ambulance!

I'd never seen John so nervous as he rushed out the door to the nearest phone box.

Within half an hour, two friendly ambulance men arrived and they helped me down the stairs and into the waiting ambulance. By this point, my contractions were every five minutes and I was struggling to cope with the pain.

"Is this your first baby, love?" one of the men asked.

"My first—and my last!" I managed to pant between groans.

"Och, they all say that but before you know it, we're back again delivering baby number two," he laughed.

****

My baby was born later that evening: a beautiful, blonde-haired little girl. The nurses nicknamed her Penny Farthing because she was so long. John and I decided to call her Susanna.

I couldn't believe she was mine and kept staring at her in wonder. John was beside himself with happiness too. He could hardly bear to put her down when it was time for him to leave the hospital.

Susanna and I arrived back home a week later. At first she seemed to settle into a routine of feeding every two to three hours. But after a few days, she started to grizzle all day long and would only sleep if I rocked her in my arms.

I paced the floor at night, desperately trying to ease her cries and soothe her to sleep, but nothing I did seemed to work. I even took her to the doctor, as I thought there might be something wrong with her, but he assured me she was perfectly healthy, "with a good pair of lungs."

John was struggling to cope with Susanna's constant crying as well. When he was working the night shift, he couldn't get peace to sleep during the day.

"I would just love one stretch of unbroken sleep," he moaned.

I suggested that while the weather was still fine, I could walk her to a café, which was a reasonable distance away, each morning to allow John time to catch up on sleep.

He picked his daughter up off the floor and laid her on his chest. "Why can't she be like this all the time," he murmured.

"I wish I had a friend to walk to the café with," I said, wanting to open up to John. "But once people hear my accent, they usually walk away."

"I'm sure you're just imagining that, Rosina," John said.

So much for sharing my troubles with him, I thought wretchedly. The exhaustion was making me feel very low.

But then I looked up and saw that both John and Susanna had fallen asleep. I smiled, wishing I had a camera to capture this rare moment of peace.

Chapter Thirty-Eight
Christmas 1946

By Christmas Day, Susanna was ten weeks old but John's family had only seen her once. I hoped that when we visited them that day, they would pay more attention to their beautiful little grand-daughter who was becoming more alert each day.

My optimism was soon squashed when we arrived and only Heather paid any attention to Susanna, offering to take her for a walk after we had our meal. I was so grateful to Heather as it meant I could just sit and relax. That was until Ethel thought otherwise. I had just closed my eyes for a minute, when Ethel nudged my legs.

"What do you think you're doing? We all pitch in here to help after dinner, but you seem to think you're above everyone else. We would all love to sit down and doze, especially Mam who's been slaving over the stove all morning to give us a lovely Christmas dinner," she snarled at me. "There's a tea towel in the drawer—use it!"

I felt so humiliated and just wanted to run as far away from these people as I could, but I picked up the tea towel and did what I was told. I didn't have the energy to fight back.

The whole time we were there, Megan never once picked Susanna up or spoke to her. I thought of my own Mamma who, if she had been alive, would have smothered Susanna in love and attention.

During Ethel's outburst, I noticed that John was oblivious to it all as he had fallen fast asleep in the chair. No-one told him to get up and help.

As soon as Heather came back, I thanked her, put my coat on and told John we had to leave before it got dark. I just about managed to choke out a thank you for the two small presents Susanna had been given.

I railed at John on the way home, spilling out all my angst at his family's rudeness and lack of interest in my baby daughter.

"What do you expect me to do, Rosina?" John retorted.

"Well, if you hadn't fallen asleep, you could have defended me when Ethel laid into me," I said furiously. I wasn't prepared to let the matter drop. "Did you notice that your sisters spoke in Welsh whenever I walked into the room, deliberately not involving me in their conversations? My family didn't do that to you!" I reminded him.

His stubborn refusal to say anything in reply infuriated me, but suddenly weariness overcame me and I too walked the rest of the way home in stony silence.

A new year arrived, but Susanna only seemed to become more unsettled, especially once she started teething.

One particular night, the crying was unbearable. I got up and took her out for a walk in the middle of the night, willing to do anything just to let peace reign.

The following morning, after I had washed and fed Susanna, I was taking the dirty water I had in the bowl to the bathroom. Out of nowhere, Idris cornered me. He wouldn't let me past and bellowed in my face, "I have had enough of that bloody baby of yours! What the hell is wrong with her? She doesn't stop crying! Get back to Germany where you belong!"

"I'm not German—I'm Belgian," I managed to squeak out but I was terrified. "I have tried everything to stop my baby crying but I don't know what else to do."

"Well, try bloody harder!" he screamed, taking a step towards me. His hands were bunched into fists and I was convinced he was going to punch me.

The next thing I knew, I was throwing the bowl of dirty water all over him. He yelped and started raving like a madman. Before he could retaliate, I dropped the bowl and ran to my room and locked the door, putting a chair under the handle of the door.

Idris started banging on the door and screaming abuse at me. "Get back to wherever you came from! You're not welcome in this country, you Belgian, German bitch!"

I put my hands over my ears. I hadn't felt so frightened since the Nazis had burst into our home in Oostende that dreadful night that now seemed so long ago.

Finally, after what seemed an age, he left and I could hear him shouting as he flew down the stairs.

I sat on the floor and sobbed and sobbed. I couldn't believe it when I looked over at Susanna, who had fallen asleep through all the shouting.

What am I doing in this horrible place? I said to myself. I thought back to when John and I had first gotten together. I had thought then that I would be happy wherever I was, if he was with me. But now, sitting on the floor, sharing a house with a stranger who hated foreigners, I wondered if I had been too hasty in allowing myself to fall in love with someone I hardly knew. I longed for my Mamma and sobbed as the loneliness threatened to overwhelm me.

John was later than usual coming home. There was a loud angry knock on the door and then John shouted, "Rosina, open this damn door!" When he came in, his face was like thunder and he came straight over to me.

"What the hell have you done? What made you throw water all over Idris?" I couldn't get a word in as John kept shouting at me. "You do realise we have a week to find somewhere else to live or we will be homeless!" he shouted.

"Do you know what he called me, John," I said, determined to defend myself. "He called me a German bitch and he was screaming at me. He raised his fists and I was convinced he was going to hit me. I threw the water over him to defend myself."

"Well, you'll need to apologise," John said. "Maybe he'll change his mind."

I couldn't believe my ears. "I'm not apologising to that man," I gasped. "He is constantly sniping at me and complaining about Susanna. I am a bag of nerves when I know he's in the house. And today, I was genuinely terrified."

"We'll end up on the street, woman," John said angrily.

"You promised Papa you would take care of me," I sobbed. "But I've never once heard you defend me when your family are rude to me. And when I told you that Idris intimidated me, you did nothing!" I paused, looking for a response from John. But instead of concern, all I could see was rage in his eyes.

"I'm leaving you, John. I'm going back home to Belgium and I am taking Susanna with me. I'm not welcome here and I don't even know if you want me anymore," I said wearily.

"You go if that's what you want," he said and I felt like I'd been stabbed. "But you will not take Susanna out of the country. She was born here and this is where she remains!"

"My daughter is coming with me," I said, trying to keep my voice steady. "Who do you think would look after her anyway? Your mother can barely look at her, never mind look after her."

"You are not in Belgium now," he said, and I shuddered at the threatening tone in his voice. "Papa's not going to help you so get used to it. Whether you like it or not you are my wife and this is your home."

Without warning, he caught hold of my arm and yanked me out of my chair then he forcefully tried to make me go downstairs. I struggled to free myself but he wouldn't let go.

"Get down that stairs now and say you are sorry!" John shouted.

"You can kill me but I will not say sorry to that man!" I screamed back. John pushed me violently and I fell and screamed as my back hit the floor. Susanna woke up crying.

"Look what you've done! You call this a home? It's nothing but a prison for me!" I picked Susanna up and quickly ran to the bedroom with a stabbing pain in my back.

About an hour later I opened the bedroom door and peeped out, hoping Idris wasn't out on the landing waiting, knowing that he must have heard our row. I crept into the living room, bracing myself for having to face John, but he wasn't there. I put my coat on, dressed Susanna and went to the shops.

By the time I got home, John was waiting for me in the living room.

"Rosina," he said, coming towards me with open arms. "I am so sorry for how I acted earlier. There is no excuse for my outburst. I know I need to take better care of you, and I hate myself for the misery I'm causing you."

His eyes pleaded with me to forgive him, but I wasn't ready to forget the violence he had shown towards me in front of our daughter.

"What really hurts, John, is you never believe me or stick up for me. You make me feel like it's always my fault." I was determined to keep my tears in check and not show him how afraid I really was.

"I'm sorry, my love. Please believe me," he said and I saw again the tenderness in his eyes that always melted my defences. I said no more, but wasn't quite ready to just walk into his arms as if nothing had happened.

Seeing that my anger had subsided somewhat, John continued, albeit hesitantly.

"I think there is an answer to the problem of where to live," he said. "I heard last week that a gentleman that works in the same factory as me is looking for a house keeper to live in and look after his bedridden mother. His name is Henry Evans, he's a bachelor. He lives on the same street that we are on now."

"It's more rooms in someone else's house again," I reminded him. "This is the fourth time we've moved since we were married and we still don't have our own place. I'm fed up of sharing kitchens and bathrooms, John."

"That's why I didn't mention it before now. And I wasn't sure how you would feel about taking on the role of looking after this man's mother. But we are desperate, Rosina, and so is he." He looked at me like a repentant child. "At least we would have a roof over our heads. And you can decorate the house to your own liking," he ventured, eager to convince me this was the answer to all our problems. I had to laugh at his comments.

"I don't know, John," I said. "You don't understand how miserable I am here. I feel so unwanted. I just want to go back to Belgium to be among my own people."

Ignoring my comments, John continued, "Will you at least consider the offer?"

"I'll think about it," I told him.

"I think you would enjoy looking after someone as frail as the old lady; it's in your nature to be caring," John said. I knew he thought he was paying me a compliment, but I was still bristling from the fact that he never acknowledged what I had sacrificed to be with him in Wales.

"You do remember we have a daughter who is very hard work. What happens if I am so busy that I am unable to get your tea ready when you come home from work? What will you do then? Create hell like you always do when things don't go your way?" I said. I wanted him to acknowledge that his treatment towards me wasn't acceptable.

"I will try and make an effort to help," he replied, but he didn't sound very convincing.

However, in my heart of heart, I knew we had no other choice, so grudgingly I agreed to visit Henry Evans and his mother the next day.

Chapter Thirty-Nine
Move Number Four

"Pleased to meet you, Henry," I said, holding out my hand to the tall, thin man who greeted us at the front door of the house that would become our new home. I received a firm handshake back.

"So you're from Belgium then?" he said with a welcoming smile which warmed my heart when compared to the usual look of suspicion I received from strangers when they realised I was foreign. "I believe you had a terrible time during the war. I used to listen to the wireless every day and the cruelty inflicted on so many people throughout Europe was horrendous."

His concern, made me feel more at home already, than I had felt in any other of our so called 'homes' in Wales before this one.

The interior of the house was very old and I could tell nothing had been replaced for a long time. As we walked round the house, I gave it a full appraisal. I couldn't help but notice how dark everything was, from the large, black granite fire grate to the tiny hallway decked in dark oak and two gas lamps, which sat high on the wall but gave out very little light. The windows were very small and any light they did let in was hindered by heavy, drab curtains.

But, I could also picture what a lick of paint could do to the bedrooms that we would occupy, and my imagination transformed the box-room into a nursery that would be perfect for Susanna. I also saw that I would have access to a deep set oven, a tin bath and a wringer which seemed great luxuries, compared to the little we had had previously.

Henry took me into the front room and introduced me to his frail, elderly mother, who was called Beatrice. She could barely lift her head to acknowledge us and her speech came in rasps, so that it was hard to understand what she was saying. My optimism was dampened as I realised that this lady would need a lot of care.

"Well, what do you think, Rosina?" Henry asked, as we walked into the hallway. "Would it be too much for you, looking after my mother and the little one?"

"No, not at all," I replied, determining to look at the positives and do my best to make this arrangement work. "I'm used to hard work." I smiled and looked at John, who seemed relieved that I was prepared to take on this new role.

We moved into Henry's home the following day and since we had very little with us, it didn't take me long to pack.

The following morning, the first thing I did was to go and see Beatrice. She was very weak; she would need to be fed and was incontinent. I opened the dark curtains and let some light into the dreary room in an effort to lift her spirits, as well as my own.

It soon became obvious that I had my work cut out for me, between Susanna, who was at a busy stage, and Beatrice, who needed my attention throughout the day. On top of that, my sleep was still being interrupted every night by Susanna, and I had begun to have nightmares again, just like after Mamma died.

One night, I woke up screaming and sweating. I jumped out of bed, not knowing where I was. My days were so busy by the time evening came, I was exhausted and just wanted to fall into bed. When John was at night shift, I had the chance to go to bed early, otherwise I was at everyone's beck and call day and night.

Life in Henry's home took on new dimension. True to his word, I had the run of the house and I was able to buy some curtains for the whole of downstairs and some small rugs for Beatrice's room and the living room. Henry helped with the purchase of the new things.

John seemed to be a lot calmer since the new move; sometimes he helped around the house and read to Susanna. She loved the garden and we had to persuade her to come in for her meals.

I had moved Beatrice's bed nearer to the window and opened the curtains wider. I asked Henry for extra pillows so that I could prop her up slightly and she could then watch the world go by, which she loved.

Rationing was still in force, so it was very difficult when feeding two grown men. John would usually moan that his plate was half full and he didn't have enough to eat but one day, I was lucky enough to buy four lamb chops. Henry was out for the evening so John had three and I had one.

John had very little to say as we ate our meal. We had just finished and I picked up the dishes to put in the sink, when out of nothing John looked at me with the evil expression I had seen in his mother's house.

"You're a glutton!" he shouted.

"What did you say, John?" I answered in confusion.

"You are a glutton," he screeched out the words.

"I gave you most of the food; I only had a small amount!" I cried, shocked by his sudden outburst. "How dare you accuse me of being a glutton! You of all people should know of the starvation our country endured. I would have gladly given you my share if I'd thought you didn't have enough. I'm used to starving!" I spat out.

"Well, you're bloody well making up for it now," he roared. He jumped off his chair and I could see the madness in his eyes. I screamed, as he came at me. The plates fell to the floor as he forced my head sideways with a brutal slap.

I clasped my ringing ear which was throbbing violently.

"What have I done to deserve this?" I cried, tears flowing down my cheeks. Fearing what he would do next, I made for the door, stepping over the broken plates.

"Bugger off!" he yelled. "Get out of my sight—you make me sick!"

I climbed the stairs to the bedroom, feeling utterly sick. I took my pillow and a blanket from the wardrobe and went into Susanna's room, hoping she wouldn't wake up.

"What am I doing putting up with John's abuse?" I asked myself over and over. "Have I made the biggest mistake of my life? Is this how my life is going to be: used as a punch bag whenever John feels like it?" His volatile moods were beginning to really frighten me.

I looked at Susanna, sleeping peacefully, and I thought I could never leave her here with him.

"Maybe it is my fault," I whispered in despair. I tried to piece together the hours before he went wild but I couldn't concentrate, my face was stinging so much. I couldn't think of anything I had said or done to upset him and I came to the conclusion there was no reason at all for his foul temper.

From that day on I vowed to make sure that his plate was covered with food even if it meant I only had a meagre portion for myself.

For once Susanna slept through the night, but when I woke up the next morning, she looked curiously at me. Stretching out her tiny hand, she asked, "Mammy's face?"

I looked in the mirror and was shocked to see a wide red mark down the side of a swollen cheek and my ear.

"Oh, mammy bumped into the door, silly me." I laughed. Though I could still feel the pain. What had happened the night before frightened me because there was no reason for it; within seconds, John had turned into a madman! There was something not right there. I was going to have to tread very carefully around him.

As the weeks and months went on, my anxiety around my husband increased. I dared not comment on the fact that after working an afternoon shift, John would usually call for a drink on the way home. Whatever I said was wrong, and I came to realise that he enjoyed my fear. Then there were days when he was the most loving of husbands and would go out of his way to help. But I was always on edge, waiting for something, anything, to upset him—it was like waiting for a time-bomb to go off.

What grieved me even more than John's treatment of me, was the fact that Susanna, who was now almost two years old, wouldn't go anywhere near her father; she too had become frightened of him.

John couldn't understand why. One day he tried to take her for a walk. "Come on, Susanna, would you like to walk to the fields and see the cows and sheep? You'd like that, wouldn't you?"

She screamed and kicked when I tried to put her coat on. "I don't want to go with Daddy! Please don't make me go, Mammy."

I took her coat and scarf off.

"We can't make her go, John," I whispered.

"I can't seem to do anything right with her. She won't even sit with me and read a book," he complained.

"What do you expect, John?" My instinct to defend my daughter was stronger than fear for my own safety and so I continued, "The tension in this house is far from ideal for a child of her age. She's listening and watching everything we do or say. You're forever shouting and swearing and she's seen you using your fists and pushing me. What sort of environment is that for her to grow up in?"

I braced myself for an angry tirade or worse, but something must have hit home, because he looked away from us both in shame.

**

The nightmares were getting worse and interfering with my days. I was becoming irritable and by late afternoon, I was almost on my knees with exhaustion.

Trying to keep on top of my daily chores was a struggle. The nightmares seemed so real: I felt like I was drowning; my throat felt on fire with the taste of salt, I couldn't breathe. It got so bad, that I was too afraid to close my eyes, yet I knew I had to try and sleep for everyone's sake. I had hoped I had left the nightmares in Belgium.

"Look Rosina, would it help if we had a week in Belgium?" John asked one day, his thoughtfulness taking me by surprise.

"Oh, John, I am desperate to see Papa and my sisters again," I cried, delighted at his suggestion. "I haven't seen them for two years and maybe by going to Belgium it will stop the nightmares. And Monica has moved back to Oostende so I would get to see them all again."

We decided that if we waited until the summer, that would give us enough time to save money. John even worked some double shifts to add more money to our savings.

Henry arranged a week off work for when we would be away so he could take over the care of his mother.

On the journey to Belgium, I was still terrified when we crossed the Channel but, I did my best to not let Susanna see how it affected me. As we came into Oostende, I could see so much had been done to repair and modernise the town.

My heart was full when we finally made it to my home and I threw myself into Papa's arms. Over his shoulder, I could see my little sister, Sara, who at sixteen, was now a young lady. I cried as I hugged her close, regretting that I had missed supporting her through her adolescence. Heli seemed very quiet but, managed a shake of the hand, which I found odd but, I ignored the cold welcome.

I missed everything about Belgium: The shops, the language and most of all Papa and my sisters. We spent as much time on the beach as we could. The sun was bright, the sea was blue and so inviting. On the road down to the sea front, memories of my hopes of freedom and for a better life came flooding back as clear as day.

I remembered all of us deep in thought, as we walked the long walk to my uncle's fishing boat on that fateful day; the children were so excited, believing they were going on holiday, and Mamma was trying to be brave, as she said goodbye to the home she loved so dearly. I knew Marie wasn't entirely to blame in wanting Mamma to leave our country, Monica and I were desperate to leave too and in the end we helped to persuade her to go. That was something I would regret for the rest of my life.

One evening after everyone had gone to bed, Papa and I sat talking about the good times when Mamma was alive and about the war years. It felt like old times.

"Are you happy in Wales, Rosina?" Papa asked, studying me intently. "How is John treating you? Is he looking after you like he promised?"

My cheeks were burning as I replied, "Yes, we're fine, Papa. We have our moments like all couples do. But Wales is not like here; they are way behind the times. There's nowhere to take Susanna. There are no nearby cafés with music to spend the morning in. Once people hear my accent, they walk away. I'm sure they think I'm German, Papa," I stressed.

"Well, don't give them the chance, tell them you are from Belgium. At least then they have the choice to stay and talk, or walk away."

"Oh Papa, I do miss our chats." I gave him a hug.

"Do you think John would move back here to live?" Papa asked.

"No. I've asked him, but he won't," I replied sadly.

I wasn't expecting Papa's next question.

"Do you still love him, Rosina?"

"Yes of course I do, Papa." I couldn't bear to burden Papa with the truth of how John treated me, and the truth was I did, despite everything, I still loved him. "I sometimes feel homesick, but it passes. I'll try and come more often to see you, Papa. This holiday has been a real tonic." I kissed his forehead.

I loved catching up with Sara and Monica, whom I had missed more than I realised. We talked about our childhoods but never about the day of the bombing in Dieppe.

The week passed much too quickly and on the day we left Belgium, I felt desolate, but I tried my best to hide it from Papa and my family.

Chapter Forty
Descent into Depression

When I arrived back in Wales, that familiar feeling of despondency took hold of me again. I knew it would be some time before I saw my family again. With that thought in mind, I found everyday life becoming more and more difficult to cope with. I couldn't stop crying and John had no patience with me. Susanna was looking at me with such sad eyes, even though I tried desperately not to show her how miserable and depressed I felt.

"For goodness sake, pull yourself together, Rosina," John would say. "This is your home now—get used to it. It's not fair on Susanna seeing you crying all the time."

I had resigned myself to the fact that John would never change from the brute that he was, though I would long for the man who showed tenderness, the man I know he was, or certainly used to be capable of being. But every day there would be something wrong: not enough food on his plate or his dinner wasn't on the table waiting for him when he came home from work.

Somehow John knew that I would never leave him, that I still loved him, even though his treatment towards me was nothing short of cruelty. And I knew that if I did leave, I would have to fight tooth and nail to keep Susanna; the thought of her being brought up by John and his family was enough to keep me in Wales. Never a day passed when I didn't think of my little sister Louisa who had drowned in Dieppe. The memories became more vivid the more miserable my life became.

Somehow, even during the horror of the war years in Belgium, I had managed to push the memories away but now, they haunted me. I became utterly convinced, that she was the child I had kicked away from me in desperation, when I was in the water at Dieppe. Self-condemnation was slowly suffocating me. I started eating less and less, but smoking more and more.

The more John screamed and used his fists, the more withdrawn I became. My confidence had reached rock bottom.

"Why do you cry all the time, Mammy?" Susanna would say, sadness etched on her little face. "Has Daddy hit you again?"

"No, Mammy's got a heavy cold; my eyes have been watering that's all, I'm fine now." That was always my excuse to her. Guilt consumed me as I watched her suffer because of her parents' destructive marriage.

I kissed her and held her close. *What would I do without you?* I thought to myself.

My therapy was sewing and knitting. I made Susanna school skirts and gave Beatrice a bed-jacket, edged with colourful daisies.

But the relief that sewing would bring would only last until John arrived home from work or the pub. He could pick a fight about anything.

After one particular day, I was exhausted because Beatrice had been feverish and needed extra attention, John started on me as soon as he walked in the door.

"When did you last see my mother?" he growled at me.

"I don't know, last week I think," I told him.

"You're a liar!" He came right up to my face.

Not tonight, I thought. I was feeling so tired after the hellish day I had endured.

He stood over me. "You haven't seen her for weeks. I've just called there and she was upset because, she hasn't seen Susanna for ages," he shouted.

I wanted to point out that his mother normally couldn't be bothered with Susanna, but I thought better of provoking him further. I just got up and quietly busied myself getting his dinner ready.

He wasn't finished with me however. "By the way, we are going to see Mam and Dad at the weekend. And I don't care if you don't want to go. You'll do what I say, you Belgic bitch."

This man I called my husband had turned into a bully that I no longer recognised. I didn't know how much I could endure.

We'd made plans to go to back to Belgium the following summer—1950, which gave me something to look forward to, if we could save enough money.

Then, just before Christmas, I discovered I was pregnant again. Before telling John, I worked out roughly that the baby would be due the week we were planning to go to Belgium. I was devastated.

My mind was in turmoil: I desperately wanted this baby but I desperately wanted to see my family too. If I went ahead with the pregnancy, I knew it would be years before I would be able to visit them again. This filled me with a sense of panic.

I was so homesick. I longed to be with Papa. I missed our long chats and his guidance through difficult times. I always felt safe under his protection. "I do miss you, Papa," I whispered. My heart had never really left Belgium.

My life in Wales, the one I had once been so excited about, was hellish. I was raising my daughter in a home where she witnessed more brutality than love. I had no-one I could turn to.

That night I lay in bed, agonising over what I should do.

The following morning I woke with a terrific headache. I could hardly move my head off the pillow.

John didn't help. "What the hell is wrong with you? Every day there is something!" he snapped.

"Please just pass me some aspirin, John. You'll need to make Susanna her breakfast," I whispered. "And please be patient with her."

After the tablets started to take effect, I managed to get out of bed. I could hear John shouting and Susanna crying. All morning he moaned until he went to work; Susanna couldn't do anything right. His language was foul and loud enough for everyone to hear. It was breaking my heart.

I knew that if Papa knew how John treated me, he would persuade me to come home to him in Oostende. I knew my safety would be more important to Papa than the shame of a divorced daughter.

I decided there and then to do the unthinkable.

If I hadn't felt so isolated and like a punch-bag for John, I know I wouldn't have contemplated doing what I did. The anticipation of seeing my Papa and sisters again had been the only thing helping me endure the agony of living in such a volatile marriage.

If I'd known the risk to my life that I was taking. I would never have done it. I lost so much blood that I ended up being hospitalised. When I woke up, I looked up into the face of a kindly-looking man and it took me a few minutes to work out where I was.

"How long have I been here, Doctor?" I eventually said.

"Two days, Mrs Jones," he answered with gentleness in his voice. "I believe if you hadn't come into hospital when you did, you wouldn't be lying in that bed now; you would be lying in the morgue."

My eyes filled with tears and my colour rose, as the shame over what I had done came back to me.

"You were seriously ill, Mrs Jones, and you are still on two-hourly injections of penicillin and on an intravenous drip," the doctor continued. "You will have to stay in hospital for at least a week and will need complete bedrest." He hesitated, before speaking again. "I don't know what problems you have at home or what drove you to do what you did, but I would strongly advise you not to go down this road again."

His words were firm but, his eyes were full of compassion and he squeezed my hand as if to silently assure me that he didn't judge me for my actions.

I was grateful for his kindness and the care he gave me during the remainder of my stay in hospital. I knew in that moment that though there had been many regrets in my life, none would be as devastating as getting rid of my baby, and that it would haunt me until the day I died. It was against my religion, against my upbringing, against everything I valued. I wept as I thought of how appalled my Mamma would have been if she had been alive. I knew I would never be able to stop judging myself.

The following July we went to Belgium, as planned. However, a black shadow of remorse hung over me reminding me of the price I had paid to see my family again.

I desperately tried to hide my guilt. When I was with my sisters, their constant chat about their social life and their sunny natures helped distract me from the darkness I felt inside. I was able to pretend all was well and join in with their laughter.

However, with Papa, it was a different matter altogether.

"Is there something you're not telling me, Rosina?" he said one night when we had the living room to ourselves. "You seem far away. You're not the happy young girl who went in search of a better life."

But I couldn't bear to burden him with the truth of what my life had become, and I was scared that if I did open up, the truth of what I had done would spill out. I couldn't do that to him. The sorrow and grave disappointment would have been too much for us both.

And so I left Belgium carrying the weight of my dark secret, not knowing if I could endure what awaited me in Wales.

Somehow, I did endure it and would wonder at what the human spirit can tolerate.

In 1952, my second daughter was born. She was a gift that I didn't believe I deserved. I named her Louisa after my sister who had died at Dieppe. It brought me a measure of comfort knowing her name was close to my heart.

Louisa was an adorable little baby with dark hair and big blue eyes. And, best of all, she slept through the night and hardly cried during the day. I found it very strange having to wake her up to feed her.

When Louisa was six months old, she developed bronchial pneumonia. There had been an outbreak of whooping cough in Susanna's school, and Susanna contracted a mild strain of the illness. However, little Louisa was more vulnerable and when she began to cough a week later, it became so bad, I thought she was choking. I nursed her throughout the day and tried to spoon feed her but she wouldn't take anything.

One day, I had just laid her down in her cot for a few minutes, I looked down at her and saw that her lips had turned blue. I immediately panicked, fearing for her life.

I picked her up and ran screaming to our next-door neighbour, who was a retired nurse. She laid her on the table and began to give her very gentle resuscitation until finally Louisa began to breathe, then cry. I've never welcomed a baby's cry so much in all my life. I was so relieved I broke down and sobbed. The neighbour, Mildred, immediately called an ambulance which came very quickly.

I couldn't thank Mildred enough. "I will be eternally grateful to you for saving my daughter's life," I said. And I meant it.

Three days later, Louisa came home from hospital. She still had a cough but her temperature was normal; however, she was still on medication.

I put her cot close to our bed, so I could keep an eye on her. I was so nervous that I couldn't sleep. I was terrified she would stop breathing again.

John was surprisingly quiet; whenever he was home, he took charge of Louisa which was a great help to me. I could get on with everything else that needed to be done including seeing to Beatrice who seemed to be failing.

One day John's parents came to visit. I was upstairs seeing to Louisa who at that moment was having a bad coughing bout. John came upstairs and demanded that I go down to welcome them.

"I want you to take Louisa down to see Mam and Dad," he said raising his voice.

"John, I can't take Louisa down to your parents—she is still not well enough and I wouldn't want your Mam to catch whooping cough. Surely they could pop their heads around the door just for a few minutes?"

"You know Mam finds it difficult to climb the stairs," he snapped.

"I'll come down once Louisa's asleep," I said. "But I don't want to leave her just yet."

I laid Louisa down in her cot but then I saw John, from the corner of my eye, coming around the bed. He grabbed my arm and pulled me towards the door.

"What are you doing? Let go of me!" I shouted as I broke free and ran back to Louisa. I saw his arm go up.

"You Belgic bastard, get down those stairs now!" Next thing I knew, he had slapped me hard across my face and I screamed out in pain.

Susanna, who had just walked into the bedroom, had seen it all.

"Leave Mammy alone!" she screamed. "You are a horrible Daddy!"

"If you think I'm going downstairs in this state, you've got another think coming," I cried out. "Unless you want me to show your parents what you are really like!"

He came right up to me and showed me his fist. "I'll have you for this, you bitch," he snarled, then turned and stormed out of the room.

God help me, I said to myself. John's abuse had become part of everyday life. I had learnt to get up each day and carry on. I could sometimes convince myself he would change. But inside, I felt like I was dying.

Susanna crept over and rested her head on my lap. My tears fell silently onto her hair as I thought of what a troubled childhood we had given her.

We stayed in the bedroom until we heard John's parents leave and then breathed a sigh of relief as we heard the door slam behind John, as he left for his night shift.

"Thank God," I said quietly.

Beatrice was deteriorating rapidly. Henry would sit with his mother for hours; sometimes he would read to her or just fall asleep himself.

It was just as well John and Henry were on opposite shifts. If Henry could have heard and seen what John did to me, I'm sure he would have thrown us out. I felt so embarrassed by the way John was humiliating me, especially in front of his family but he just didn't care.

One night after the girls were settled and I made sure Beatrice was tucked-up with her pillows all around her, I took the opportunity to have an early night, as I was shattered. John was on night shift.

I woke about two o'clock in the morning, immediately sensing something was wrong. I quickly checked the girls but they were both sound asleep. I then went down to see to Beatrice.

When I walked into her bedroom, I turned the lamp on beside her bed to change her. As soon as I touched her, I felt the deathly chill of her flesh. I tried to check her pulse. There wasn't one.

"Oh, my dear Beatrice, you've slipped away with no one to hold your hand or sit with you. I'm so sorry I wasn't here for you," I whispered.

I crept upstairs to henry's room, hesitating before knocking his door. I broke the news as gently as I could. He remained calm and dignified until he got to his mother's bedside, where he knelt down, clasped her hands and wept.

A week after Beatrice's funeral, Henry approached John and I.

"I don't know how to tell you, but I'm going to sell the house," he said looking genuinely sorry. "I can't bear to stay on in this house without mother here. She was the reason I didn't move sooner. I always wanted something smaller and brighter, but she loved this house."

Henry reassured us that there was no rush for us to leave but he had wanted to give us plenty of warning.

"I know it can't be easy with two children," Henry said and reached down to pick Louisa up. But she turned away, stretching her hands up to her father.

Unlike Susanna, Louisa was a daddy's girl, having not witnessed as much as her big sister. Henry smiled and then looked over at me.

"You have been amazing with my mother, Rosina," he said, coming over and taking my hand. "I don't think she would have lasted this long if you hadn't cared for her so attentively."

Only I noticed John's look of disgust as he left the room, taking Louisa with him.

Chapter Forty-One
A Home of Our Own

A week later, John came home from work and told me he had called into the council offices to put our name down for a council house, and that we had been put on a priority list.

From then on, everything happened very quickly: within a month we were allocated a three-bedroom council house in another village. We had very little furniture so used our little savings to buy the bare essentials.

The distraction of moving and setting up the house had meant John was kept busy and I had a reprieve from his bullying. I dearly hoped that now that we finally had our own place, our marriage would become a happier one.

However, after we had been in the house about a fortnight, John started his antics again.

My next door neighbour had asked me if I would like to come around for a cup of tea. It had been such a long time since anyone had offered any hospitality to me that I gladly accepted. But I couldn't relax and only stayed for a short time. The fear of John's reaction if his dinner wasn't ready on time gnawed at me the whole time I was in the neighbour's house.

When John did arrive home, I was just waiting for his lamb chops to cook, but assured him dinner wouldn't be long.

I only got a grunt in response. To try and clear the air, I thought I would tell him about the new friend I had made, but I regretted it the instant the words were out of my mouth.

"That's why my dinner wasn't on the table when I got home, then," he snapped. "This better not be a habit. I'm out working all hours while you are yapping in other people's houses!" He pushed me aside to wash his hands. "Get out of my way, you bloody woman!"

"John, keep your voice down," I urged. "The walls in these houses are so thin and the neighbours can hear everything."

"I don't bloody care who hears! This is my house and I'll do what I like!" he yelled in my face.

As the months passed, John's lack of patience became intolerable and Susanna, too, was now getting the brunt of his temper and the sting of his slaps.

She was now eight years old and had started in a new school which she didn't like and couldn't settle into. Susanna had always been shy and withdrawn, especially with children she didn't know. There was also the stigma of my nationality; some people still thought I was German or French. They would take it out on Susanna, calling her names such as 'French-fries'. One day she came home crying as some of the children had told her to "Go back to Germany where you belong! You're not wanted here!" There were many days when I had trouble getting her to go to school at all. It grieved me to see my little girl so unhappy, both at school, but also at home, which should have been a haven for her.

I missed Beatrice and gentle Henry. I had felt safe when he was around and John had always behaved himself when Henry was there. Now John was free to shout and create hell whenever he wanted to.

As the girls got a little older and needed less attention, I had more time on my hands. Time to think. Time to long for the company of my family, whom I desperately missed. Time to delve into the painful memories of the war and of my missing child.

The nightmares began to raise their ugly heads again. When sleep eventually came, it would be troubled and inevitably I would wake up screaming.

Mamma's face was always so near to me and I would reach out but just as I did she would drift away from me. Little Louisa's small hands gripped my legs tightly, and in my dreams, I tried to reach down to pull her to safety, but all I would see is the terror in her eyes as she sank out of my grasp.

Depression had a firm grip on me. I didn't want to get up in the morning and I had no appetite and no will to live. Daily life became unbearable and my girls were suffering but, I didn't know what to do about it.

Louisa hadn't started school yet, so she was with me all day which helped in some ways. She would climb up onto my lap and ask me, "Why are you crying all the time, Mammy?"

"Mammy has a nasty cold," I would tell her, lying again. However, she would wipe my tears with her little hands and snuggle in closer. I knew it was her childlike way of letting me know that John's treatment of me didn't go unnoticed by her.

Once Louisa started school, I found the days very long, but lacked the motivation to take up sewing and knitting again. I lost my pride and I couldn't be bothered to wash. I became irritable and would snap at the girls for the least little thing.

They were going through hell and I knew it wasn't fair on them, being like this. Many times it felt like they were the caregivers. They would often say, "Mammy, you must eat," as they brought me a sandwich and sat on the bed until they saw me eating it.

John had changed his job and he was now working for the County Council on the Highways. There was no more shift work, so he expected tea on the table at four-thirty every day. There were many days when I couldn't find the energy to get out of bed and make a meal, even though I knew what the consequences would be. Some days he would physically drag me from my bed and force me into the kitchen.

All my dreams of what a home of our own would be like were shattered into pieces with every item of crockery thrown, every foul insult shouted at me and every vicious blow that came my way.

I felt that I was suffocating and no longer had the strength to stand up to John.

For the first time I contemplated suicide. I was immediately ashamed and pushed the wicked thought aside.

A few days later, my neighbour Helen called around, when John was at work, for a cup of coffee. She told me that the landlord of our village pub was looking for someone to clean and wash the glasses. I thought, *Why not?* He can only say yes or no. Fortunately, he said yes and he offered me a part-time job. I jumped at the opportunity. I knew it would give me fresh motivation to get up in the mornings.

My job didn't only bring in some extra money, but it gave me a sense of independence and I began to make new friends. Maybe things were looking up, I thought.

My optimism didn't last long.

One night I woke up with terrible pain in my left groin. The pain had been grumbling away for a few days but that night it was unbearable. I nudged John and asked him to get me an aspirin. Grudgingly, he did so, telling me to go and see the doctor the next day. I knew his advice was less about concern for me and more in the hope that the doctor could fix the problem so that his precious sleep wouldn't be disturbed.

However, seeing the doctor proved to be a waste of time. He dismissed the pain as nothing more than colic, despite me flinching in agony whenever he pressed on my groin. He gave me some stronger pain relief and told me I would be fine in a few days. I left the surgery with no peace of mind at all.

The doctor's appointment meant I was late for work. By the time I got there, the pain had increased. I didn't want to let Ralf down, so despite having an empty stomach, I gulped down two of the new pills.

About an hour later I began to feel sick and dizzy. Ralf immediately saw that I was in agony and, after getting one of the other girls to make me some toast, he insisted on driving me home in his car.

I went straight to bed until the girls came home. That evening when John came home from work, he announced that his mother was coming to visit us. I didn't want her here at the best of times, but especially not today when I felt so ill.

"If my mother wants to come and visit us, she damned well will!" John said when I tried to protest. "And you'd better not be rude to her!" he demanded as he turned to leave the kitchen.

"Me be rude to her?" I shouted back, the pain obviously clouding my judgment and making me forget the consequences of answering back.

John was over to me in a flash, grinding his teeth and showing his fist.

"Shut your bloody mouth or I'll shut it for you!" he roared.

Yes, you are good at doing that!" I shouted back at him.

Susanna came running in between us, screaming.

"Stop it! I'm sick of you shouting and fighting all the time. Stop it!"

John caught hold of Susanna's arm and threw her on to the chair. "You shut up or you'll have a hiding too!"

"Don't you dare put your hands on her," I screamed, jumping up to protect her. Without warning, he gave me a backhander that sent me flying to the floor. He went to lay into me again with more fierce blows.

But Susanna screamed. "No Daddy! No! Stop hitting Mammy!" He raised his arm but stopped in mid-air.

"You make me sick, the lot of you!" he bellowed as he turned to walk away.

The pain in my side was throbbing and I could hardly breathe. I took two more of the strong painkillers and as I did so, unwelcome thoughts swept across my mind again. *It would be so easy to end it all now*, I thought bleakly. A knock at the front door distracted me from my dark contemplation.

I tried my best to be as civil as I could to John's parents, and made them tea and brought them a plate of cakes. Only John's stepfather said thank you.

The only time Megan spoke to me directly was to ask, "What's that mark on your face?"

I looked at John, who turned his head away. "Oh I bumped into the door while carrying the washing out to the line," I lied. Knowing I could never confide in this woman, who was anything but a mother to me. It all compounded the misery I was feeling. I couldn't wait for them to go.

I visited the doctor on three more occasions, but to no avail. I could not convince him that I was in terrible pain and he eventually tried to suggest it was caused my homesickness.

"Maybe by going to see your family, you might feel more relaxed, and it may take your mind off the pain you have in your side," he said, getting up from his seat and showing me to the door.

I was speechless, angry and upset.

I didn't feel like going straight back home so I called in to one of the Italian cafés for a decent cup of coffee. After I had put my order in, a young lady approached me, smiling.

"Hello, I hope you don't think me rude but would you mind me asking where you are from?" As soon as she spoke, I knew this wasn't a racist local about to tell me to go back to where I came from. My heart leapt as I recognised her accent immediately.

"I'm from Belgium," I said eagerly. "And you?"

"Belgium as well!" she replied, pulling up a chair and sitting across from me. "I'm Lana and I'm delighted to meet you!"

That was the start of a close and precious friendship. Lana was an oasis of friendship in what was otherwise a barren wasteland of pain and rejection. For the first time since arriving in Wales, I was able to confide in someone about my unhappy marriage. Lana also understood fully what it was like to be a foreigner in a less than welcoming country.

It was a Sunday morning when things reached a climax between John and me. His foul mood got worse as the morning went on.

As usual, it was something petty that ignited his rage.

I was sitting by the fire, drinking a coffee and smoking a cigarette, when he came up to me and snarled in my face, "Smoking your fags, again, you Belgic bastard!"

"I'm not a bastard!" I screamed; something inside of me had snapped. I punched him in the arms and on his chest, but he was too strong for me. He pinned me up against the wall then grabbed me by the throat.

"Why don't you sod off back to Belgium, you bitch!" He screamed in my face.

"Why don't you kill me and be done with it. You've been trying to ever since I came to Wales! You're no better than the Nazis!" I was choking and coughing, as I struggled to free his hands from my neck. "The girls and I would be better off without you," I spat out. I just didn't care what he did to me anymore.

His eyes were red with rage.

"You can sod off back to where you came from but the girls stay in this country. Do you hear me?" he shouted, as he let go of my throat.

As he stormed out of the room, a crushing weight of despair descended on me.

I looked out the window and saw the girls playing outside. I was utterly exhausted with the shouting and the violence, and I couldn't stand the girls having to witness such acrimony anymore. I decided they would be better off without me. Adding to the fact my doctor did not believe how ill I was, I wondered what was the point in living.

"Forgive me, my darling girls!" I whispered as the icy fingers of suicidal thoughts took a tight grip of me.

I found some stockings, tied them together and took a chair into the passage. I tied the stockings to the top of the banister then made a loop and put it around my neck.

"This is the right thing to do," I told myself, even though my heart was breaking at the thought of leaving behind my precious daughters.

As I went to kick the chair away, the passage door swung open and I stared down in horror at my daughters.

Susanna started screaming and tried to shield Louisa from what I was doing.

The sight of my girls and the pain in their eyes was enough to loosen suicide's grip on my mind. I took the stockings from my neck and collapsed into a chair beside the fireplace.

I must have dozed off because, the next thing I knew, someone had their hands on my shoulder. I got up quickly thinking it was John.

But it was Lana.

"What has he done this time?" she asked, as I buried my head in her shoulder.

I told her the whole story, between sobs and gulps.

"I'll make you a cup of tea," Lana said. "And I'll fix some lunch for the girls." I looked behind her and saw my two frightened girls crouching in the doorway. I realised that they had been the ones to bring the only person that they thought could help me.

I held my arms open and they both ran over and we held each other close. I whispered again and again, "I'm sorry, I'm so sorry, my precious, precious girls."

Chapter Forty-Two
Seeking Help

The following day I couldn't face going to work. I caught an early bus down to the doctor's and vowed I would not leave the surgery until I got some answers.

Since I hadn't made an appointment, my usual doctor wasn't available, but a Doctor Bevan was.

After he examined me, he didn't say anything and he went to sit back down behind his desk and began to write.

"How long have you been suffering with this pain?" Doctor Bevan asked.

"I have been coming to this surgery for almost two months with this same complaint, but it has only been getting worse," I explained.

"I'm going to refer you to a specialist urgently. Don't be alarmed but I think the pain you are suffering is coming from your ovary. I suggest you go home and rest."

Rather than alarm, I felt relief that finally I was being taken seriously. I thanked him and left.

When I got home, the pain suddenly became worse but as the doctor had given me a thorough examination, I thought that was why. I began to get the dinner ready but I started to feel faint and then everything went black.

The next thing I knew, I was laid out on the settee and the pain in my side was so horrendous, I could hardly breathe. Helen, my neighbour, was peering over me holding a glass of water.

"What happened?" I asked.

"I called around to see if I could borrow some salt and it's a mercy I did, because I found you on the floor," Helen said giving me a sip of water.

Helen's husband, Bill, arrived a short while later and he had brought Doctor Bevan.

"I 've called the specialist and he should be here soon," Doctor Bevan said. "I'm going to give you a morphine injection which will make you feel drowsy but it will help control the pain."

Within two hours of the doctor leaving, the specialist was knocking on the front door.

He introduced himself, "I'm Dr Cunningham. I can see you're in a lot of pain, Mrs Jones, but would you mind if I examined you?"

I winced in pain even though I could see he was being as gentle as he could.

Eventually, he stopped and looked at me kindly, before saying, "I'm almost certain you have a cyst on your ovary and you will have to be operated on today?"

"Today…" I looked up at the specialist. Just at that moment John walked into the room. Doctor Cunningham explained the situation to him and John looked genuinely shocked and worried. It had been a long time since he had given me any help, but that afternoon he excelled himself and helped get me ready for hospital. He assured me the girls would be fed and bathed before bed.

Being admitted to hospital at such short notice left me overwhelmed but as they carried me out to the ambulance on a chair, I tried not to cry. I was eager to see the two girls but knew they wouldn't be allowed to visit me that night.

"John, will you bring the girls to visit tomorrow?" I asked, as the ambulance doors closed.

The following morning, having had the operation, I woke as the light came on in the ward and I could hear the noise of the nurses seeing to other patients. I tried to sit up but found it very painful.

Doctor Cunningham appeared at my bedside later that morning.

"Well, Mrs Jones, how are you feeling today?" he asked with a smile.

I told him how much pain I was in.

"I'm not surprised," he said with concern. "We had to remove your whole ovary because you had a very large cyst which had damaged it badly."

He gently checked my wound and then told me that I would be in hospital for a week.

"And no lifting or carrying anything heavy for at least six weeks once you get home," he said. "Leave that to your husband or your children because the wound could start bleeding again."

I smiled weakly but inside the old fear crept back. There was no way John was going to cope with working and making meals and seeing to the girls. I knew the brunt of the work would fall on Susanna.

Louisa was still only six and wouldn't be able to do much to help.

John and the girls came to visit most nights and even John's mother came to visit some afternoons; however, her visits were very awkward as we had nothing to talk about.

When I arrived home a week later, I went straight up to bed because I felt so weak. Susanna followed me upstairs and sat on the bed. I noticed her eyes were red-ringed.

"What's wrong, sweetheart?" I asked.

She burst out crying. "Oh Mammy, I was so scared you were going to die in hospital. I thought you might never come home," she sobbed and I embraced her tightly, my heart aching for all the suffering one so young had had to endure.

"Well, I didn't die and I'm home and will soon be up on my feet again," I said in attempt to reassure her.

John had told the school that Susanna would be taking the rest of the week off to help look after me. They all did their best to take some of the work load from me, even little Louisa, who was a tonic.

"I missed you, Mammy," she said. "Susanna has been bossing me, so I'm glad you are home now." She planted a massive wet kiss on my cheek.

Despite John stepping up to helping in the house, his bad temper was still bubbling under the surface and I wondered when it would next erupt.

As I started to feel stronger, I thought I would see if I could manage to wash some dishes. John wasn't happy and pushed me aside when he saw what I was doing. "I'll do them in my own time," he snarled. I crept back to bed, exhausted by the exertion of going down the stairs, but also by the reminder of John's true colours.

Chapter Forty-Three
Coping with Depression

After six weeks, I went for a check-up and the specialist was pleased with the healing of the wound but told me to still take it easy.

With the operation out of the way and the pain no longer ruling my life, I expected to feel much better in myself, but I didn't.

All the old familiar feelings and emotions slowly began to surface again. Our hostile life style returned as soon as I was able to do a bit more about the house. I tried my best to avoid conflict but, John would always find fault.

During a coffee morning with Lana, I confessed how I was feeling and that the nightmares were ruling my life.

"I can't shake off the tiredness I feel when I wake in the morning. I struggle to get out of bed. I'm irritable with the girls and in John's eyes, I can't do anything right."

Lana poured us a second cup of coffee.

"Rosina, why don't you ask the doctor for a course of antidepressants? He also may be able to help you, or arrange for you to talk to someone," Lana suggested.

And so on her advice. I went to see Doctor Bevan again who started me on a course of anti-depressants.

After a few weeks, I started to feel that life was worth living again. I began to take an interest in my home, which had been neglected, and I bought material and made some new cushions.

However, I decided to not tell John about the pills I was taking, and he continued to be abusive towards me. Deep down I knew the pills were only a sticking plaster, and that the root of my misery would be much harder to deal with. Before long, the old feelings of despair crept back and took hold.

I went back to Doctor Bevan and ended up being more truthful about the daily reality of my home life. His sympathy and understanding made me open up more and I told him about my past and the nightmares which haunted me.

"I'm going to try you on another tablet," he said, glancing at me over the rim of his glasses. "It's called Valium. I'm going to put you on a month's trial just to see how you respond to them."

My reaction to the pills was not the one the doctor had anticipated.

When I was on my own, the darkest thoughts would insinuate their way into my mind. One dank and dreary morning, after John had left for work and the girls had gone to school. I sat on the edge of my bed with the Valium by my side. Guilt and self-hatred was swallowing me up. My life seemed pointless. I wanted to be free.

I picked up the Valium bottle and gulped down several pills at once. Then I lay down on the bed, closed my eyes and waited to die.

But I didn't. Instead, I woke to the awful sensation of a thick tube being forced down my throat.

"Wake up, Mrs Jones," I could hear a voice saying through a haze. A doctor was peering at me over the side of the bed. "Do you remember what happened?" he asked.

"Yes. I do. I shouldn't be here," I cried. "I don't deserve to live."

"Your life is very valuable, Mrs Jones," the doctor said softly.

He introduced himself as Doctor Matthews and he spoke to me at length. He had already been told some of my medical and mental health history by Doctor Bevan. He knew this wasn't my first attempt to take my life.

"I would like to transfer you to another hospital just for a few days. It's a psychiatric hospital and it is where I am based most of the time," he explained.

"I'm not mentally ill doctor," I said, mortified at his suggestion.

"You can't fight this on your own," he said. "We need to try and get to the bottom of your troubles."

"Couldn't you just give me stronger antidepressants?" I asked, horrified at the stigma of being admitted to a psychiatric hospital.

"We can't risk you taking another overdose, Mrs Jones." The doctor glanced at me with a worried frown. However, he decided to give me two weeks of stronger tablets. He patted my hand gently and that small act of tenderness broke through my defences.

I agreed to attend his clinic and he made me an appointment for two weeks later.

"Thank you, doctor," I said as he left my bedside.

He turned around and said firmly, but with a smile, "My pleasure, Mrs Jones. I will see you soon."

I was discharged from hospital that afternoon and when I arrived home, the girls were back from school.

"Mammy's home! Mammy's home!" Louisa ran towards me shouting and I opened my arms to catch her. "I'm so glad you're home, Mammy." Little Louisa put her arms around my neck.

Susanna remained quiet.

As I hung my coat up in the passage, John arrived home from work. "You're home then," he said.

There was no welcoming hug or smile. "Are you well enough to make the dinner?" was all he said, as he pulled his coat off and hung it in the passage.

The following morning I woke with a terrible headache and I felt dizzy when I tried to get up. I called on Susanna. By the time she came up the stairs, my vision was blurred.

"Are you alright, Mammy?" Susanna asked.

"I'm okay, darling. Mammy's just feeling a little dizzy because of the tablets I got from the hospital. Do you think you could stay home from school today? I'm really going to need your help." I felt terrible burdening Susanna with such responsibility but I had no other choice.

I stayed off work for a week. As the days passed, I began to feel a little better but often walked around as if in a trance. A fog came over my brain, which often left me confused and my ability to do even mundane chores was restricted.

When the day came for my appointment with Doctor Matthews, the psychiatrist, I arrived early at the clinic. As I waited to be seen, the realisation of what had become of me began to sink in. I started to berate myself for allowing myself to fall victim to physical abuse. But then, my mind went down a different path and I started to feel angry, not with myself, but with John. If he had cherished me and cared for me as he once promised to do, instead of inflicting violence and fear on me, then surely I wouldn't have fallen into such a pit of depression.

My mamma had brought me up to be independent and to stand up for myself. These lessons had allowed me to face the enemy and horror of war with resilience and courage. So, why, I asked myself, did I crumble when John so much as raised his voice at me? Mamma would have been horrified to see me sink so low.

"Mrs Jones." The doctor's voice broke into my troubled thoughts.

"Come in and take a seat," he said, smiling. "How are you today?"

Doctor Matthews's gentle manner helped me feel at ease and I spoke to him at length, about how I had been since he had seen me in hospital after my attempt to take my life.

He asked about my day to day life and I told him, about how I enjoyed the social interaction but, found it tiring, especially on top of my household duties. He soon discovered my main help at home was from the girls and that John didn't offer much assistance.

"Is your husband coping with your illness?" Doctor Matthew's asked.

"Not really," I admitted. "He can't understand why I'm feeling this way and he tells me to snap out of it and to pull myself together. He hasn't got much patience with me or the children."

"Was your husband in the war?"

"Yes he was. He was at the Normandy Landings and he saw many of his friends die all around him," I explained. It really only dawned on me in those moments that John too was a victim of trauma. "We've both been left scarred by the war."

"It must have been horrendous," he said. "Do you think you could tell me about the nightmares you are having? It will give me a better idea of how to treat you."

I told him everything: about the bombing of the boat and how I was convinced that I had, unknowingly, kicked my younger sister to her death and how the guilt of that day was slowly killing me. I couldn't hold back my tears. "There's not a day that goes by that I don't think of her," I said in anguish.

The doctor looked up from the notes he was writing, his gaze intent and full of compassion.

I spoke for the first time about my abortion. More guilt, more shame, more endless torment.

The doctor's eyes still displayed only understanding and concern. No condemnation. "I think the best course of treatment for you would involve a stay in hospital," he said.

"I can't, Doctor; I have a family to look after. I can't leave the girls alone," I replied but reluctantly. I felt safe with this doctor and he gave me hope that he could help, but I couldn't risk leaving Susanna and Louisa on their own for such long periods.

Doctor Matthews hesitated, but thought better of exerting any more pressure on me. He had probably read between the lines and suspected John was violent. And understood why I couldn't trust him with the girls.

"I think then we'll keep you on these tablets," he said. "It's early days yet, so I'll see you back here in a month. Any changes, go straight to your doctor and he will arrange for me to see you earlier." He shook my hand warmly as I left his office.

I felt lighter as I walked to the bus stop, but my mood was dampened when I saw the bus pull away before I could get it. I knew John would be in a rage if his dinner wasn't ready when he got home.

Sure enough, John was waiting for me and the shouting started straight away.

"The dinner isn't even on the stove, woman, and why is the fire out?" he ranted. "I'm slogging my guts out all day and you're either in the hospital or at the doctors. What the hell is wrong with you all the time?"

I looked over to where Susanna was sitting and I snapped at her, "Why couldn't you have put the dinner on, you know what he's like if he hasn't got half a dozen lamb chops on his plate waiting for him."

"I'm sorry, mammy, I didn't think," Susanna replied meekly. I immediately regretted taking out my frustration and fear on her. She deserved better.

As I turned to hang my jacket up, I saw John coming for me. He caught hold of my upper arm and pulled me into the kitchen.

Without warning I felt the slap, then the sting across my face. Susanna got up screaming and tried to push him away from me.

"Leave Mammy alone! You are a horrible, nasty father and I hate you!" she yelled.

John swung his arm out and caught her on the side of her head. She screamed out in pain.

I picked up my largest China flowerpot and hit him as hard as I could across his head, scattering flowers and dirt everywhere.

"It's about time you had what you dish out every week," I screeched at him. John stared wildly at us like a maniac, grinding his teeth, and frantically trying to get the dirt out of his eyes.

I grabbed both of the girls and we ran upstairs and locked the bedroom door.

I heard him yell, "I'll have you, you Belgic bastard!"

The girls were sobbing uncontrollably by this point and Susanna gulped out, "Why don't you leave him, Mammy? Why put up with his violent temper? It's so humiliating for Louisa and me—everyone must hear the shouting and fighting. And we have to go to school the following day. I can hear the girls talking about me; it's so unfair."

Her words felt like a stab to my heart. Susanna was right: enough was enough.

However, Louisa put her arms around my neck and cried, "Please Mammy, don't leave Daddy, he'll be on his own. I know he's got a temper but he doesn't mean it." Louisa had never suffered the wrath of her father in the same way that Susanna had. He had shouted at her many times and smacked her bottom. But that was all.

"He's hitting mammy and me all the time now, Louisa," Susanna said, putting her arms around her little sister. "It's not fair."

I don't know how long we sat there for. Eventually, I told the girls I was going downstairs to make their tea. Susanna protested. Still too scared on my behalf about what her father might do.

"If I hear him shouting, or hitting you, I will come down," Susanna said bravely.

"And I will too," Louisa said.

"Your father will have calmed down by now, don't worry," I assured them both.

To my surprise, I went down to discover John had cleaned up the mess of flowers and dirt and the table was laid. I was even more shocked to see the dinner was on the stove cooking. John was sitting by a roaring fire, reading the paper.

"Dinner's nearly ready," was all he said when he saw me.

"How can you be so calm after what you have just done?" I said, unable to stop myself, but knowing I might provoke another outburst. "The girls are most probably too upset to eat anything. You'll have to change, John."

He didn't reply but just went to the bottom of the stairs and called the girls down for dinner, acting as if nothing had happened.

We ate our dinner in silence.

After the girls went to bed, I sat in the kitchen, smoking one cigarette after the other while John sat watching his favourite programmes on the television, with not a thought for me.

One day, when John came home from work, I could see there was something on his mind. I braced myself, not knowing what to expect. As I poured him a cup of tea, his eyes softened and he glanced up at me.

"Why don't you go to Belgium for a few weeks?" He said.

Caught off guard by his unusual behaviour, I just stared at him.

"You haven't been well lately and I think it will be good for you and the children," John continued, and he actually smiled at me, something I hadn't seen for a long time.

"Are you sure, John? I don't want to write to Papa then you change your mind."

"I won't," he said. "We have a little money saved and I will send you money every week." I was shocked and thought I must be hearing things.

I wrote to Papa that very night. The girls were off for six weeks holiday soon and we planned to go then. I felt a weight had been lifted off my shoulders.

When Papa wrote back, I started to make the necessary arrangements and told the girls about the trip.

Later that night, I spoke to John. "Why have you done this? Are you feeling guilty because of the way you have been treating me?"

"No, but it's been a few years since you saw your family and I thought it may do you good to see them again. I just hope that when you come back home, you will begin to settle down here," John replied, glancing at me.

"My goodness, John, what's come over you?" I asked and he laughed.

Chapter Forty-Four
Back Home

Papa met us at the docks in Oostende. I was so happy to see him and after all the hugs and kisses were done, Papa flagged a taxi for us all.

Much had changed in Oostende since my last visit: Heli had passed away the previous year after a long illness. Monica was married with a son called Randall. Sara, my little sister, was also married and she had a little, fair-haired boy called Richard.

My sisters and I often met at the beach when the weather was warm enough. Randall and Richard would dive in and swim confidently in the water, but Susanna and Louisa would hang back nervously.

"By the end of this holiday, my two girls will be swimming too," I said confidently.

"Good luck," Sara said.

"All the best," Monica replied and we all burst out laughing.

"I do miss this," I confessed to my sisters.

I had opened up to them in my letters over the years about how John was treating me and they took the opportunity of seeing me in person to try and persuade me to leave him.

"You can't carry on living the way you are; it's not fair on the girls to see what John is putting you through," Monica said, expressing her fears.

"I know you're right, Monica, but I still love him, even though I don't think he loves me," I said.

"He can't do, if he's treating you so badly," Sara said frowning with worry in her eyes.

I wasn't so truthful with Papa during our many late night chats. I did admit to feeling terribly homesick and was honest about the lack of help and support I got from John's family but, I couldn't bear for him to know just how miserable my marriage was.

I told him about my Belgian friend, Lana and what a tonic she was to me. "It's great to have someone to drink coffee with," I told him. "Not many people in Wales drink coffee."

We talked of the war years and wondered how we had managed to survive the poverty and starvation. Papa said he often congratulated himself for the fact that he had lived to tell the tale.

I was enjoying every minute of my stay. I was sorry to have missed Jack but he was married and living away in Brussels.

On the last day I went to the cemetery alone. I wanted some private moments with my brother Joseph.

"Why did you do what you did, Joseph?" I asked him through my tears. "It was madness, thinking you could cycle all the way to Dieppe. Oh, my darling brother, rest in peace. I miss you, your wicked grin and your teasing words. You would be a grown man now, with a family of your own if you'd lived." I stayed for over two hours, lost in the memories and regrets of what could have been.

All too soon, the holiday was over. I hated saying goodbye to everyone.

"Don't leave it so long until next time," Papa said, hugging me.

***

I had been home about a week when the nightmares began to disturb my sleep again. I woke one night terrified and screaming, with visions of the boat sinking and people screaming.

John shot up in bed. "Don't tell me the nightmares are starting again? I thought your trip to Belgium would have cured them."

"I'll be okay, John. Go back to sleep," I said and he promptly rolled over and was soon snoring.

I got up and made myself a cup of coffee and had a cigarette. My head was pounding and my heart was racing. Suddenly, everything became clear: The visions of Mamma and the bombing seemed to be a sign to me that I should have died with my family. I swilled down the last of my coffee and told myself off for having such morbid thoughts.

The following morning, after John had gone to work and the girls had gone to school. I made a cup of coffee and sat on the settee staring at my bottle of tablets. It seemed hours that I sat there contemplating my future. I wanted to let go of the past and forget about all that had happened, but the memories were too vivid to forget. I was desperate to get well but again, I felt I had failed miserably. I didn't know which way to turn.

"Oh, Lord, help me to be strong," I cried.

I longed to sleep and the only way I knew how was to take some extra tablets. I didn't count how many tumbled into my hand, but I gulped them down. I lay down on the settee and closed my eyes.

When I woke, I was back in hospital again with another thick tube down my throat. I tried to struggle and pull the pipe out but there were too many hands around me.

Later Dr Matthews came to see me.

"Rosina, Rosina, why didn't you go back to your doctor? He would have referred you back to me," he said studying my face.

"I only took the extra tablets to help me sleep, not to die," I sobbed. "The nightmares are horrific but I can't get anyone to listen to me. I cannot go on like this. I am absolutely worn out."

He pulled a chair up alongside my bed. "Do you know where you are now?"

"In hospital?" I answered.

"Last night I had you transferred to the psychiatric hospital," he said. "This is the second time you have been admitted to hospital for trying to take your own life; this time you almost succeeded. Your GP has also told me that you tried to hang yourself. On your last visit to the hospital, I wrote in your notes that if it happened again you were to be admitted to this hospital," Dr Matthews informed me.

"I am too exhausted, Doctor, to argue with you," I said wearily. "My children deserve better than what I can give them, and my husband has no patience with me. I am just a nuisance to everyone."

"I don't think for one minute that your family thinks you are a nuisance," Doctor Matthews smiled. "I'm certainly not giving up on you."

John and the girls arrived a few minutes after the doctor had left.

"Mammy, mammy!" Louisa jumped up on the bed and put her arms around my neck and kissed my cheek. "When are you coming home?"

"Not just yet, but tell me, how are you both?" No one answered.

Susanna sat on the edge of the bed with her head hung down; she looked very sad.

"Mammy, why do you take so many tablets? Don't you want to live with us anymore?" she said and I felt so ashamed.

"My darling girls, I am sorry I caused you so much pain. Of course I want to live with you. I love you both with all my heart." I put my arms around them to reassure them. "Mammy's not very well, but I will get better, you wait and see. Here's some money for you to get some chocolate from the shop downstairs."

After the girls had left, I struggled to look John in the eye.

"When is this going to end, Rosina?" he said. "The girls are upset all the time. Susanna is off school again, as someone has to be there for Louisa when she comes home from school. She gets the tea ready and when I come home, I do the rest."

"Why can't you always be like you are now, John? Instead of the hurtful words you keep shouting at me," I implored.

Ignoring my accusation, he continued, "Rosina, you can't keep taking extra tablets. One of these days you won't wake up and what will happen to the girls then?"

"You are part of the reason I'm here, John." I lowered my voice. "You threaten me, bully me, humiliate me. There is only so much a person can take. I didn't take the tablets to kill myself; I took them to try and get some sleep. I'm desperate to have a peaceful night's sleep. You can believe me or not," and I cried.

Before he could say anything, the girls returned. The rest of the conversation was about mundane matters such as what I would need John to bring up for the rest of my stay in hospital.

"I thought you weren't staying long," Susanna queried.

"I'm not—just until the end of the week." I caught hold of her hand. "It will go quickly, darling. Try not to worry." I turned to her little sister. "Louisa, you be a good girl for Daddy and you must help Susanna as well," I said.

"We will, Mammy," they both chorused as they left. John gave me a peck on the cheek and they were all gone.

After they'd left, I got up to go to the toilet but was promptly sent back to bed by a very stern nurse, who informed me that I wasn't allowed to go without supervision.

"Doctor's orders," she said briskly. "I'll take you shortly, when I'm finished what I'm doing."

When the nurse finally came, she took me out of the ward and down a long corridor with plain white walls. I could see straight away that this was no ordinary hospital. There were bars on the windows and every door was locked with only the staff having keys.

On my way back, I heard a woman's pitiful cry as it echoed along the corridor. *Another lost soul*, I thought.

Dr Matthews was already on the ward speaking to the sister and he made his way over to my bed.

"Please Doctor, let me go home! I don't want to stay here. I'm not as bad as these people! Please let me go home." I was sobbing and shaking. The nurse pulled the curtain around my bed while the doctor sat by my bed and held my hand.

"Rosina, you do want to get better, don't you?"

"Yes I do. I want to be well to look after my family, but I'll not get well in this hospital," I wailed.

The doctor's eyes softened. "The treatment we are hoping to give you cannot be done in another hospital. You are suffering from a severe depression and the facilities we use here will hopefully help you to get well." He paused and waited until my sobs had subsided. "Have you ever heard of ECT? The full name for it is Electroconvulsive Therapy."

When I told him I had never heard of it, he explained that it is an effective short-term treatment for depression, where I would be given an anaesthetic and a muscle relaxant. The doctor would pass a pulse of electric current through two electrodes on each side of my head for several seconds.

"On my head?" I squealed.

"You won't feel anything and we will monitor your heart throughout the procedure," he tried to assure me. "When you wake up, you may experience some confusion and memory loss but that will soon disappear."

"How is this going to help me?" I asked.

"Well, I'm hoping that, in time, this treatment will help to blur some of the memories which have been making you ill. The nightmares won't be so vivid, but you will need more than one session."

"How many"? I enquired.

"That remains to be seen. I would like to keep you in hospital until the end of the week but how many sessions you need altogether will depend on how you react to the treatment."

I trusted Doctor Matthews but this new treatment was so unknown and I felt fearful about the week that lay ahead.

The following morning I was dressed and ready for theatre before eight o'clock. I was glad to be first going down for the treatment, although I was shaking with nerves. I was given a pre-med that helped to calm me a little, then I was taken down to the theatre in a wheelchair. I was asked my name and age then told to count to ten.

I woke up back in my bed feeling very disorientated and confused, with my arms and legs twitching uncontrollably. I felt as if I was floating above my bed and my head wasn't where it should be. It was a bizarre and frightening sensation, like nothing I had ever experienced before.

I must have slept for most of the day, and when I woke again the twitching had disappeared and I could work out where I was, which was a great relief to me.

I had just finished a cup of tea, when John and the girls came to visit.

"Oh, Mammy, you look awful; what's happened?" Susanna observed.

I had to think quickly which was difficult because I didn't want to frighten them.

"The doctor has given Mummy a very strong medication to help block out some of my bad memories. Do you remember me telling you both about the boat when Mammy was a young girl?" They both seemed to be satisfied with my answer.

John gave me a peck on the cheek,

"I thought you weren't coming tonight?" I said.

"I was going to come on my own but the girls wanted to come. When are you coming home?" he asked, more with irritation than concern.

When I told him that I would be in for a week, and then back in as an outpatient for at least another week, John's eyes told me he was fed up.

"How are you managing with the food and the washing and ironing?" I asked.

"We're not," was his curt reply.

"No, Mammy, we're okay," Susanna said, eager to reassure me. "I put the dinner on and when Daddy comes home from work, he does the rest and then serves it. I've even done some ironing today as well."

"Good girl," I replied with a smile.

Louisa suddenly came and sat right up close to me; there were tears bubbling in her eyes. "I miss you, Mammy. It's not the same with Daddy making the food," she said.

"Hopefully, I will be home on Friday, Louisa, then Mammy will make you a nice meal."

"What are you going to make me, Mammy?" Her big blue eyes shone with excitement, just like I remember my little sister Louisa's shone when she was excited.

"Oh I don't know yet, I'll have to think about that," I answered, squeezing her close.

I looked at both of my girls and knew they were my reason for living. They loved me and needed me, and I had to endure this strange new treatment for their sakes.

The Electroconvulsive Therapy was exhausting and it always took a few hours to regain any sense of equilibrium. The gruelling treatment wasn't all I had to endure.

Many of the other patients' behaviour was distressing. One night, a woman came over to me and tried to drag me out of bed, screaming, "That's my bed— get out!" It took two nurses to pull this mad woman off me.

"If I don't get out of this place soon, I will be as crazy as them," I told the nurses. They settled me back in bed but sleep evaded me. I asked the nurse if I could go to the toilet myself. I had obviously gained her trust as she let me go.

As I walked down the long corridor, there was a woman standing on a chair underneath the lights. Her hands were dripping wet. I gasped in horror as she reached up and took the bulb out of the socket and put her hand on the live wiring. I screamed as she fell to the floor, hitting her head on the chair on the way down. Nurses came running to her and one guided me back to bed, doing her best to calm me down.

I couldn't wait for Friday.

When Dr Matthews came to visit me at the end of the week, he told me that he was pleased with how I had been tolerating my sessions of ECT.

"Does that mean I can go home today," I begged.

"Yes, but you will need to come back for at least four more sessions as an outpatient starting next week," he explained. "Then I will see you for a follow-up appointment in a month. You will need to stay on anti-depressants just now,

Mrs Jones. It's going to be trial and error to know which ones are suitable for you." He got up and shook my hand and told me to take care.

I arrived home early in the evening, to a wonderful welcome from the girls but not so much from my husband. I told them that I needed help for the first few days and that didn't go down well with John. "I'm worn out seeing to everything. Having to go shopping after work, trying to keep the girls in order; it's been hard work, Rosina," he complained.

"Tell me about it, John," I said bitterly. "That's what I've been doing every day, and on top of all that trying to cope with this illness I'm suffering from."

He grudgingly went over to help Susanna, who had already started to get dinner ready. I reminded myself that she and Louisa were my motivation for getting better and tried to not dwell on John's lack of concern for me.

Over the next month, I had six more sessions of ECT as an outpatient and I started to see their benefit.

I was able to go back to work and everyone was happy to see me.

"Oh, Rosina, it hasn't been the same without you," said Barbara, one of the barmaids, as she gave me a big hug and a lovely bunch of flowers.

"Thank you so much, all of you. I'm so glad to be back," I said, feeling the most relaxed and happy I had felt in a long time. I had started to put on a bit of weight so was looking healthier as well.

Then one day, I received a letter from Sara that brought a dark cloud back over my brighter moods. Somehow I knew as I opened this letter, that this was not just a newsy epistle, and dread crept over my heart. I wept as I read the words telling me that my beloved Papa had died. It had happened quite suddenly after a short illness and there had not been time to let me know and give me time to visit him. I sobbed quietly into the letter, mourning this man who had been so precious to me and deeply regretting that I had not been able to say goodbye.

When I told John, he was surprisingly sympathetic and was insistent that I go back to Oostende for the funeral. By this time, Susanna had left school and was working and would not be able to take time off to come with me. However, it was decided that ten-year-old Louisa would accompany me.

***

I arrived at the docks in Oostende with a heavy heart. Sara was there to greet me and we held each other for a long time, not being able to express in words the sadness we both felt.

Sara's husband drove us home and Sara prepared supper for us.

After a sleepy Louisa had gone to bed, Sara and I sat drinking coffee.

"At last proper coffee," I said, gulping it down with pleasure. "It's so wonderful to see you again, Sara, but I'm sorry it is under these circumstances."

I glanced around her sitting room, trying to distract myself from the tears I could feel welling up in my eyes.

"You have a lovely home, Sara, "I said. "Such gorgeous furniture and look at that dining table—it's so big with such detail in the glass covering—I've never seen anything like it." I sighed. "I've often wondered over the years if I had made the biggest mistake of my life marrying John. I often wish I had never left Oostende."

"How bad is it, Rosina?" Sara asked, reaching out to hold my hand.

The floodgates opened and I told her everything: about my depression and admission to a psychiatric hospital; about how John was such a brute to Susanna and me; how Louisa seemed to know how to get round John and didn't suffer at his hands in the same way.

"The trouble is, Sara, I still love him but why I'll never know."

Sara was appalled and called him every name under the sun. In a way, I was sorry I had told her.

"Please, Sara, keep this to yourself," I begged.

"Don't worry, I will," she replied. "Oh, you poor thing, why don't you stay here and leave him?"

"That's what Susanna keeps telling me to do. She hates him but I just can't leave him," I explained, ashamed of what I felt was weakness.

"You're a fool to stay, Rosina," Sara answered sternly.

The day of the funeral came. It was in the same church that Mamma had worshipped in. I was dreading it, but as soon as I entered the church, I could feel her presence. The coffin was an open affair, as was the custom in Belgium, so that we all could say our goodbyes. When I bent over to kiss him goodbye, I noticed how much he had aged. My only consolation was that he was now with Mamma.

Chapter Forty-Five
Days of Change

As the months passed, after my return to Wales, our house took on an quieter ambience of its own: there was no shouting or fighting and the girls seemed more relaxed. I felt better than I had for a long time and was able to keep on top of my work in the house and do my job at the pub, which I loved.

However, I wasn't foolish enough to think that it could last.

One Saturday night before John went out, he was in an argumentative mood; it didn't matter what I said or did, it was the wrong thing. I was glad to see the back of him. Susanna, who was now eighteen, had gone into town with her friends and Louisa was upstairs with her friend.

I was in the parlour watching television, when, at about ten o'clock, Louisa's friend went home. "I'm going to bed, Mam," she said, kissing me on the top of my head.

About an hour later, John came home; I could see he had had a skin full.

"Are you still up?" he groused. "Whatever you're watching, turn it off. I want the football on."

"Let me see the end of this, John. It's almost finished," I said. Despite knowing he was drunk, he had been more reasonable of late, so thought he would let it go.

I was wrong. He walked up to the television, turned it over and said, "Go and make me a cup of tea and a sandwich."

As my health had started to return, so had my feisty spirit. "You want something to eat, make it yourself, I'm going to bed!" By this point I was in the dining room and I didn't hear him behind me.

"I told you to make me a cup of tea," he breathed down my neck, which he then grabbed and started to squeeze my throat. I tried desperately to prise his hand loose, but I fell over with him on top of me. I was gasping frantically for a breath.

Anger flooded my being and I managed to tell him to "Finish it, why don't you! Do it, finish it once and for all!"

I felt I was drifting in and out of consciousness when suddenly he stopped. Without saying a word, he got up and walked into the parlour.

I lay there for a minute, panting heavily with breathlessness and coughing. I heard John go up to bed and I managed to get up and drag myself into the kitchen, where I made a coffee and lit a cigarette to help calm me down.

The old familiar self-doubt came rushing back and I started to ask myself what had I done for him to be so violent? I was convinced John would kill me one day. I couldn't face going up to lie in the same bed as him.

At about half past one, Susanna returned home.

"Why are you still up, Mam?" she said.

"I couldn't sleep," I lied but she wasn't that easily fooled.

"What's that on your neck? Let me see." She came closer and took my chin gently in her hand, tilting my face to the side. "Did he do that?" she spat out. "Mam, one day that bugger is going to kill you. You've got to leave him! How can you love someone that does that to you?"

I couldn't answer her. I felt pathetic and ridden with guilt that she had endured this throughout her whole life.

"I hate him," she whispered. "I'm ashamed to say he's my father." She put her arms around me and we wept together.

The incident set me back and the black cloud of depression began to loom over me. For the first time in ages, I had to take time off work.

It also made Susanna's and her father's relationship deteriorate even further. For years John had taken his aggression out on her but as she got older, she became braver and stood up to him.

One of her ways of coping was to stay out of the house as much as she could. We knew she had met a young man—Daniel—and as the months went by, it was him she spent most of her time with.

One evening, after being out, Susanna walked into the parlour and announced to John and I that she and Daniel were planning to get married.

"We've booked the wedding on my birthday next month," she said. Then she looked at her father. "I'll be out of your way soon. You won't be able to pick on me anymore."

John said nothing—his default setting when he couldn't be bothered to fight.

I was happy for Susanna but I encouraged her to wait a little longer so we could save more money to help pay for the wedding.

"I'm not happy here, Mammy," she said. "I don't want a big wedding and Daniel and I have saved enough between us."

I could see she had made her mind up, so said nothing more, other than to bid her goodnight when she came to kiss me on the cheek.

About a week later, John was sitting in the lounge with a faraway look in his eyes. Suddenly, he looked at me and said, "Rosina, I've been thinking about the wedding. What if I take redundancy from the council? They're looking to make some cutbacks and they are offering good pay-outs at the moment. I've been going over it and over it in my head; it's the only way we can provide her with a decent wedding."

I stared at him. "Am I hearing right? After all you've done, you go and make a statement like that. You do realise what you're giving up?"

"Yes, I've thought long and hard about it," he said. "I can take a job at the lemonade warehouse; I know they're looking for new workers."

"You better think this through thoroughly, John. You'd be sacrificing a job you love to give Susanna a wedding," I said, still shocked by this out of character generosity and thoughtfulness.

"Yes, I know," John replied.

"Well, I hope you know what you're doing? Don't you dare take it out on me, when you come home from work miserable because you don't like your new job," I warned him.

We waited until John's redundancy pay came though before we told Susanna.

"Susanna," I began, "if you were willing to wait until Christmastime to get married, your father and I would be willing to pay for the whole wedding."

She looked over at John, obviously thinking this was all my idea and expecting him to protest.

Susanna's eyes grew wider as John explained what he had done so he could fund her wedding.

"Are you serious, Daddy?" she breathed, not sure whether she should laugh or cry.

"Yes, I am," John smiled and his eyes softened. I was reminded of the man I had fallen in love with all those years before. "Look, I know we haven't seen eye to eye over the years but I am trying to make amends for it now." He actually said, for the first time as far as I could remember, and looked ashamed of himself.

Susanna said very little, and I knew she would find it hard to forgive her father so quickly, but she did come over and kiss him on the cheek before saying thank you to us both.

The wedding was set for 17 December, which was John's birthday. Everything went to plan and onlookers would never have guessed the harmony between the bride and her father was the exception rather than the norm.

Susanna and Daniel rented a flat about fifteen miles away from us, but they would come over regularly for their tea.

Life seemed to be improving again. I honestly believed John had turned over a new leaf.

My hopes were soon extinguished, once again.

One day I was working late in the pub. I had reminded John the night before that there was an afternoon party booked and I would be late home.

At five o'clock I was behind the bar, washing out the glasses, when John came in.

"Hello, have you come up for a drink before I finish?" I smiled.

He didn't answer but came behind the bar and as he looked at me I immediately saw the old John; his eyes were like slits and he was grinding his teeth. He grabbed hold of me by the top of my arm and yanked me away from the bar.

"What are you doing, John?" I cried. "Don't you realise there are people watching? Let go of me."

"I don't care who the hell is watching, woman! Get home and make my sodding dinner now!"

Harold, the boss was watching. "Leave her alone, John," he told him sternly.

"You mind your own bloody business—she's my wife," John shouted as he pushed me out of the main door onto the pavement. He wouldn't even let me get my coat.

"Get down that road now and make my dinner, you Belgic bugger," he snarled, continually shoving me in the back.

Crying tears of humiliation, I spun around to face him.

"What is wrong with you? It's your new job, isn't it? You're not happy there and you're taking it out on me. I should have known this would happen!"

"You're finishing in that pub," he yelled back.

"No, I'm not!" I shouted back. "I love my job and you can't make me leave."

"You'll do what I say, woman! I'm the man of the house and I'm fed-up of having to make the dinner."

"Stop making excuses, John! This is the first time in months that I've been working late! This is just another excuse to use me as a punch bag!"

He pushed me into the kitchen, shouting, "Make my dinner now!"

"What's happened, Mammy?" Louisa came running into the kitchen. "What has he done now?"

I told her what had happened but immediately regretted it as she turned around and marched into the parlour.

Louisa caught hold of him by his shirt and pulled him out of his chair.

"If you put one finger on Mammy again, or humiliate her in front of others then you will have me to deal with." I couldn't believe how brave she was and feared what John might do. She felt no fear, however, and continued to berate him. "How dare you do that to her! I'm older now and I won't stand by and watch you treat her the way you do! Father or no Father, I'm warning you. You want dinner? Make it yourself!"

Suddenly, there was a knock on the front door,

"Don't you dare open it!" John shouted from the parlour but Louisa ignored her father and opened the door.

It was Harold.

"I had to come and see if your mother was alright. I was so worried for her," I heard him say to Louisa.

"I'm here now, Harold. Nothing will happen to Mam," Louisa shouted, loud enough for her Father to hear.

"Shut that bloody door!" John shouted from the lounge.

"Would you like me to call the police, Louisa?" Harold asked.

"No, you don't have to do that," Louisa told Harold. "We'll be fine. I've dealt with it."

I was scared Harold's visit would enrage John further, so headed upstairs out of his way. Louisa followed me.

"Do you mind if I sleep with you tonight?" I asked her.

"Of course you can, Mammy," Louisa answered. "I know I have always asked you not to leave Daddy, but I was wrong. I'm scared he'll end up killing you. Susanna has escaped and it won't be long until I'm old enough to leave too, but I can't bear to leave you on your own with him."

"I honestly think he can't stand seeing me happy. He knows how much I love my job," I said, wondering when Louisa had gone from being a little girl, to this young woman I could confide in. "Please, Louisa, don't say anything to Susanna. It will only worry her and the baby is due any day now."

"I won't, Mam. At least when the baby does come, you will be able to get away from here for a couple of weeks, when you go to help Susanna with the baby," Louisa said.

Susanna and her husband had recently moved house sixty miles away; Daniel had been offered a new job that provided a house.

"It will be a welcome break," I admitted. "But I'm going to miss you, my darling."

"If he puts a hand on you again, he'll be sorry, Mam. He's not getting away with hitting you anymore," Louisa said.

***

Two evenings later, at nearly midnight, there was a knock on the front door. It was Daniel.

"Could you come quickly, Rosina," he gasped. "The baby is on its way!"

My bag was already packed so I could be ready to leave at short notice. After hastily wakening Louisa and John to tell them what was happening, we jumped into the car and set off.

By the time we got to the hospital, Susanna's baby had been born. It was a boy! We were overjoyed.

I rang from a coin box and spoke to Harold in the pub and asked if someone would call at the house to give the good news to John and Louisa.

It was hard work living with Susanna and the new baby but I loved being with my grandson. I didn't mention to Susanna that her father was up to his old antics and that my health was suffering as a result. I wanted to leave my problems where they belonged back home.

At the end of my two weeks, I found it difficult to say goodbye to Susanna and my little grandson who had stolen my heart.

I came home to a spotless house: Louisa had kept the washing up to date and got the shopping in. I threw my arms around her, thankful that I had her to come home to.

Before Susanna's baby was born, I had made an appointment with the doctor. My nightmares had returned and I couldn't face sinking back into a pit of despair.

My GP, Doctor Freeman, took blood tests which revealed that, despite being only forty-one, I was going through menopause.

"That might explain part of why your mood has dipped again," she said, "but I have referred you back to your psychiatrist again. With your history I don't want to take any risks and see you as low as you were before." She glanced over the rim of her glasses with concern. I breathed deeply, thankful that I was now blessed with a GP who actually listened and took me seriously.

Within a few days I was back in Dr Matthews clinic. I couldn't help but wonder, what good had all that shock treatment done for me, if I was back here again?

"How have you been Rosina?" he asked in his soft Welsh brogue. He always put me at ease and I was able to tell him about when I'd started to feel the depression come back again. As we were talking, I realised that when I was with Susanna and the baby, my mood had improved.

"I suppose I felt good when I was kept busy and I had no time to think about my problems." I knew that the real problem was John, but despite how comfortable I felt with Doctor Matthews, I was too ashamed to admit everything about what John was really like.

Doctor Matthews asked me at length about my nightmares: had they changed, were they worse?

"I see my little sister still, only now, I can hear her crying for help. I want to help her but she is out of my reach. In the visions of my Mother her arms are open, calling me to come to her and I try to but I can't." I began to weep.

"You've been taking your tablets regularly?" the doctor asked.

"Yes," I told him.

"Rosina," he said gently, "I am going to have you admitted into hospital again. I think you need to have more ECT treatment. I could put you on a stronger antidepressant but you need more immediate help."

I sighed deeply, but I trusted this man and agreed to go into hospital the following week.

Chapter Forty-Six
Older Years

Almost two years after the second round of ECT, I began to turn a corner and life became happier for a spell. Susanna made me a grandmother again, this time giving birth to a beautiful, blonde, curly-haired girl.

Louisa was also due to get married, and a year later, she too gave birth to a cute little daughter. Since Louisa lived nearby, we got to see her and her baby daily. Two years later, Louisa gave birth to another beautiful daughter.

These little girls were such a blessing to not just me, but they won their grandfather's heart too.

John still had his moods but he had mellowed quite a lot since the grandchildren were born.

As the grandchildren grew, so did John's love for them. When I wasn't always well enough to go and stay at Susanna's house for the weekend, John would go down instead. I wouldn't have believed a few years earlier that Susanna and her father would be able to get on as well as they now did.

***

The years continued to roll on, and life became more difficult again. I watched both of my daughters go through divorces. In time, they met new partners and entered into happier second marriages.

I was still having recurring nightmares; the tragic events that happened during World War Two had haunted me all of my life, and as life became less busy, I found that I had just been suppressing the feelings of worthlessness and depression. With more time to think, these unwelcome enemies pounced once again.

I turned once again to that little bottle of pills that were meant to make me feel better.

Once again, I ended up back in hospital having my stomach pumped.

"Why do you keep saving my life? Please, just let me die," I implored the doctors.

More ECT and more anti-depressants followed. Susanna and Louisa asked if their father had triggered this latest episode, but I shook my head "No".

"You might as well face it, girls, I'm never going to be well," I said in despair. But they wouldn't give up on me and when I eventually got discharged from hospital, they brought my grandchildren to visit as often as possible.

By some miracle, I picked myself up again. I applied for another job, this time as a carer in the community. It was my salvation. I loved every minute of it, looking after the elderly and the disabled, as I had long ago with Beatrice.

John had somehow managed to lay his demons to rest and it had been many years since he had shouted abuse or physically hurt me.

He was lucky enough to walk straight back in to his old job with the council on the highways.

We started to holiday in Spain with our daughters and their families. The black cloud that had always been lurking nearby now seemed to have finally gone.

It was physical illness that became my new enemy.

I started to experience abdominal pain and was struggling.

In the New Year, I asked the doctor if I could have an x-ray, as I had been complaining about the pain in my side for over six months and felt I was being fobbed off every time I visited the surgery.

In February 1988, a bowel scan showed nothing that the doctors were concerned about, but I was still having severe pains in my back and I had no appetite.

One particular night the pain was so unbearable that I couldn't sleep. The painkillers I was given did nothing to alleviate the pain. By seven o'clock the following morning, I couldn't stand it anymore.

The doctor was called and after he examined me, I knew, by the look in his eyes, that something was gravely wrong. He had me admitted to hospital straight away.

I sat on the edge of the bed, my hands still tightly gripped around my cup of coffee, the contents long grown cold. I stared out of the window, not seeing the rolling green hills dotted with sheep, nor hearing the muffled rumble of traffic from the nearby motorway. I caught a glimpse of myself in the dressing table mirror and thought how gaunt I looked. My small frame had become even smaller; I must have lost more weight, but that didn't matter now. The priority was my daughters.

"How am I going to tell them?" I asked myself over and over. "They need to know the truth."

The End

Epilogue

I am Susanna and I am writing about the death of my beloved mother.

My sister and I were delighted when our mother finally seemed to have broken from the chains of depression. She was able to enjoy her grandchildren and her relationship with my father was the most harmonious that we had ever known it.

After all the attempts she had made to take her own life, it was cancer that snatched her from us in the end. We were told she had ovarian cancer. She was operated on but the cancer had spread too far.

My sister and I went to the hospital daily to wash her and make her comfortable, and to shield her from the fact that she was dying. Our hearts were breaking.

I rang her sisters in Belgium and they immediately came over, as they wanted to say their goodbyes. I will never know if Mum realised she was dying, when she saw her sisters and her brother Jack sitting around her hospital bed together.

Just four weeks after their visit, at four o'clock on a beautiful spring afternoon, Mum left this world where she had suffered so greatly. She was sixty-one years old.

Her family in Belgium all came back for her funeral.

We were left with this massive void in our lives. It would take a long time for us to come to terms with mum's death.

Two years after her death, I decided to write her life story. To do that, I had to go to Oostende in Belgium several times for information about her life.

My husband and I met up with Mum's two sisters, Monica and Sara, and they gave me so much information. It was wonderful to hear about mum as a child and I will always be grateful for that. But then we spoke about the bombing in Dieppe, and as my aunties spoke of the devastation caused that day, I discovered that Mum's sister, little Louisa, had died in the hold of the boat. She was never in the open water at all.

I came to the conclusion that Mum had gone to her grave falsely thinking that she had killed her little sister, Louisa. Marie and my grandmother, Hanna, were also found in the hold of the boat, their injuries making them almost unrecognisable. They had never been in the open water either, as Mum had believed.

I was horrified to think that all these years, Mum had suffered the torment of those terrible nightmares and had carried a burden of guilt, all for nothing. She had not seen her Mamma in the water and if someone had tried to grab her legs, it was not the hands of her little sister Louisa.

She suffered a lifetime of torment based on false memories, born in a moment of great distress and trauma.

It is obvious that when Mum visited her family in Oostende, they never once spoke about the day that they had lost most of their family.

They spared no mercy
Life hung by a thread
Lost in a sea of blood
Many bodies lay dead
Echoes of the night
Unleashed shadows from a watery grave
Haunting memories ridden with guilt
Her sanity she endlessly fought to save.

THIS IS A LEGACY TO YOU, MUM.
REST IN PEACE.
YOU WELL AND TRULY DESERVE IT.

When Mum died, my father came to live with me for eighteen years. We don't condone what he did, but we learned to forgive him for his terrible behaviour. We realised that he too was a victim of that horrifying war. He died in his eighty-ninth year.

Appendix 1

Figure 1 Hanna Callens (Rosina's mamma)

Figure 2 Jakop Callens (Rosina's papa)

Figure 3 Joseph (Rosina's brother)

Figure 4 The Callens family home

Figure 5 Sara (left) and Rosina

Figure 6 Photograph showing the aftermath of the bombing

Figure 7 Rosina with the hotel staff